A SHORT HISTORY OF
THE WEST INDIES

The University College of the West Indies
[*Photo: Packer, Kingston*]

A SHORT HISTORY OF
THE WEST INDIES

by

J. H. PARRY

and

P. M. SHERLOCK

SECOND EDITION

LONDON
MACMILLAN & CO LTD
NEW YORK · ST MARTIN'S PRESS
1963

Copyright © J. H. Parry and P. M. Sherlock 1963

First Edition 1956
Reprinted 1957
Reprinted (with alterations) 1960
Second Edition 1963

MACMILLAN AND COMPANY LIMITED
St Martin's Street London WC 2
also Bombay Calcutta Madras Melbourne

THE MACMILLAN COMPANY OF CANADA LIMITED
Toronto

ST MARTIN'S PRESS INC
New York

PRINTED IN GREAT BRITAIN

INTRODUCTION

THE BOOK WHICH FOLLOWS is an account of the history of the islands in the Caribbean Sea: the four great islands of Cuba, Jamaica, Hispaniola and Puerto Rico, and the hundreds of smaller islands which form an arching breakwater against the Atlantic, from the scattered peaks of the Virgin Islands in the north to Curaçao and Aruba lying off the coast of South America. It attempts to treat the story as a connected whole, though, being particularly addressed to readers in the British Caribbean, it pays somewhat more detailed attention to places of English speech. It is not concerned directly with the history of the lands bordering the Caribbean, except for areas such as British Honduras and the Guianas, whose development was closely connected with that of the islands.

The recorded history of the West Indies does not grow gradually, as most Old World histories grow, out of a more remote mythological or archaeological past. It begins abruptly with a definite event: the arrival of the first European discoverers in Columbus's fleet in 1492. The present aspect of the islands has been shaped largely by events which took place after that date.

The peoples who inhabit the West Indies — with a dwindling handful of exceptions — migrated or were deliberately transplanted from the Old World. They came from Europe, Africa and Asia, bringing with them their religious beliefs, their language, their social habits. Today the evidence of this transplanting of social institutions can be seen on every hand in the West Indies. Not only the people, but their physical surroundings, are largely transplanted. All the domestic animals and most of the useful plants came from the Old World. Even the wild animals and the wild plants were, many of them, introduced, and have driven out or modified the native plants and animals.

The West Indians, then, are imported people in a largely imported environment. There is nothing unique about this. The same is true, in varying degrees, of many other peoples in the New World. But the West Indians were much slower than most American peoples to grow away from their Old World origins and to form characteristic communities of their own. This difference was due partly to economic dependence: the early settlers set themselves deliberately to produce precious metals and tropical crops for sale in Europe, and their economy developed accordingly. Partly the difference was due to the deep divisions between the immigrants: divisions of language, religion and political allegiance between the European groups who settled in the various islands; and divisions in each island between European, African and Asian. These divisions were complicated and emphasised by the separateness of the islands themselves, small as most of them are, and scattered in a great expanse of sea. Until the steamship and the aircraft brought them some measure of freedom, the West Indians were at the mercy of the winds and currents which governed the movement of sailing ships. For sailing ships, the Caribbean is easy to enter from the east, but hard to leave. Almost any gap in the Antillean break-water will serve for a west-bound ship; but one east-bound must beat out against the north-east trade wind, which blows steadily for most of the year, and relatively few exits are safe and con-venient for that purpose. For the early settlers, bound to their respective origins in Europe by sentiment, by political discipline and by economic dependence, the most useful harbours were naturally those which lay near the best exits. The principal settlements of the West Indies therefore grew up along well-defined sea-lanes to Europe. To this day, sea-borne communi-cations between the islands are difficult and haphazard, while inter-island air travel is limited by high cost and inadequate airports.

The Caribbean has sometimes been likened, in its historical role, to the Mediterranean; but the likeness is superficial. The Mediterranean is an enclosed sea which for millennia linked, in peace or war, the cities, the empires, the cultures of the peoples living round its shores; and for millennia those peoples had no need to look far beyond the boundaries of their sea. The Carib-bean has been less a meeting and crossing place than a corridor. The gravitational pull of Europe to the east was balanced by a corresponding pull to the west. The islands, for much of their history, were valued not as citadels or dwelling places for their own sake, but as the outlying barbicans of a gate. The gate to the South Sea, to India and Cathay, proved to be an illusion; but Vera Cruz and Nombre de Dios were real gates to great empires, and in our own day, since the Canal was cut, the islands have become barbicans again, manned once again in time of danger by forces from outside. The Caribbean waterways have linked Europe with Latin America, Spain with the Philippines, New England with California. They have divided the Caribbean countries, shore from shore and island from island; and most of the traffic passing through has passed the islands by.

Hundreds of ships, thousands of men and great stores of treasure have passed through the Caribbean, bound either east or west, but, in the early days at least, relatively few people and little wealth settled voluntarily in the islands. Even when West Indian planters found, in sugar, a crop which could make them rich by European standards, their growing wealth — especially in the French and English islands — served only to facilitate their return to Europe and to emphasise their dependence on the outside markets where their sugar was sold. It failed to stabilise the impermanent, makeshift fashion of their life. Sugar, also, entailed slavery. The introduction of plantation slavery in the sixteenth and seventeenth centuries and its abolition in the nineteenth were social revolutions severe enough to alter the foundations of West Indian society and rob West Indian history of what little continuity it possessed. Both revolutions were brought about by movements originating outside the West Indies. To this day West Indian history tends to follow similar patterns. Major events are still largely the product of outside circumstances. Even the modern concepts of nationalism and self-government are European in origin, and those West Indians who profess them most vehemently seem uncertain about the scale on which they are to be applied.

All these facts help to explain why most of the West Indian islands were slow to develop a clear sense of community, even within their own shores, and why a sense of community between island and island has hardly developed at all. They explain, too, why West Indian history appears disjointed and unreal to West Indians today. It is a story told from someone else's point of view. The political history of the islands has been written in terms of the struggle of Europeans (or North Americans) for possession or control; their economic history in terms of crops for export — of sugar and tobacco, not of yams or cassava or salt fish; their constitutional history in terms of greater or lesser degrees of imperial supervision. Obviously these factors must be understood by anyone who seeks to understand the West Indies; but there is another, a hidden, aspect of West Indian history — the accumulated experience of people who lived in the West Indies and could never seriously contemplate living anywhere else. In the last century, or century and a half, periods of neglect following upon periods of great if flimsy prosperity have driven West Indians back upon their own social resources and compelled them, belatedly, to develop a consciousness of their own separate existence. The stories of the different islands, though distinct, are in this respect closely parallel, and may legitimately be treated together within a single book. The area, politically and historically disunited, is a natural geographical unit. The modern communities within it, though widely scattered and differing one from another, have many broad characteristics in common. They are all mixed societies. They are remarkable in that they have accepted their mixed character and so have avoided the worst of the tensions which, in many mixed societies, have attended the determination of one race to oust or dominate the others. Their history is worth studying for its own sake and not merely as an appendix to the history of their several European, African or Asian homelands, or of the United States. Such a study, of the history of the West Indies in its own right, is the object of this book.

AUTHORS' NOTE

SINCE THE FIRST publication of *A Short History of the West Indies*, major political changes have taken place in the Caribbean area. The Trujillo régime in the Dominican Republic ended in assassination. In Cuba, a drastic change of government was brought about by armed revolution. The Federation of the British West Indies broke up, and Jamaica and Trinidad became independent states. The second edition contains a brief account of these changes, and traces the story down to the summer of 1962: the eve of the discovery by the United States of Russian missile bases in Cuba, which brought the West Indies once again to the forefront of the international scene.

J.H.P.
P.M.S.

CONTENTS

CONTENTS

LIST OF ILLUSTRATIONS

LIST OF MAPS

CHAPTER I

DISCOVERY

THE RECORDED HISTORY OF the West Indies begins with a definite event, the arrival of Columbus. To say that Columbus discovered America is a misuse of words. Columbus revealed to Europeans the existence of continents and islands which were inhabited already, and had been so for many centuries. Columbus did not discover a new world; he established contact between two worlds, both already old. More important, he did so at a time when the peoples of western Europe had recently developed ships and navigating instruments good enough to maintain that contact in regular voyages, so that people, plants and animals began to flow in a steady stream from the world of Europe to the world of America. In most parts of Latin America, and even to some extent in North America, the two worlds met and mingled. In the West Indies, however, there was little or no mingling, because the shock of conquest proved too much for the weaker race. In the greater islands the native peoples soon dwindled before the impact of an aggressive alien culture. They could not adapt themselves to living beside Europeans; they could not retreat, as the Plains Indians were to retreat centuries later, with the dwindling buffalo herds; there was nowhere for them to go. Within a century they were extinct, and a new society of immigrants from Europe and Africa had taken their place.

Today the Arawaks are hardly even a memory. They had no writing; their only records took the forms of carving in wood and stone and of rude graffiti on natural rock faces. Our knowledge of them is derived partly from the accounts of sixteenth-century Spanish writers, and partly from examination of burial caves and middens. All the witnesses agree that they were a kindly and peaceful people. They had no reason to be otherwise. Except in eastern Puerto Rico they had little or no contact with warlike

I

enemies; and though they got some of their food by hunting, their quarries — the aguti and the iguana — were not beasts which put much tax upon the courage and endurance of the hunter. Fishing was more important to them than hunting. They rarely went far from the sea. Their sites are often marked by great mounds of conch shells. For more adventurous kinds of fishing they fashioned dug-out boats of considerable size from the trunks of silk-cotton trees. They had some agriculture. Oviedo says that they used maize, though the absence of grinding-stones from their pre-Columbian sites suggests that they knew only a soft variety; hard types of maize, from which bread flour could be made, came later from the mainland. Their only bread-stuff was cassava; the discovery of a method of leaching out the poisonous juice of this root must have been, for so primitive a people, an economic event of the first importance. Cassava will flourish where little else will grow; it has spread from the Americas to parts of the Old World, in particular to West Africa, but has never commended itself greatly to European taste. Today, in remote and arid parts of Jamaica, 'cassava without salt, coffee without sugar' is proverbial diet in times of drought and hardship. In addition to food crops, the Arawaks grew tobacco, which they used as a drug, as an ingredient in ritual, and as a means of exchange. Tobacco is the only native crop which became an important article of export from the West Indies after the European occupation. It has made more fortunes than all the silver of the Indies.

The Arawaks made good baskets, and serviceable pottery, which has a rough and distinctive beauty and is often decorated with incised patterns. They made polished stone tools — knives, scrapers, axes and adzes — which compare with the neolithic artefacts of the Old World. They had no knowledge of hard metals, but in some of the islands used gold, washed from the streams and hammered into trinkets for personal ornament. Like most New World peoples they had no beasts of burden and no wheeled vehicles. Though they used caves for burial pur-poses, and probably sometimes for shelter, they made their own dwellings of thatch, and lived in settled villages. They slept in hammocks, made either of woven cotton or of string open-work. This habit much impressed the Spaniards, and was one of the few Arawak contributions to European material culture as it developed in the West Indies and elsewhere. Of Arawak government and religion relatively little is known; but some of the chiefs reigned over considerable tracts of country and seem to have kept some state. The Spanish writers often remarked on the loyalty and devotion which these *caciques* drew from their people.

In Columbus's time the Arawaks occupied all the greater islands of the Caribbean; but in the easternmost island, Puerto Rico, they were already suffering from the raids of an intrusive and far more warlike people, to whom the Spaniards gave the name of Caribs. Carib means cannibal; and cannibalism, whether for ritual purposes or merely for food, was one of the characteristics of these canoe-borne marauders who were pushing north along the line of the lesser Antilles and enslaving or destroying the earlier inhabitants in their way. Though a handful of Caribs still survive in Dominica, even less is known of their early culture than of that of the Arawaks, from whom, probably, many of their skills were originally derived. They were dangerous enemies, and after the first few encounters the Spaniards left them and their islands alone, to their own great disadvantage, as later appeared; for other Europeans were to seize the islands which the Spaniards had passed by.

The world which these simple peoples inhabited had two characteristics which it still retains — breath-taking physical beauty and, in parts, great fertility. Columbus wrote to his king from Cuba: 'The banks of the rivers are embellished with lofty palm trees, whose shade gives a delicious freshness to the air, and the birds and the flowers are uncommon and beautiful. I was so delighted with the scene, that I had almost come to the resolution of staying here for the remainder of my days; for believe me, Sire, these countries far surpass all the rest of the world in beauty and conveniency.' Many later travellers, in different parts of the West Indies, have echoed his words. Geographically and geologically the islands fall into two great groups, the division corresponding almost exactly with the ethnographical division at the time of the conquest. The Greater Antilles rest on a common submarine bed and form parts of a partially submerged continental tract which once extended continuously from Cuba to the Virgin Islands. They are traversed by an abrupt and lofty mountain range, of which the peaks are nearly 12,000 feet high, culminating in Hispaniola and falling off on either side in Cuba, Jamaica and Puerto Rico. They are composed mostly of limestones, with outcrops of other rocks, all much older than the eruptive rocks of the Lesser Antilles, and nowhere showing traces of recent volcanic activity.

The Lesser Antilles in the north form two parallel chains, of which the outer, terminating in Marie-Galante, represents an area of upheaval on the seaward slope. Except for Antigua, its members are of marine origin, coral below and limestone above. The inner chain, which runs through to Grenada, is a partly submerged peninsula. The existing islands represent old volcanic cones, culminating in Dominica at a height of 5,340 feet. Trinidad and Tobago, and probably Barbados, belong geologically to Venezuela. The nomenclature of these island groups is confusing. Today the name Leeward Islands is applied to the northern portion of the chain, from the Virgins to Guadeloupe; the Windward group includes Dominica, Martinique, St. Lucia, St. Vincent, the Grenadines and Grenada. In early Spanish times the whole chain from the Virgins to Trinidad was called the Windward Islands — Islas de Barlovento — the name Leeward being confined to the other islands off the South American coast; a logical and descriptive distinction, considering the prevailing north-east wind.

Vegetation is exuberant in all the islands, and most of them in Columbus's time must have been covered in forest to the water's edge, except perhaps on the south-east coast of Cuba, where early voyagers reported the same harsh xerophytic plants — cactus and the like — which grow there today. Now the islands are largely deforested except in the higher mountains. The larger fauna is poor in species, except for birds. Most native species differ from those of the mainland, owing to the length of time that the islands have been separated from the continent, but the fauna of Trinidad and Tobago, as might be expected, is South American in character. Fish and turtles abound everywhere, and land reptiles, including crocodiles, are common in the larger islands; but, except for the fer-de-lance in Martinique and St. Lucia, and for the Trinidadian species, there are no poisonous snakes.

As if to compensate for their great beauty and for their comparative freedom from animal pests, the West Indies are peculiarly subject to natural cataclysms: hurricanes, earth-quakes, and, in some of the Lesser Antilles, volcanic eruptions. These recurrent disasters have played a considerable part in the history of all the islands, and are still a serious danger. Columbus on his first voyage escaped the evidences of these visitations; but he was to have his full share of hurricanes later.

Columbus's first irruption into the terrestrial paradise of the Arawaks was a mere reconnaissance, though a well-planned and ably executed one. Making, by good fortune, the best of the North Atlantic wind system — it was not the least important of his discoveries — he sailed from the Canaries to the Bahamas before the north-east trades, and later returned to the Azores in the zone of the westerly winds of winter. His first West Indian landfall was at San Salvador in the Bahamas. During his stay in the West Indies he explored Santa María de la Concepción, which later and less pious sailors renamed Rum Cay; the north-east coast of Cuba; and part of the north coast of Hispaniola — La Isla Española — modern Haiti. Almost everywhere the new-comers were received by the natives with hospitality and respect — respect due, it may be, to belief in their divine origin. In Hispaniola they obtained by barter a number of gold nose-plugs, bracelets, and other ornaments; small trinkets, but valuable enough to attract fresh expeditions and to seal the fate of their over-trustful owners.

Columbus claimed, and believed until his death, that he had found islands lying off the coast of eastern Asia, and possibly part of the mainland too. The name West Indies is testimony to his belief. We cannot be sure whether these claims agreed with Columbus's original intentions and promises, nor whether Ferdi-nand and Isabella entirely accepted them. Some intelligent contemporaries certainly did not; and doubt in the minds of Columbus's own men is suggested by the alternative name of Antilles, from Antilla or Atlantis. But beyond doubt Columbus had found an extensive archipelago of hitherto unknown islands which yielded some gold and were inhabited by a peaceful and tractable, though primitive, people. These islands might prove to be merely another Atlantic group, like the Canaries, over which Spain and Portugal had been bickering for many years; they might prove easy stepping-stones to India. In any event, they were worth careful investigation.

B

The first voyage, though successful, had been expensive. Columbus had lost his flagship and had been compelled to leave half his men behind in Hispaniola to face an uncertain fate. The plunder he had secured was negligible in proportion to the cost of the enterprise. It was now essential to follow up the discovery and to produce a return on the investment. Immediately upon receipt of Columbus's first report, the sovereigns commanded him to begin his preparations for a second voyage. Shortly afterwards they embarked on negotiations with the Papacy and with Portugal in order to secure a monopoly of navigation and settlement in the seas and lands which Columbus had discovered.

The negotiations with the Papacy presented little difficulty. Alexander VI was himself a Spaniard, already under heavy obligations to the Catholic monarchs and looking to them for support in his endeavour to create a principality in Italy for his son. His predecessors had conferred on Portugal the monopoly of exploration and missionary activity in West Africa, and Alexander was willing to do as much for Spain. He issued a series of four bulls, each successively strengthening and extending the provisions of the previous ones, in accordance with successive demands made by Ferdinand and Isabella, upon Columbus's advice. The first two granted to the sovereigns of Castile all lands discovered, or to be discovered, in the regions explored by Columbus. The third, the famous *Inter Caetera*, drew an imaginary boundary from north to south a hundred leagues west of the Azores and Cape Verde Islands, and provided that the land and sea beyond the line should be a Spanish sphere of exploration. The fourth, *Dudum Siquidem*, extended the previous grants to include 'all islands and mainlands whatever, found or to be found . . . in sailing towards the west and south, whether they be in regions occidental or meridional and oriental and of India'; further, all grants previously made in the regions mentioned were cancelled, even if they had been followed by actual possession.

Whatever the international force of these enactments — and Catholic opinion was divided in the matter — the four bulls constituted for Spaniards the basic legal claim of the Spanish Crown to the lands of the New World. As instruments regulating relations with Portugal they were superseded, it is true, by the Treaty of Tordesillas in the following year. By that treaty the

Spaniards unwittingly signed away their claim to the real route
to India, the imaginary land of Antilla, and (as later appeared)
the real land of Brazil; but the treaty did not affect the West
Indies, and Columbus was back in the islands long before it was
signed. He left Cadiz in September 1493 in command of a large
fleet, ships, caravels and pinnaces, seventeen sail in all. The
composition of the fleet, no less than the instructions which the
admiral carried, indicated the purpose for which it was sent. It
contained no heavily armed fighting ships; it carried no trade
goods, other than small truck for barter with savages. Its chief
cargo was men — priests, gentlemen-soldiers, artisans, farmers,
twelve hundred people in all — and agricultural stock — tools,
seeds and animals; a whole society in miniature. The immediate
object of the voyage, then, was not to open a new trade or to
conquer oriental kingdoms, but to settle the island of Hispaniola,
to found a mining and farming colony which should produce its
own food, pay for the cost of the voyage by remitting gold to
Spain, and serve at the same time as a base for further exploration
in the direction of India or Cathay. There had been no lack of
volunteers. For men-at-arms, unemployed through the decline
of private war and the fall of Granada, the Indies offered adventurous service, plunder, and the possibility of landed ease; for
humbler folk there was the hope of escape from the harsh uplands
of Castile, overrun by the privileged flocks of Mesta, to a place
where soil and climate were kind and native labour cheap and
plentiful; and who knew what golden dreams might lie beyond?

The fleet made a prosperous passage and a good landfall, at
Dominica, and passed along the beautiful arc of the lesser
Antilles, through the Virgin Islands, past Puerto Rico, to the
north coast of Hispaniola. There Columbus's good fortune
ended. The settlement of Navidad, planted on the first voyage,
had been wiped out; in selecting as a site for his second settlement the unprotected, unhealthy shore which he named Isabela,
Columbus made his first serious blunder. Isabela never prospered. It would have taken a leader of commanding genius to
maintain discipline among those early Spanish settlers — touchy,
adventurous and greedy as they were — to compel them to clear
the forest, build houses, and plant crops instead of roaming
about the island in search of gold or of slaves. Great explorer
and sea commander, brilliant navigator though he was, Columbus

had neither the experience nor the temperament of a successful colonial governor. He was, moreover, a foreigner and the son of an artisan tricked out with an empty title and a new coat of arms. It soon became a question whether he and his officers could keep his men in hand until the relief fleet arrived.

The search for India could not be delayed, however; and after sending some of the most troublesome away to explore the interior, Columbus again set sail with three caravels, to explore the south coast of Cuba and to discover Jamaica. On his return to Isabela, he found his people weakened by sickness and at open enmity with the natives. The peaceful Tainos had been exasperated to the point of war by the incessant demands for food and women. Columbus turned upon the Indians, hunted them through the forest with armed men and savage dogs, and imposed upon them a poll-tax of gold dust which they could not pay. The captives in this pitiful warfare were enslaved. Columbus shipped some hundreds to Spain, where most of them died. The remainder were released and sent back by the orders of the queen, so that even the slave trade brought no profit. Meanwhile, at Isabela, the surviving Indians left their land untilled. Columbus's fleet had brought a stock of food from Spain, but not enough to feed the colony for any length of time. Over-optimism about the extent to which Europeans could live off the country in the tropics was a common feature of all these early explorations. War with the Indians caused a scarcity of local food supplies; and famine threatened the Spaniards in their fever-ridden camp.

Matters were in this state when, in the spring of 1496, Columbus sailed for Spain to deal with the complaints which had been carried there by malcontents from Isabela. In his absence, but with his approval, his brother Bartolomé, whom he left in charge, organised the removal of the settlement from Isabela to a better site on the south coast. There, in 1496 or 1497, the colonists began to build the town of Santo Domingo, which was to be for half a century the capital of the Spanish Indies, and which survives as a thriving city today.

The Catholic monarchs still trusted Columbus. With their support and at their expense he returned to the Indies in 1498; but this time there were few volunteers, and men had to be pressed or released from prison to sail with the admiral. Columbus sailed to the south of his former course, to discover the island of Trinidad and the mouths of the Orinoco, by far the largest river then known to Europeans, whose great volume of fresh water proved the new-found coast to be part of a mighty continent. By ill-luck he missed the pearl-bearing oyster-beds off the Venezuelan coast, but sailed directly north from Margarita, by a remarkable feat of navigation, to Hispaniola, to the new city which his brother had founded.

At Santo Domingo Columbus found half his settlers, under the *alcalde* Francisco Roldán, in open revolt against the authority of Bartolomé. Columbus could not — or did not — suppress the revolt by force, but bought off Roldán and his followers by concessions — pardon, restoration to office, and free land grants. Besides consenting to these humiliating terms, the admiral made at this time another and more significant concession to the rebels — the division of the Indians of the island among the Spanish settlers as servants and estate labourers. This *repartimiento* system later became general in a modified form throughout the Spanish Indies. For a time, the arrangement served its turn in pacifying the leaders of the rebellion, and Columbus was able to suppress subsequent minor Spanish revolts with a severity probably overdue. The damage was done, however. Where Columbus's policy had been weak, malcontents returning to Spain were able to represent it as tyrannical. In the spring of 1499 the sovereigns appointed Francisco de Bobadilla to supersede Columbus and to investigate the complaints against him. Bobadilla sent the admiral home in irons. Though his sovereigns restored his titles and property and treated him with all courtesy to the end, Columbus was never again allowed to exercise his offices of admiral and viceroy or to interfere in the government of his island of Hispaniola.

The real beginnings of settled government in the Indies date from the arrival of Bobadilla's successor, Frey Nicolás de Ovando, Knight Commander of Alcántara. It was characteristic of the time that this task should be entrusted to a high officer of an order founded to garrison Christian outposts in Spain against the forces of Islam. Ovando arrived with a great fleet of thirty ships and brought 2,500 people to reinforce the 300 or so surviving settlers. He governed Hispaniola for six years with a severity far harsher than Columbus had ever dared to exercise.

Discipline, indeed, was what the settlers chiefly needed. As for the Indians, Ovando secured a royal decree in 1503 giving legal form to the *repartimientos* begun by Columbus. From the subjugated Indians the invaders exacted tribute and forced labour in return for conversion and protection. Against the wild Indians they waged relentless war. Probably the Tainos were doomed already and Ovando's severities only hastened their extinction. Forced labour drove some of them to despair and suicide; European diseases, smallpox especially, killed many; and the Spaniards loosed against them yet other destructive enemies. A primitive agricultural people, tilling unfenced clearings in the forest, cannot live close to an aggressive pastoral community, such as the Spaniards formed in both the Old World and the New. The Indians were defeated not only by armies of down-at-heel swordsmen, but by greater armies of wandering beasts which rooted up their cassava and trampled and grazed their corn. The Spaniards, for their part, achieved a modest prosperity, pasturing great herds of pigs and horned cattle upon open range and washing for gold in the streams. The production of gold increased steadily, and reached by the second decade of the sixteenth century a quantity sufficient to attract the interest and the cupidity of Ferdinand and his advisers. It reached a peak in 1518, but thereafter declined sharply. By the middle of the century the silver of New Spain and Peru had become the main interest of government, and the gold of the islands was relatively insignificant.

Lack of labour was the chief hindrance to the development of Hispaniola. The settlers resorted to slave-raiding in the Bahamas to replace the dying Tainos, but the captured Lucayos also died or killed themselves rather than face the harsh conditions of forced labour in mines and fields. To men of the temperament of the early Spanish settlers land was useless without hands to work it; even gold-mining was tedious work which called for unskilled labour. It was lack of labour as much as greed for gold, missionary zeal, or simple restlessness which drove many Spaniards on from Hispaniola to settle in other islands and mainlands, where the native population might prove more numerous and more hardy. Hispaniola became, as its founder had intended, the base for further exploration and the source of bacon, dried beef and cassava bread to victual the exploring expeditions which

sailed out in ever-increasing numbers during the government of
Ovando's successor, the old admiral's son, Diego Colón.

In 1509 Juan de Esquivel began the settlement of Jamaica, or
at least of the area round New Seville, near what is now St.
Ann's Bay, where Columbus had beached his worm-riddled
caravels five years before. Jamaica yielded no precious metals.
It supported a small population of Spaniards who lived by
cattle-ranching, but was never of much importance in Spanish
times. The much larger enterprise of settling Cuba was undertaken shortly after. Sebastián de Ocampo, sent out by Ovando
to reconnoitre in 1508, circumnavigated Cuba and proved it to
be an island, contrary to what Columbus had asserted. In 1511
Diego Velázquez, who had been lieutenant-governor of Hispaniola under Ovando, began the work of settlement, as a private
investment, but with official approval. Oviedo, who knew
Velázquez, has related the story of the conquest in detail. Like
Ovando, Velázquez was a disciplinarian and an administrator of
considerable ability. With a small force of personal followers he
put down native resistance and occupied the whole island — or,
at least, desirable sites throughout the island — within three
years. He showed remarkable foresight and skill in selecting the
best localities for the establishment of Spanish settlements;
during the first five years of his governorship he founded seven
towns, and though both the names and the precise sites of
several of them changed more than once, they all survived in the
districts where they were founded. Santiago in the south-east
was the first, and remained, by virtue of its proximity to Hispaniola, the chief settlement, until a shift in Caribbean trade
routes brought Havana into prominence. Cuba produced considerable quantities of gold; and being more fertile and less
mountainous than Hispaniola, it offered better opportunities for
ranching, tobacco-farming and sugar-planting. As in Hispaniola,
the labour for mines and farms was procured in the early years
by *repartimientos* of the native population. Cuba attracted many
settlers from Hispaniola, and for a time at least Velázquez
succeeded in making himself practically independent of the
governor of the older colony.

The fourth major island settlement, that of Puerto Rico, which
began in 1512, was less immediately successful. Intrusive groups
of Caribs from the Lesser Antilles had already established

themselves in Puerto Rico, and offered a much more formidable resistance to the Spaniards than the natives of Hispaniola had done. The attention of the first governor, Juan Ponce de León, was, moreover, divided between the island itself and the peninsula of Florida, where he made an unsuccessful attempt to settle in 1514. The settlement of Puerto Rico, in consequence, was slower, more sanguinary and less complete than that of the other islands, and the colony did not attract large numbers of Spaniards in the sixteenth century.

Hispaniola had been the base for the conquest of Cuba and for all subsequent settlements down to 1519. In that year Cuba in its turn became the base for a greater conquest. Ever since Columbus's fourth voyage, expeditions, sailing either from Hispaniola or from Spain itself, had been exploring and settling in Castilla del Oro, as the Isthmus of Darien was called. Balboa, the first of the great *conquistadores* of the mainland, was a soldier of fortune from Hispaniola. In 1513, following up an Indian report, he led an expedition through the dripping forests of the Isthmus to the shores of the Pacific. Balboa's discovery not only revealed to Europeans the existence of the 'South Sea'; it revealed also how narrow a strip of land separated the two oceans, and so gave a new encouragement to those who hoped to find a strait through Central America and a westward all-sea route to India. It was partly that hope which prompted the exploration of the coastline of the western Caribbean and the Gulf of Mexico. The conquest of Central America was thus in a sense an incident in the race between Spaniards and Portuguese to reach the East. In the same year — 1513 — that Balboa crossed the Isthmus, the first Portuguese ships reached the true Indies, the Moluccas, whence the spices came. In the same year — 1519 — that Cortés sailed from Cuba to conquer Mexico, Magellan left Spain on the voyage which was to reveal both the true western route to the East and the daunting size of the Pacific. Magellan's voyage also revealed that the Spaniards had lost the race; but in tropical America they had a reward of a different sort. Though they failed to find a strait, they founded a great empire. The Caribbean was the highway to that empire, Cuba and Hispaniola its gatehouse towers.

CHAPTER II

THE SPANISH INDIES

THE EXPEDITIONS WHICH SAILED from Hispaniola to settle Golden Castile, and from Cuba to conquer Mexico, made heavy demands upon the resources of the islands. Cortés' departure in particular, with 600 armed men, eleven ships and sixteen horses, weakened seriously the fighting strength of the Spaniards who stayed behind; and the victualling of so large a force must have imposed a severe strain on the economy of the island. In the following year a hurricane destroyed trees and crops on the south coast of Cuba; a smallpox epidemic swept both Cuba and Hispaniola, killing some Spaniards and many thousands of Indians. The process of depopulation went on, as tales of plunder and high adventure drew settlers in a steady stream from the islands to Mexico. The mainland provinces soon overshadowed the islands in population, wealth, and royal estimation, especially when the small quantities of alluvial gold in Cuba and Hispaniola showed signs of becoming exhausted. The islands, however, were not deserted. Spanish settlement had struck deep roots. Santo Domingo was already a place of some importance, by virtue of its early settlement and its central position. It was, and for some years remained, the administrative centre for the Caribbean area, including the mainland coast of South America. Other towns were useful as ports of call for shipping. Outside the towns, undeveloped estates and great ranges of wild pasture, deserted by their owners in the rush to Mexico, were bought cheaply by less adventurous but more business-like people who were content to produce relatively humdrum commodities: provisions for sale to passing ships, hides and tallow, sugar and tobacco, for export to Spain. Settlers continued to come to the West Indies, and made a modest living. Most of them were relatively humble folk; the great *conquistadores* went elsewhere. A few Portuguese came from Madeira and the Azores, and a sprinkling of German artisans settled in Hispaniola in Charles V's time, when the Welsers maintained an agency at Santo Domingo; but the great majority of settlers were, of course, Spaniards. Of the four greater islands, Cuba, Puerto Rico, and the larger part of Hispaniola remain Spanish in character and language to this day.

The Spanish communities in the West Indies lived by a predominantly pastoral economy. In the arid uplands of Castile, from which most of them came, pastoral pursuits, the grazing of semi-nomadic flocks and herds, had long been preferred to arable farming. The preference was social and military as well as economic; it was the legacy of centuries of intermittent fighting, of constantly shifting frontiers. The man on horseback, the master of flocks and herds, was well adapted to such conditions, whether in the Old World or the New; the peasant, conversely, was economically vulnerable and socially despised. The labour of tilling the soil in Spain was left, wherever possible, to the *moriscos*. In America it was left to the Indians, so long as there were Indians to do it.

The raising of cattle, though it called for daring horsemanship and occasional bursts of great energy, required no careful or sustained effort. The beasts were turned out on the virgin savannahs and multiplied prodigiously. Cattle-grazing properties were very loosely defined, usually in terms of a radius from a fixed spot, and little attempt was made to survey boundaries. Cattle were sorted, and calves branded, at periodic round-ups, but many escaped the branding and took to a completely wild existence in the forests. These *cimarrones* were so numerous that *montería* — the hunting of wild cattle — became an established right held in common by the settlers in each locality. The chief value of the beasts lay in the hides. Leather was in constant demand in Europe, both for saddlery and for protective clothing, for an ox-hide jerkin would turn a knife-thrust. Tallow also was a marketable commodity, for making candles and for coating the hulls of ships as a protection against marine borers. When hides and tallow had been removed, the carcasses of slaughtered cattle were often left to rot where they lay. Much of the fecklessness of the early settlers throughout Spanish America can be attributed to these circumstances; whatever the economic difficulties of the time, no Spaniard need starve, when beef could be had in abundance for the trouble of slaughtering it.

Grants of grazing land for cattle went chiefly to the wealthier settlers, who could afford to stock them; though lesser people sometimes sought and obtained grants merely in order to sell them. The Crown itself operated ranches in Hispaniola, by means of overseers, down to the middle of the sixteenth century. The ranchers, with the owners of gold-mines, were the principal capitalists in the early days. Agriculture — until sugar became important — was the recourse of those who lacked capital to undertake more lucrative enterprises. Of course beef was not the only subsistence of the settlers, nor leather and gold their only exportable products. Cassava remained the principal bread-stuff throughout the sixteenth century, with maize occupying second place, for the islands were too poor to import wheat flour from Europe in any quantity. Tobacco, the other important native crop, was also taken over to some extent by Spaniards. It was characteristically the small planters' crop. Its production and export did not reach significant proportions in any of the islands until the last quarter of the century.

Both Columbus and Ovando during their respective govern-ments had tried to settle European farmers in Hispaniola, and had introduced Old World crops to supplement tobacco and cassava. Their efforts met with varying success. Vines, olives and European cereals all failed; rice did moderately well in suitably wet areas. Fruit trees were an immediate success. Spaniards are fond of orchards and skilled in their management — one of the gracious characteristics, perhaps, inherited from the Moors. They introduced bananas from the Canary Islands, figs, oranges and lemons from Spain, all in the first two decades of the sixteenth century. All these trees flourished in cultivation, and soon no monastery, and few private houses of any size, lacked the amenity of a walled orchard.

The most important crop introduced by the Spaniards, how-ever, was sugar. The story of sugar is a continuous thread running through the whole history of the West Indies. In later years the fortunes of the islands were to rise and fall with the price of sugar, and the requirements of the sugar industry were to determine the nature of their population. In the Spanish islands the story of sugar began modestly. Hispaniola was the only island which produced an exportable surplus in the sixteenth century, partly because it had very much better communications with Spain than had the other islands, partly because it obtained, at government expense, the services of a number of Canary Islanders who understood the peculiarities of sugar culture. Sugar-cane is highly perishable, and must be milled within forty-eight hours of cutting. The sugar producer, therefore, must be a manufacturer as well as a cultivator; or at least cultivator and manufacturer must be in very close touch. The planting and the reaping of cane are both heavy undertakings demanding considerable labour. The manufacture of sugar — even by the crude small-scale methods of the sixteenth century — required a crushing mill, and power to turn it. A small mill might be turned by a mule or an ox, or even by man-power; a larger one needed a water-wheel or windmill. Coppers and furnaces were needed for boiling, and pots for crystallising the juice. Carts, and beasts to pull them, were necessary for transporting cane; and the manufactured product, being full of molasses, had to be shipped in casks. The production of sugar in quantities large enough for export, therefore, required considerable initial capital and a large labour force, including unskilled hands for field work and skilled men for the processes of manufacture.

Shortage of capital does not seem to have been the main difficulty of the Hispaniola planters. A sugar estate was a good investment, provided that the crop could be shipped to Europe, where demand was high; and the government itself was prepared to make loans for the construction of mills. The first mill was built in 1508 or 1509, and the first samples of sugar sent to Spain about 1515. Oviedo says that by 1523 there were twenty-four mills of various types working in the island, which must have represented a considerable capital investment. Shortage of labour was a more serious limitation. Free labour was out of the question, and the supply of forced labour was limited. The local Indians, as we have seen, were quite unequal to the task, even when reinforced by captives from the Bahamas and from Pánuco. The only alternative seemed to lie in the import of slaves from the Old World. The chief source of slaves at that time, and for several centuries to come, was West Africa, where the Portuguese had long been established as the possessors of a trading monopoly with the coastal chiefs who dealt in slaves. Many Spaniards possessed African household slaves, and a few negroes were brought out by their masters in Ovando's fleet. In 1510 the government in Spain ordered its agents at Seville to send out 250 slaves for the gold-mines of Hispaniola; and from 1518, in order to forestall Portuguese smuggling, the Crown began to grant licences to private traders for the import of slaves into the West Indies. In this way the third racial element was added to the West Indian mixture. By the late fifteen-twenties all the disciplinary problems of plantation slavery had made their appearance: shortage of European supervisors — partly due, in this instance, to the exodus to Mexico; servile mutinies; bands of runaways hiding in the mountains and emerging at intervals to attack the settlements. Even so, the planters constantly clamoured for more slaves. There were never enough. Import was by individual licence, though sometimes a monopoly for a period of years might be granted, with the right to sell individual licences to sub-contractors. The licensees had to buy their slaves from Portuguese dealers; the supply was haphazard and irregular; and the island buyers had to compete with larger producers of sugar on the mainland. The only satisfactory solution, from the settlers' point of view, lay in a firm contract for a regular annual supply; and such a contract did not become possible until the union of the Spanish and Portuguese crowns later in the century. Labour shortage, and the difficulty of shipping to a distant market, combined to limit the development of sugar production. Though important in the sixteenth century, it did not become the predominant occupation of West Indians until a much later date; and for the same reason negroes never came to outnumber Europeans in the Spanish Indies as they did elsewhere.

The main economic undertakings of Spanish West Indians all required intermittent supervision rather than constant personal attention. Cattle-ranching and sugar-making were both to some extent seasonal occupations. Even the mines were left by their owners largely in the care of overseers. The leading settlers did not care to live permanently in the country, among the sullen, resentful Indians or the mutinous negroes, whose labour they employed. They preferred to live, for most of the year, in the towns. Spanish life, in the colonies as in Spain, was strongly urban in character, and the corporate town rather than the great country house was the characteristic stronghold of the ruling class. The contrast with the later English settlements is obvious

even to a casual observer today; for English wealth, in the West
Indies as in England, liked to keep its state in the country. The
towns of the Spanish islands are well planned, dignified, and
often architecturally distinguished, unlike the haphazard and
often mean collections of buildings in the British colonies; but
Cuba and Puerto Rico have nothing comparable with the
Georgian 'great houses' of Jamaica and Barbados.

The foundation of towns was always the first care of the leader
in charge of a new Spanish conquest or settlement. The business
of foundation was attended with considerable ceremony. After
the selection and formal marking of the site, the first step was
to trace the lines of the central square and the main streets,
which were laid out usually with the rectilinear rigidity of a
Roman camp, even though the buildings might for years be mere
huts of adobe or thatch. The next step — subject to eventual
royal confirmation — was the creation of a municipal governing
body — a *cabildo*. The towns of Hispaniola first secured the
formal privilege of municipal incorporation in 1507. *Cabildos*
exercised administrative and judicial authority over wide tracts
of surrounding country, and in the early days were the only
formal institutions of law and order in newly settled areas. The
cabildos of large towns could become very powerful bodies. They
corresponded directly with the Crown, either by letter or by
accredited representatives (*procuradores*) and were at times both
outspoken and effective in their criticism of royal policy. The
members of a *cabildo* — the *regidores* — might vary in number
from four in a small place to twenty-four or more in a great
provincial capital. They were appointed initially by the commander of the settlement, the governor, from among his own
associates, and the officers of the conquest; thereafter they usually
appointed their own successors annually, subject to the governor's approval. In some small towns some or all of the *regidores*
might be elected by the whole body of householders; in Havana,
for instance, popular election was the rule at the beginning and
survived intermittently until about 1570. To many sixteenth-
century Spaniards, however, popular election was a dangerously
anarchic proceeding, and the Crown discouraged it. Even where
it existed it appeared in practice to make little difference to the
character of municipal bodies. Respectable citizens understood,
and expected, that offices should circulate among the heads of

the leading families of the neighbourhood. The concentration became narrower still when, in the fifteen-twenties, persons who had claims on the royal gratitude began to ask, and to obtain, appointments to membership of colonial *cabildos* for life. Such life appointments might, with further royal permission, be sold or bequeathed; and in the last decade of the sixteenth century the Crown itself began to sell life *regimientos* by public auction. These practices, of course, put an end to any form of election. There was, therefore, nothing democratic about the constitution of the *cabildos*. Municipal government was the perquisite of local magnates, who, in most places, formed a close and jealous oligarchy.

The *cabildos* supplied the means whereby groups of associates — who, it must be remembered, had undertaken conquests and settlements at their own risk and expense — recouped themselves for the hardships they had undergone. *Regidores* received no salary, but might have many unofficial perquisites. For example, the leading settlers, as private individuals, required land; as *regidores* they were responsible for distributing land. As ranchers they produced the beef and other provisions with which the towns were fed; as *regidores* they fixed the prices at which those provisions were to be sold. As land-owners and mine-owners they needed labour; as *regidores* they were responsible — at least in the early days — for the administration of native labour under the *repartimiento* system. As private individuals they could be sued by those whom they wronged; but as *regidores* they elected, from among men of their own type and interests, the *alcaldes ordinarios* — the municipal magistrates before whom, in first instance, the suits would be heard. Their local authority — so long as they agreed among themselves — could be lawfully challenged only by the governor — who was often an interested party — or the Crown itself.

Naturally the settlers, the missionaries and the governors failed to agree among themselves: and the Crown was willing enough to intervene. It was financially interested in the produce of the mines; it was extremely sensitive to any suggestion of local independence, whether quasi-feudal or municipal, and became more so after the revolt of the *Comuneros* in Spain in the early fifteen-twenties; it was responsible for defence and for the protection of trade, which naturally called for the regulation of trade. Finally, the consciences of succeeding rulers were troubled by the plight of the native peoples, and demanded closer supervision, with a view to the conversion and civilisation of the Indians and their protection against the rapacity of the settlers. Closer control was to be achieved partly by appointing salaried governors to replace the original self-appointed leaders and investors; and partly by creating judicial, administrative and financial machinery under more or less direct Crown control, to assist and also to check the work of the governors.

Ovando had been the first effective royal governor in the Indies, except for the brief interlude under Bobadilla. Ovando's administration, efficient though it was, had not given complete satisfaction; his native policy had been notoriously harsh and there had been talk of financial irregularities. After Ovando's retirement to Spain, full of riches and honours, the Crown once more recognised the claims of the Columbus family by sending Diego Colón out to Hispaniola as governor and viceroy. The new viceroy was a thoroughly Hispanicised Italian who had married into a great and ancient family. He brought with him a considerable retinue of both sexes and maintained a viceregal court whose elegance must have contrasted strangely with the squalid background of pioneering in the tropics. Despite this makeshift pomp, however, Diego Colón exercised much less personal power than Ovando. His authority was expressly confined to the islands; and during his government the foundations were laid of a whole system of courts and offices which was to limit the powers both of governors and of settlers in the future.

It was characteristic of Spanish ways of thought that the system of colonial government created in the second and third decades of the sixteenth century should be primarily judicial rather than administrative in character. Spain had carried over from the age of feudalism into the age of sovereignty the notion of jurisdiction as the essential function of authority. The king was still regarded primarily as a judge, an umpire. His authority was most directly and characteristically represented by the high courts of justice, and in the government of his dominions the school-trained lawyer was his most useful servant.

The professional lawyer was an admirable agent of centralised government. Though not always devoid of adventurous qualities, he had no excessive family pride, and as a rule no great ambition for military glory. His training gave him a deep respect for authority and a habit of careful attention to detail, while it discouraged any tendency towards rash or unauthorised action. A judge, moreover, representing the jurisdiction of the monarch, preserved a certain impersonality which helped him to control truculent *hidalgos*, who would have resented the authority of one of their own type. The *audiencias* of Valladolid, Galicia and Granada, courts of appeal representing the royal jurisdiction in their localities, had rendered valuable service in the unification of Spain under the Catholic monarchs. The conquest of the Indies represented to the legal mind an immense expansion of the area requiring unification. A direct branch of the royal jurisdiction was needed to control disorderly and avaricious colonial factions. The task was naturally entrusted to benches of professional judges.

The central Council of the Indies, established in 1511 as a permanent committee of the Council of Castile, and constituted as a separate organ of government in 1524, was a predominantly legal body. It combined, in the manner characteristic of Spanish institutions, the functions of a supreme court of appeal with those of an advisory council and a directive ministry for the supervision of colonial affairs. A corresponding institution on a smaller scale was established at the same time in the Indies. In 1511, after three successive governors had failed in the hopeless task of pleasing both missionaries and colonists, the Crown appointed an independent royal tribunal empowered to hear appeals from the decisions of the local magistrates, and in some cases of the governor himself. The court was modelled upon the *audiencias* of Spain, and may be regarded as the direct predecessor of the *audiencia* of Santo Domingo, formally established fifteen years later. Though the authority of Diego Colón did not extend to the mainland, the appellate jurisdiction of the *audiencia* did. In 1526 — the year of Diego Colón's death — the convention was established that the lawyer-president of the *audiencia* should also be governor and captain-general of Hispaniola. With him served — as judicial associates and as administrative advisers — the four judges (*oidores*) of the court, and the staff of lawyers — procurator-fiscal, advocates, notaries, clerks — which the cumbrous procedure of all Spanish courts made necessary. The services of such a tribunal, in checking the

c

ill-treatment of natives by the colonists, in keeping watch upon the activities of colonial governors, and in sending home reasonably impartial reports and recommendations, proved so valuable that the institution was quickly extended as more provinces were conquered. Ten *audiencias* were created in the sixteenth century, representing royal authority in the more important and populous centres throughout the Americas. The settlers, accustomed in the early years of conquest to a life of independent idleness, intrigue and rapine, found themselves confronted by active bodies of professionally trained judges, the colonial counterparts of the conscientious, scholarly, unbending men who were administering Castile. No doubt most *oidores* adapted themselves to colonial life, developed local contacts, demanded local (and illicit) perquisites; but they always represented peninsular ideas and interests, and their appointment created a tension which lasted throughout the colonial period, and burst into open rebellion in the nineteenth century.

One of the most urgent tasks of the young administration was to regulate the relations between the conquering Spaniards and the conquered Indians. In this, account had to be taken of an interested third party — the Church. The Spanish settlement was a spiritual as well as a military conquest, and the principal local opposition to the rule of swordsmen came from the soldiers of the Church — the friars of the missionary orders. The conversion which the missionaries sought to achieve was more than a mere outward conformity. It was necessarily associated with social organisation, and the policy of the orders necessarily interfered with the control of Indian labour upon which Spanish economic activity depended. The campaign against the reckless exploitation of the natives began with a Christmas sermon preached by Fray Antonio de Montesinos at Santo Domingo in 1511, which gave great offence to Spaniards in the island and caused a great stir in Spain. Montesinos was sent home by his fellow Dominicans to plead the cause of the Indians at Court, and after much deliberation the king's advisers produced the Laws of Burgos of 1512, the first European colonial code, which among a mass of detailed regulation enunciated three clear principles: the Indians were free men, not slaves; they were to be converted to Christianity by peaceful means, not by force; and they were to be made to work. The *repartimiento* or *encomienda*

system introduced by Columbus and regularised by Ovando
was to be continued, but the demands for labour and tribute
made upon Indians by Spaniards were to be limited, and the
encomenderos were to carry out their side of the bargain —
protection and religious instruction — and to observe a whole
series of rules designed to prevent ill-treatment. This definition
of native rights was, for the Dominican agitators, unsatisfactory,
and inadequate; but at least the Crown had admitted, by a formal
enactment, that the Indians had rights. The enslavement of
Indians was forbidden by law from then onwards, and the royal
conscience was not allowed to slumber. Montesinos, having
made his protest, relapsed into silence, so far as is known, but
other religious took up his work, urging better treatment and
greater liberty for Indians and closer control over the Spaniards.
Most prominent among these followers of Montesinos was the
great Dominican missionary and polemist Bartolomé de las
Casas, whose *Brief Relation of the Destruction of the Indies* is a
horrifying catalogue of atrocities perpetrated during his time in
Hispaniola. Las Casas devoted the rest of his long life to the
cause of Indian liberty, continually urging the Crown, in his
sermons and writings and by personal agitation at Court, to enact
more humane legislation and to make the *audiencias* enforce it.
He was himself appointed Protector of the Indians in 1516, and
over the next ten years sponsored a whole series of social experiments designed to show that free Indians could be induced, by
preaching and force of example, to form civilised Christian
communities, without compulsion or enslavement. The experiments merely demonstrated, in fact, that the Spanish settlers
could not live without Indian labour, or some substitute for it;
and that Indians would not work without coercion. The change
of policy inspired by Las Casas — though it bore striking fruit
on the mainland later — came too late to save the doomed races
of the Antilles.

Las Casas is sometimes accused of having suggested the sub-
stitution of African slaves for the dwindling Tainos. There is no
evidence for the accusation; but it is true that even those
Spaniards who insisted most strongly on the personal freedom
of the Indians saw nothing inconsistent in negro slavery. The
African, of course, made a better slave than the island Indian
because he was stronger, less primitive, and more adaptable; but

to the sixteenth-century mind the two cases were in all respects widely different. The objections to the enslavement of Indians were primarily on legal grounds. The Indians were the subjects of the King of Castile and were entitled to protection. Africans, on the other hand, were the subjects of independent kings. Europeans visited West Africa as traders, not as overlords. If the local rulers made war among themselves and sold their prisoners to slave dealers, that was not the fault of the King of Spain. The enslavement of prisoners of war was a normal proceeding in most parts of the world. In the Moorish wars and the constant fighting against the corsair towns on the Barbary coast prisoners were regularly enslaved on both sides, and all the naval powers of the Mediterranean employed slaves to row their galleys. The incidental suffering made little impression upon people accustomed to sudden death by violence or disease. The slave trade was carried on under Crown licence, and although some Dominicans had misgivings about it there was no serious opposition from the missionaries in general, or from government. The sixteenth century was not a tender-hearted age. In the West Indies the voices raised on behalf of the Indian, though loud, were largely ineffective. For the negro, no one spoke at all.

Consideration of the slave trade, and the official attitude towards it, leads naturally to the question of the regulation of trade in general. The Crown of Castile assumed as axiomatic its subjects' monopoly of trade and navigation in the Atlantic west of the 'line of demarcation', and its own right to draw a direct tribute from its American possessions. Both for the defence of monopoly and for the efficient collection of taxes and customs a tight regulation of transatlantic shipping was necessary. A subsidiary, but important, motive for regulation was the desire to prevent persons with Jewish or Muslim connections from going to the Indies, where they might cause considerable trouble both to the civil and ecclesiastical authorities. Muslim slaves from North Africa were particularly suspect. For these reasons trade to the Indies, almost from the beginning, was forced through a narrow bottle-neck — the harbour of Seville, seventy miles up the winding, muddy Guadalquivir. As early as 1503 a royal 'house of trade' — the *Casa de Contratación* — was established at Seville. It never actually traded, but developed as a government bureau for inspecting and licensing ships, cargoes, merchants, passengers and crews passing to and from the Indies. The *Casa* collected duties and licence fees and enforced regulations for the conduct of trade. It also contained within itself a court for the settlement of maritime disputes and a hydrographical department for the construction of charts and the training of navigators.

In the Indies there was no separate organisation for the regulation of trade, and in the early days none was needed. The royal treasury officials in the colonial capitals collected duty on incoming commodities, such as salt, which were the subject of Crown monopolies, and collected and despatched the Crown royalty on precious metals. There were no other receipts of importance; tithes were mostly devoted to ecclesiastical purposes in the islands, sales tax was a much later introduction, and such tribute as the island Indians could pay was not worth collecting. Santo Domingo was the western terminus of transatlantic trade; goods and passengers for the other islands made their way from there by means of local shipping.

So long as Spanish settlements in the New World were chiefly concentrated in the West Indian islands their trade could be concentrated in the port of Seville without hardship, since its total volume was small. The preservation of the Castilian monopoly presented no great problem. Occasional cargoes of hides and sugar were not sufficiently valuable to tempt interlopers to cross the Atlantic; the only danger lay in sporadic acts of piracy in European waters. The islands themselves were protected from foreign attack by their remoteness. The conquests of Mexico and, later, Peru, however, created a different situation. An insistent market soon grew up in the mainland provinces for flour, oil, wine, manufactured goods, and slaves. The volume of shipping increased rapidly, and the port of Seville could neither adequately supply the demand nor conveniently handle the shipping. The value of shipments also increased; after the discovery of the great silver-mines, eastbound cargoes contained a large and ever-growing proportion of specie. All this shipping, with its precious cargoes, had to pass through the West Indies. The legal bottle-neck at Seville was matched by a geographical bottle-neck in the West Indies, for the Florida Channel was the only convenient exit from the

Gulf of Mexico. Ports such as Santo Domingo, on the south coast of the island chain, lost in commercial importance, while Havana, commanding the western approach to the Florida Channel, began to take its place as the chief port of call. Santo Domingo remained an important administrative centre — it had over a thousand householders in 1540 — and ships from the Isthmus continued to call there until the fifteen-sixties, when they shifted to Havana; but shipping from Mexico had used Havana from the beginning.

The danger in this change of commercial routes lay in the fact that the north coast had never been effectively settled. Havana, in the first half of the sixteenth century, was a small and squalid settlement, with an almost unpeopled hinterland. Its *vecinos* produced beef and bacon for sale to passing ships, and for export to the mainland. It had a good natural harbour, and sprang into activity whenever a ship put in; but it was un-defended, and when defences began to be built in 1540 there were not enough people in the district to man them. Havana could offer little protection to the increasing volume of shipping which called on passage to Spain.

Spanish shipping to and from America in the middle decades of the sixteenth century was thus both valuable and vulnerable. It offered great temptations to interlopers and pirates in time of peace, and to all enemies of Spain in time of war. Its concentration in narrow but largely undefended channels made it easy to intercept. An early indication of what Spaniards could expect was given in 1523, when part of the loot sent by Cortés from Mexico to Charles V was captured off the Azores by the French privateer Jean Fleury. The value of this capture astonished Europe and concentrated envious attention upon the Spanish monopoly. The West Indian islands, relatively poor in themselves, soon began to attract the interest of foreigners, either as possible entrepôts for a smuggling trade with the Spanish empire, or as vantage points for attacks on Spanish shipping. To the Spanish government, on the other hand, they became bastions to be fortified and held at all cost.

CHAPTER III

THE CHALLENGE TO SPAIN

FOR THE FIRST FORTY years of their existence the Spanish settlements in the West Indies remained unmolested by other Europeans, chiefly because of their remoteness and their poverty. From the 'thirties of the sixteenth century, however, as their harbours began to handle an increasing volume of Spanish shipping en route to the mainland, and to supply goods and services which earned mainland silver, they began to attract foreign attention and to suffer increasingly from foreign interference. This interference took two distinct forms. One form was smuggling — illicit but peaceful trading in slaves and European goods in exchange for sugar, hides and silver. The other consisted in armed raids on harbours and shipping, carried out by enemy ships in time of war, but also to some extent in peace-time, either by professional pirates or by vessels which were neither warships nor pirates, but unauthorised, unavowed privateers whom the Spaniards called *cosarios*.

To the Spanish government these distinctions were unimportant. Foreign ships, whether pirates, smugglers or men-of-war, in war or in peace, were all unwelcome in the Indies and were all to be treated as enemies and seized whenever possible. To the settlers, on the other hand, the distinctions were vitally important. Throughout most of the sixteenth century the inhabitants of the West Indian ports lived in constant anxiety, never knowing, when a strange sail appeared, whether it was to be welcomed officially as a Spaniard, received discreetly as a foreign trader, or fired upon as a raider. On the whole the West Indians welcomed smugglers, and the cheap goods which smugglers brought; while they resented the high prices charged by the Seville monopolists. They both feared and resented the constant outbreaks of war in Europe, which loosed fleets of privateers upon the West Indies. They deplored a naval policy which was largely ineffective against raiders, but which treated peaceful smugglers as if they were raiders, and so encouraged them to go armed and take to raiding. Even at this early date, therefore, there appeared a conflict of commercial interests between settlers and home government which was to remain characteristic of the West Indies throughout their history as European colonies.

Down to 1580 the principal smugglers were Portuguese and the most important contraband trade was in African slaves. From 1532 (when the four-year contract given by Charles V to the firm of Ehinger expired) down to 1580 the supply of slaves to the West Indies was officially managed by Spanish dealers who held licences from the Crown, each licence permitting the import of a stated number of slaves. The dealers were not, in fact, all Spaniards. Some were Flemish or Portuguese sub-contractors; but the essential thing was the possession of a Spanish licence. The dealers usually bought their slaves from Portuguese middle-men, who got them from the Portuguese-owned 'factories' and barracoons on the Guinea coast. Individual settlements in the West Indies habitually entered into contracts with licensed dealers for the supply of cargoes of slaves at a flat rate per head, the slaves being retailed on arrival to planters by the local officials. So many licences were issued that checking was difficult and fraud comparatively easy, especially as most local officials in the Indies connived at it. Slaves on passage, in those days of rudimentary medical and hygienic knowledge, formed a highly perishable cargo, and common sense as well as desire for profit recommended a direct voyage, without the delays imposed by Spanish commercial regulation. Despite the severe penalties imposed for such evasions, many Portuguese slavers carried shipments from Guinea to the West Indies without bothering to secure licences. These unlicensed slaves were unloaded in the smaller harbours of the islands, and naturally sold cheaper than the licensed imports. Isabela, Columbus's early foundation on the north coast of Hispaniola, was a favourite and characteristic haunt of smugglers. The place had dwindled to a mere hamlet, but behind it lay a fertile region of ranches and sugar plantations known then as La Vega, where slaves were in high demand and where return cargoes of sugar and hides could be obtained. The area was separated from Santo Domingo

by a wide stretch of rough country, and the danger of official
interference was very small. The activities of smugglers, by
their nature, are not officially recorded so long as they are
successful, so that evidence is scanty; but there is little doubt
that considerable numbers of slaves entered the West Indies by
such channels; and with the slaves came cargoes of European
goods — wine, oil, tools, cloth, paper, and so on — from Tene-
riffe, Las Palmas, or Lisbon itself.

These activities were of benefit to the West Indian settlers,
and the people engaged in them were mostly Portuguese, who,
though they might break the law, would not resort to arms against
their best customers; or else Germans or Flemings, who, though
not Castilians, were still subjects of the emperor and unlikely
to engage in piracy against his colonies. The settlers could deal
with them without running any danger other than the wrath of
their own government. A very different situation arose, however, when, in the fifteen-thirties, French ships began to make
voyages to the Caribbean. Some of them were traders and
smugglers like the Portuguese; but France and Spain were intermittently at war throughout Charles V's reign, and many French
privateers cruised the Caribbean in search of plunder rather than
of trading profit. Their first appearance in serious numbers was
in 1536, and was caused by two European events — a fresh outbreak of Franco-Spanish hostilities, and a defensive alliance
between France and Portugal. This was the Treaty of Lyon,
whereby the French government undertook to forbid its subjects
to attack Portuguese shipping or to poach upon Portuguese trade
preserves in Africa. Accordingly, instead of cruising off the
Azores to intercept Portuguese Indiamen, the more enterprising
French privateers removed to the Bahamas to cruise against
Spanish shipping. The myriad cays of the Bahamas were well
suited to the purposes of piracy; for two hundred years they
were to harbour fast, predatory craft, lying in wait for heavily
laden ships beating out through the Florida Channel. The
French took a number of prizes in the winter of 1536, enough
to encourage Jean Ango, the great shipping magnate of Dieppe,
to organise and finance a much bigger enterprise: an attack on
an armed fleet which was known to be returning to Spain from
the Isthmus carrying the spoils of the conquest of Peru. The
Spanish fleet was commanded by the redoubtable Blasco Núñez

Vela, later viceroy and captain-general of Peru. Ango had been the backer, fourteen years before, of Jean Fleury, who had captured part of Cortés' loot from Mexico. Ango's people were successful again. They captured nine Spanish ships out of a total sailing of twenty-odd, and sacked or held to ransom a number of the smaller ports of Hispaniola, including Yaguana, modern Port-au-Prince. They did not venture to attack Santo Domingo; and their attempt against Santiago, the capital of Cuba, was beaten off.

The truce of Nice in 1538 brought a respite from organised fighting; and when in 1542 war broke out again, the Spanish government was ready with a plan, the same plan that every beleaguered maritime power has used to protect its shipping against attack. All shipping to the Indies was to be sent by pre-arranged routes under convoy, and the principal harbours were to be fortified. From 1543 the long conflict between Spain and the interlopers in the West Indies took on its characteristic form: on the one side a defensive policy relying upon weight and strength, on the other a policy of attack relying upon manœuvrability and speed. The conflict revealed yet another divergence of interest between the settlers and the home government; the authorities in Spain were chiefly concerned with the safe passage of the silver fleets, the settlers with the protection of their homes and harbours and with the safety of the local shipping among the islands and to the mainland. The generals of the fleets demanded heavier escorts and the support of cruiser squadrons; the colonial governors and *cabildos* begged the Crown for stronger fortifications and soldiers to man them. In the event, the fleets were better protected than the port towns, and the West Indians suffered most in the long series of Caribbean encounters. In the war of 1542-44 the convoys were well supported by frigates, which in the spring of 1543 succeeded temporarily in clearing the route of the silver ships through the islands; but the privateers merely transferred their activities to the coast of Venezuela, and later, when the fleets had passed and the war-ships were withdrawn, they returned to cruise for prizes in the Florida Channel and Mona and Windward Passages, so that Santo Domingo, Santiago and Havana were again put in constant fear of attack until the Treaty of Crespy in 1544 again gave some relief. By that treaty Francis I formally recognised the Spanish monopoly of Caribbean settlement and trade; but again, in 1552, a fresh war gave occasion for Caribbean raiding, and this time the privateers deliberately aimed their attacks at the principal harbours of the West Indies.

Havana was the pivot of the Spanish convoy system, at least for the homeward passage which chiefly interested the enemy. The system was not worked out in all its details until the fifteen-sixties, but the general idea remained the same from 1543. The fleet from the Isthmus started early in the year. It first put into Cartagena, where it remained for a week or so and then steered north-west — usually a comfortable reach with the wind on the starboard beam — until it could round Cape San Antonio and put into Havana. Meanwhile the Mexico *flota*, having waited until the 'norther' season was over, in April or May made its tedious three-week beat against the trade wind from Vera Cruz. From Havana the two fleets sailed in company for Spain in the course of the summer. Annual sailings out and home were intended, but not always achieved. While assembling in Havana harbour the ships refitted and provisioned for their Atlantic passage. During their stay the town was naturally crowded and full of activity, and considerable sums of money were spent — or lost in gaming — in a place which then had very little to offer in return. There was no regular water supply; fresh water was lightered from the Almendares river, just west of the town. There was little accommodation, and only a handful of the houses were built of stone. There was little government — only a *cabildo* of two magistrates and four *regidores*, until in 1550 the governor, Angulo, removed to Havana because — so they said in Santiago — he had private business interests there. Probably he had; one of his first acts was to build the first public slaughter-house in Havana — a matter of some importance for a town which lived largely by selling salt or dried meat to ships — and presumably the governor's cattle were to be slaughtered there, in the normal way of public life in the Indies. The change of capital was obviously sensible from a strategic point of view, and the Crown eventually approved it, despite bitter protests from the older and larger settlement. It was one more victory for general imperial considerations over local West Indian interests.

The facilities and attractions of Havana, then, in the early years of the convoy system were quite inadequate for the functions which trade and geography thrust upon the place. Its defences were equally inadequate, as events were soon to demonstrate. In 1553 François Le Clerc, whom the Spaniards called *Pie de Palo* — Timberleg — crossed the Atlantic with a fleet of ten French warships and began systematically to pillage and burn the port towns of the West Indies. In 1554 he took Santiago — the strongest settlement so far attempted by the French — and drove its inhabitants inland to comparative safety at Bayamo. In the following summer his lieutenant Jacques Sores, with two ships, captured Havana and razed it to the ground.

Sores' exploit naturally caused a great stir in Spain, and panic throughout the Indies. In France it gave rise to the first of a long series of comprehensive but abortive schemes for a large-scale naval expedition, which was to sack Santo Domingo, sail on to the Isthmus, seize Panama and capture the South Sea fleet, then intercept the Mexican *flota*, and return home by the Florida Channel. Probably Coligny was the author of this plan to ruin the war potential of Spain; Drake, Piet Heyn and Cromwell were all to entertain the same idea in later years, but none of them ever succeeded in carrying the whole programme into effect. For Spaniards, the sack of Havana pointed a more immediate and practical lesson. No one reading the records, then or now, could fail to be struck by the contrast between the importance of the event and the scale of the operation. Sores had anchored in the San Lázaro inlet, and landed his assault party in boats for an overland attack, thus outflanking the defences, such as they were. We do not know how many men were with him; but they cannot have been more than a hundred or so, and the Spaniards could only muster thirty-five, of whom nine were mounted. There were no Spanish ships in the area. The land defences consisted of a look-out post on the headland where the Morro now stands, and a small square fort on gently rising ground on the edge of the settlement, probably near the site of the present Foreign Office. This fort had been built on contract, with Crown money, by Juan de Lobera, who was a local rancher and a *regidor*. When the fort was complete Lobera had got himself appointed *alcaide* — commandant — at an annual salary, and had taken up rent-free residence inside. Those who disliked him insinuated that the place was designed for comfort rather than defence. It mounted six small guns, chiefly for the defence of the harbour. The guns, incidentally, were bronze pieces cast in Seville, using samples of Cuban copper sent from the Cobre mines near Santiago, in which Lobera had an interest. The only other weapons in the fort, apart from the defenders' own swords, were four crossbows. To do him justice, Lobera resisted for some hours, until the French set fire to the doors of the fort and smoked him out. He then surrendered, and soon reached agreement with Sores on the amount of his personal ransom. After his surrender the governor, who had withdrawn inland with most of the population, returned with such fighting men as he could muster to make a counter-attack which failed. Negotiations for ransom of the town ensued; but Sores refused the thousand *pesos* or so which were all the townspeople could offer, set fire to the buildings, and withdrew after a stay of nearly three weeks.

The capture of Havana, then, was a trifling operation in itself; but its details are of interest because they are typical of hundreds of similar episodes through a century and a half of West Indian history. Even the governor's march inland, an act not of cowardice but of common sense, was part of the normal pattern. Often the best defence of more or less unfortified settlements was an orderly withdrawal of the settlers, with their families, their cattle and their movable valuables, to hiding-places in the bush, from which ransom negotiations could be undertaken. The enemy, anxious to be gone, would usually accept a reasonable cash offer. Havana, however, had become too important a place to be 'defended' in this passive way; and Santo Domingo, Cartagena or Vera Cruz might any day suffer the fate which had befallen Havana. It is true that the Treaty of Câteau-Cambrésis in 1559 settled, mostly in favour of Spain, the questions over which the two powers had officially been fighting; but the Spaniards could not be sure that peace would endure for long, or that the French government would be able, or even willing, to control such of its privateer captains as chose to take to piracy on their own account. Imperial safety, therefore, demanded not only powerful escorts for the fleets but also powerful defences for the chief harbours and towns of the West Indies, and mobile cruiser squadrons, permanently based there, which could keep the sea-lanes clear throughout the year. Co-ordination of the land and sea defences was urgently necessary, and could be achieved only by unification of command in the West Indies. The establishment of such a unified command was entrusted, in the fifteen-sixties, to Pedro Menéndez de Avilés, one of the ablest sea.commanders of his time.

Before Menéndez took up his task in the West Indies, however, matters took a new turn, due to the arrival on the scene of a new group of interlopers, the English, led initially by the versatile and ingenious John Hawkins. Hawkins organised four trading voyages to the Caribbean between 1562 and 1568, and commanded three of them himself. He carried cloth and general merchandise from England, and slaves, whom he purchased directly from dealers on the West African coast. He proposed to sell his goods and slaves to Spanish settlers in the Caribbean, and to secure cargoes of sugar, hides and silver for the return voyage to England. Hawkins's plan thus anticipated the triangular voyage of later times, and defied the monopolistic regulations both of Portugal and of Spain. He did not, however, intend mere tip-and-run smuggling; still less, open piracy. He seems to have entertained serious hopes of securing licences from Spain which would legitimise his activities. England and Spain were at peace, and traditionally friendly. Hawkins was known in Seville and had friends and business correspondents there. He was prepared to pay all lawful dues; and in return for a licence to trade he offered his services to the Spanish Crown as a privateer, to assist in clearing pirates and foreign smugglers from West Indian waters. In particular, he appreciated the strategic importance of the Florida Channel and knew that the French were trying to establish a settlement on the coast of Florida, under René de Laudonnière, which could become very dangerous to Spanish shipping. Hawkins hoped to demonstrate the value of his services by destroying this colony at the beginning of its career.

Hawkins's plan failed completely in its larger aspect, though as business ventures his first two voyages were highly successful. He was right in assuming that Spanish planters and minor government officials would be glad to do business with him. On the first voyage — the only one to the islands — he passed along the north coast of Hispaniola, sold his slaves at Isabela, Puerto Plata and Monte Christi, paid the duty on them, and secured certificates of good conduct from the local officials. Prudently he kept well away from Santo Domingo. The other voyages were to mainland ports where the officials proved less amenable and had to be threatened before they would trade. On the last homeward trip Hawkins was driven by continued bad weather into the Gulf of Mexico and obliged to seek shelter at San Juan de Ulúa, the port of Vera Cruz. Here he was caught by the *flota* arriving from Spain. Most of his fleet was destroyed in the ensuing battle, and he himself eventually reached England in January 1569 after great hardships, with only fifteen surviving companions. The whole episode made clear that the Spanish government would tolerate no interlopers of any kind in American waters; any foreigner was a pirate and would be treated as such if caught. Foreign traders in the West Indies, therefore, must go secretly or go well armed. Meanwhile — and this may have been one of the reasons for Hawkins's failure — Admiral Menéndez's dispositions in the West Indies showed that the Spaniards could do for themselves what they refused to allow Hawkins to do for them.

Pedro Menéndez de Avilés served his king in high naval commands for nearly twenty years. For the greater part of that period Spain was nominally at peace with other European powers; though by that time what passed for peace in the West Indies demanded the services of a great admiral. No fair estimate can be formed of his skill as a naval tactician because he was never called on to command a fleet in any large-scale action against an adversary worthy of his steel. His dispositions in the West Indies, however, reveal him as a strategist of the first order, with a rare gift for appreciating a situation as a whole and for reconciling immediate necessities with the demands of long-term planning. He was remarkably successful in explaining naval needs to landsmen in high office, so that he enjoyed — and deserved — the confidence and support of Philip II throughout his career of command. He was a good, though exacting, disciplinarian; and as a naval administrator he was unsurpassed in the sixteenth century. His views on strategy and logistics had, curiously, something in common with those of Hawkins — who, at one stage in his career, was a very capable director of the queen's dockyards. Menéndez's appreciation of the West Indian situation resembled Hawkins's, though his ideas on remedial action were more comprehensive in their naval aspects, and naturally less flexible on their political side. To complete a sketch of a forceful and somewhat sombre character, Menéndez was honest, fearless, entirely loyal, and ruthlessly impatient of lesser men.

Menéndez's first important appointment was the command of the escort of the homeward-bound fleet of 1555-56. In 1561 he was appointed captain-general of the *Armada de la Carrera de Indias*, and in that capacity he took out and back, in 1562, the largest fleet which up till then had left Spain — forty-nine sail, of which six were men-of-war. During the next two years he was engaged in advising the Crown upon the regulations for the Indies trade, which were promulgated between 1564 and 1566. His proposals fell under three main heads: all sailings between Spain and the Indies were to be in convoy, except for urgent sailings of fast and well-armed ships which might be made licensed exceptions; *armadillas* — cruiser squadrons — were to be permanently based in the West Indies to seek out and attack corsairs upon their arrival in the area and to patrol the main trade routes all the year round; the principal harbours were to be strongly fortified and provided with regular garrisons. The most important harbours were Cartagena, guarding the eastern approach to the Isthmus; Santo Domingo, the administrative centre of the islands; Santiago; San Juan del Puerto Rico; and, most important of all, Havana. Havana was to be made, as nearly as possible, an impregnable fortress, to provide a safe place of assembly for all homeward-bound convoys. To complete the defence and control of the Florida Channel, another fortified base was to be constructed opposite Havana, on the coast of Florida itself. Menéndez made this suggestion early in the discussions, in anticipation of French attempts at occupation of that area; the actual settlement under Laudonnière naturally gave added force to his arguments. Philip II and the Council of the Indies accepted his comprehensive and very expensive plans in their entirety; and to establish the unity of command needed to carry them out Menéndez was made *adelantado* of Florida in 1565, and governor of Cuba in 1567.

The years which Menéndez spent in the West Indies were years of intense activity and, on the whole, conspicuous successes; for to achieve any co-ordinated defence at all at that time was a success. Although internecine religious war had removed

France temporarily from the international arena, French corsairs were still active on their own account; and the revolt of the Netherlands and war with England were soon to bring the war-ships and privateers of the two strongest North Atlantic maritime powers to the West Indies in formidable strength. Menéndez shared with Drake and Nelson the strategic genius that treats all seas as one. His West Indian dispositions were only part of an over-all plan, in which the long-term remedy for the menace of Caribbean privateering was a Spanish base in the Scilly Isles — a bold and brilliant anticipation of eighteenth-century strategic ideas. He was not allowed time to create the admiralty organi-sation which these plans required, for he died in 1574, in one of those swift epidemics that often ravaged the fleets of his time. Nevertheless, his work, in fortifying bases and drilling and organising the transatlantic convoys, was carried on by a series of able and energetic successors, and enabled the Spanish colonies to survive intact, their communications with Spain unbroken, through a long and wasting naval war. For sixty years the treasure fleets reached Spain safely and regularly, losing a few stragglers now and then, but never — until Piet Heyn's great exploit in 1627 — losing the major part of a shipment. From the point of view of peninsular Spain, Admiral Menéndez did all that could be expected of a master of his trade.

From a strictly West Indian point of view Menéndez was less obviously successful, because the islands were, in his mind, of secondary importance. He made of Havana an almost impreg-nable fortress, safe against enemy attack for over two hundred years, with a dockyard capable of building efficient light warships from local timber and of refitting any class of ship. He destroyed the French settlement in Florida and built a Spanish fort in its place. Santo Domingo and Santiago, on the other hand, though much more important as local centres of population, received relatively slight additions to their fortifications, sufficient to stand off casual raids, but not to face attack by organised fleets. Similarly, in operating against corsairs in the Caribbean, Menéndez and his successors were compelled by war and financial shortage to concentrate on the immediate problem of getting the *flotas* through, and to postpone the secondary task of protecting local shipping throughout the year. The 'Wind-ward Squadrons', based on Cartagena and Santo Domingo, whose establishment Menéndez had advocated almost from the beginning, were not commissioned until 1582, eight years after his death. Light oared vessels were employed in this service, and proved very effective; but the expense of keeping the squadrons permanently in commission was very great, and their effectiveness was frequently impaired by shortage of funds for their maintenance.

Menéndez's whole policy, the very nature of his appointment, emphasised the decline of the island settlements in relation to the mainland, and their relegation to the position of mere ports of call. In Cuba Menéndez was heartily disliked. He sternly refused to allow settlers in Cuba to leave for the mainland: yet — so they complained — he did nothing for them in Cuba. His fortifications at Havana, his dockyard developments and ship-building activities, meant little or nothing to planters whose estates were mostly at the other end of the island. His troops — the few hundred men who formed the garrison at Havana — were a constant source of dispute: for the local people wanted them under local command and stationed at Santiago. Menéndez's appointment as governor and *adelantado* was a high-handed remedy for his bad relations with local governors and *cabildos*, who neither liked nor understood his policy, and obstructed him whenever they could. It was idle, of course, for small and relatively poor island settlements to urge their own local interests against the interests of Old and New Spain represented by a commander-in-chief of Menéndez's ability and vigour; especially since the works which he initiated were not paid for by the islanders. Cuba at this time contributed practically nothing to the royal treasury, and Hispaniola relatively little. The great works at Havana were paid for by *situados* from New Spain — subsidies sent by royal order from one provincial treasury to another. The West Indians had no control over the spending of this money, which was intended chiefly to protect the fleets. Despite Menéndez's vigour and success, therefore, despite the fifty-odd corsair ships which he captured during his career, the minor harbours of the West Indies were never safe from raiding. Even the principal cities, though safe enough against mere pirates, were still vulnerable to attack by organised fleets in time of war. Their situation grew worse as relations with England worsened, as religious bitterness came to reinforce the rapacity of the corsairs, and as that other naval genius, Francis Drake, was loosed upon the Indies in independent command of voyages of reprisal.

The place of Drake in the history of the West Indies is hard to assess in precise terms. He became the central figure in the attack upon the Spanish Indies, as Menéndez was the central figure of their defence. He personified in his day, and afterwards, the maritime genius and the Protestant religion of his countrymen. He created the legend of the bold corsair and the rich, defenceless Spaniard, which was to affect English policy in the Caribbean for many generations. He was the hero and the model of a host of poor gentlemen in England, small landlords who had been driven by inflation and social change to take to privateering, to 'get a ship and judiciously manage her'. For Spaniards, 'El Draque' was a name to frighten children. In sober fact, Drake evolved a coherent strategic West Indian plan in place of a series of small and uncoordinated raids; he carried his plan into effect with great, though not complete, success; he did great damage, acquired great booty and seriously weakened the fighting power of Spain, without, however, breaking the Spanish monopoly of territorial possession in the Caribbean.

Drake began his acquaintance with the West Indies as an illicit trader; he was with Hawkins at San Juan de Ulúa, and in 1570 he went out again with two small ships taking cargoes of slaves to the islands and returning with hides and silver. On this voyage, and on a subsequent one in 1571, Drake also carried out a reconnaissance of the shores of the Isthmus and established contact with local wild Indians and with groups of *cimarrones* — 'maroon' or runaway slaves. The illicit trader was becoming perforce a more or less authorised privateer, and the savage alliances he made were to become a traditional part of English policy. In 1572, the year of the expulsion of the Spanish ambassador from England, Drake sailed on his first privateering raid, the famous voyage on which, with two small ships and seventy-odd men, he took Nombre de Dios by surprise and captured three mule-trains crossing the Isthmus loaded with treasure from Peru. The booty was enough to make every man in Drake's company rich for life. It arrived in Plymouth in 1573, the same year that Menéndez laid his plan for a Scilly Island base before Philip II.

In 1574 — the year of Menéndez's death — the English and Spanish governments patched up a grudging reconciliation. English captains continued to visit the Caribbean, trading with the smaller settlements and with the maroons, cruising with letters of reprisal, or making minor raids. None of them achieved successes comparable with Drake's. Their government left them to fend for themselves as pirates, and a number of them — notably Drake's friend John Oxenham — were caught and hanged by the Spaniards. Menéndez had succeeded, if not in making the Caribbean a Spanish lake, at least in making it a dangerous cruising-ground for mere raiders. Drake, who never regarded himself — nor was regarded, even by his enemies — as a pirate, kept away from the West Indies in those years. His great voyage of circumnavigation of 1577–80 had only an in-direct bearing on West Indian affairs. He did not appear again in the Caribbean until 1585, when war between England and Spain was already certain.

Drake's 'Indies voyage' of 1585 was no mere raid, but a full-scale naval operation carried out by a fleet of more than twenty sail. The plan was similar to that which the French had pro-jected thirty years before, but never put into effect. It included, first, an attack on Santo Domingo and on the port towns of Tierra Firme, in particular Cartagena; then a land attack on Nombre de Dios and Panama in conjunction with the maroons, in order to control both ends of the land route across the Isthmus; and finally the capture of Havana. Drake hoped to hold both Havana and Cartagena with permanent English garri-sons. Success would break up the whole communication and supply system of the Spanish Indies. It would deny to Spain, for years, perhaps permanently, the means of making war in Europe, and would throw the Indies open to English exploita-tion. The conception of such a plan is evidence, already by the end of the sixteenth century, of the importance of the West Indies in the international rivalries of Europe. Over and over again, for more than two hundred years, English, Dutch and French admirals and statesmen mounted plans similar, in whole or in part, to that of Drake. Some achieved partial and temporary success, as Drake did; but the Caribbean proved too big, the islands too scattered and too wild to be mastered in a single campaign. The commander of a large-scale amphibious operation, moreover, faced more serious health difficulties than the tip-and-run raiders of earlier times, for his men had to live and fight ashore in large numbers for a considerable length of time. Armies and navies, coming fresh from Europe, wasted away in the fearful mortality of tropical campaigning. The Spaniards, the mosquitoes and the climate worked together to defeat every attempt.

Santo Domingo, the administrative capital for the West Indies and Tierra Firme, was one of the largest cities in the Spanish empire, impressively laid out with stone buildings and spacious streets and plazas. It was fortified, and had a small garrison of trained soldiers. Its capture was by far the most ambitious feat yet undertaken by an English commander in the West Indies. Drake employed tactics similar to those used earlier by Sores at Havana, but with a force more than ten times the size of that of Sores. A successful surprise attack by a party landed some miles down the coast synchronised with the frontal assault upon the harbour by the main body of the fleet. Parties of maroons from the mountains helped the attackers. Once inside the walls Drake's people entrenched themselves in the main plaza and opened negotiations for the ransom of the city. The bargaining lasted over a month, during which time the invaders carried out a systematic programme of looting and destruction in order to hasten the governor's decision. The plunder and ransom were both disappointing; but the damage to the prosperity of the city was heavy and permanent. All the principal buildings were gutted, the guns and stores of the fort taken away, and the ships of the island guard squadron burned in the harbour.

Drake's next major objective, Cartagena, was a much smaller town than Santo Domingo, but strategically much more important, and likely to be a richer prize, for it was a collecting depot for goods and treasure to be loaded for Spain. It was well defended, and Drake's attack, in the teeth of brave and well-organised resistance, was perhaps the most brilliant of all his amphibious operations, involving intricate and dangerous pilotage and synchronised landings through heavy surf. As at Santo Domingo, he forced a way to the centre of the town, dug himself in in the plaza, and systematically destroyed buildings while awaiting the result of ransom negotiations. Again the loot, though considerable, was disappointing, because most of the valuables in the city had been sent inland before the fighting began. The negotiations lasted for six weeks, and at the end of that time the English forces were reduced by casualties and sickness from their original number of 2,300 to about 800 fit men. There could now be no question of holding Cartagena with an English garrison. Drake decided to abandon his attempt on the Isthmus, and to make for the Cayman Islands and thence for Cape San Antonio, where, with his ships refitted and his men refreshed, he hoped to intercept the *flota* from New Spain. The weather in May was bad, however, and the *flota* slipped through unmolested. Judging Havana too strong to be attacked, Drake sailed for home in June 1586, only pausing to destroy the fortifications which were being built at St. Augustine, on the site of the ill-fated French settlement in Florida.

The 'Indies voyage', though it failed in its larger aims, did great material damage to Spanish possessions and even greater damage to Spanish prestige. The Spanish authorities did not fail to note the lessons of their defeats. They concluded that Menéndez's appreciation of the West Indian position had been accurate, but that his policy had not been pursued vigorously enough. They set to work to remedy the weaknesses of his system; and in spite of the defeats which they suffered in their operations against England in Europe, they achieved remarkable success in the Caribbean. In the fifteen-nineties the defence forces of the Indies were all greatly strengthened by both land and by sea, despite the urgent need for ships and troops in Europe. A beginning was made by Antoneli, the best military engineer of his day, on the immense fortifications of Puerto Rico, the windward bastion of Caribbean defence — not so much because of the direct importance of the place to the Spaniards as because of the vital necessity of denying its use to Spain's enemies. At the same time, communications between the Caribbean bases were greatly improved by the provision of fast despatch boats. When in 1595 another great fleet left England, under the joint command of Drake and Hawkins, on what was to be for both their last Indies campaign, they found the Spaniards ready and able to resist. The English were defeated at San Juan del Puerto Rico (though, curiously enough, a less able leader, Cumberland, succeeded in taking the place — but not in holding it — three years later). They abandoned their project for a second attack on Cartagena. On the Isthmus — where the Spaniards had abandoned Nombre de Dios for the more defensible harbour of Puerto Bello — a picked party of 750 men set out overland for Panama, but were driven back to their boats by a combination of heavy rains and Spanish ambushes. After Drake's death off the coast of Veragua, Sir Thomas Baskerville, his successor in the command, was intercepted in the Florida Channel by a powerful fleet under Pedro Menéndez Márquez and had to fight his way out in a running battle, the first naval action between regular fleets to be fought in the West Indies. The action was inconclusive; but it cleared the Caribbean of the invaders at a time when Spain was suffering heavy defeats in Europe and could not have spared ships or men to reinforce the West Indies.

The attempts made by the French and the English in the sixteenth century to break the Spanish monopoly of trade and territorial power in the West Indies were thus, on the whole, failures; or, at least, their successes were only temporary. Sporadic raiding continued, and an extensive but still risky smuggling trade had developed; but Spain, exhausted as she was, lacking the men, the ships and the money to back her vast responsibilities and claims, still would not consider the open admission of foreign traders to her Caribbean preserves. In 1596, at the Treaty of The Hague, France under Henry of Navarre, England and the Netherlands formed an alliance against Spain which seemed strong enough to dismember the Spanish empire; and a joint English and Dutch fleet promptly destroyed a whole American convoy lying in Cadiz harbour, thus stopping communication between Spain and the Indies for nearly two years. The alliance failed to fulfil its promise, however; the French backed out and made their peace separately in the Treaty of Vervins in 1598. According to later accounts, Henry IV tried to secure a share of the American trade in this treaty. There is no contemporary evidence of these attempts; if made at all, they were unsuccessful, for the treaty is silent on the subject. The English and Dutch fought on; but in 1604, the pacific James I having succeeded Elizabeth, England also made a separate peace — the Treaty of London. In the negotiations for this treaty, however, a new and important principle was put forward. James announced that he was prepared to respect Spanish monopolistic claims in all territories effectively occupied by Spain, but that he recognised no Spanish rights in unoccupied parts of America. This contravened the basic assumption of Spanish imperialism in the Indies, and it was only after considerable haggling that the Spaniards agreed to a silence which their enemies might interpret as consent. In the Truce of Antwerp of 1609, which ended for twelve years the war between the Netherlands and Spain, and which recognised the Dutch as an independent nation, the same principle was embodied in a formal, if ambiguous, clause. So at the outset of their independent existence the Dutch gave notice of the role they were to play in West Indian history. Their West India Company was to be the foster-parent of the French and British empires in their West Indian aspect.

The Spanish attack on Saint Kitts, from the painting by Eugenio Caxes
in the Prado

CHAPTER IV

THE SETTLEMENT OF THE OUTER ISLANDS

AT THE END OF the sixteenth century, as at the beginning, the only settled colonies in the West Indies were those of Spain. No other European nation had achieved anything, or indeed seriously contemplated anything worth achieving, in the way of permanent settlement. In all successful colonisation two sets of factors are necessary for success: the private, spontaneous, largely economic urges; and the directing, protecting, sometimes limiting policy of government. The two are equally essential; without the one the other can accomplish nothing. Neither was present in sufficient strength, either in France or in England, in the sixteenth century. Patrons, prospectors, merchants, emigrants, alike failed to see their interest in colonial ventures overseas. It is true that in England a land-labour problem existed and was growing more acute; but homestead emigrants found an outlet in Ireland rather than in the Americas. The West Indies certainly attracted adventurers; but they found scope for their activity in smuggling and raiding rather than in settling, and individual adventures lapsed easily and naturally into something closely akin to piracy. The hope of booty was high enough to cause a lack of capital for more constructive ventures, and the outcome was further to handicap the settler and the merchant by making them liable for the raids of the privateers. At the same time a long-term constructive policy of settlement appeared unattractive to governments when compared with the quicker returns and greater dividends to be gained by raids on Spain and the Spanish colonies. Governmental support and organisation, therefore, never advanced in the sixteenth century beyond the primitive urge to oppose Spain wherever she claimed to rule. Colonies and settlements were merely flanking movements in the attack on Spain, of secondary interest. In addition, settlement anywhere in the Caribbean was still, at the end of the sixteenth century, a dangerous proposition, in which investors might lose their capital, and settlers their lives or liberty, in one stroke of Spanish retaliation.

The rise to prominence of a third group of interlopers — the newly independent Dutch — materially altered the Caribbean picture. The Dutch were more deeply committed than either French or English, both to a commercial livelihood and to hostility to Spain. They were already the principal sea carriers of the Atlantic coasts of Europe. The contraction of their trade with Spain and Portugal which resulted from the war caused them serious loss and drove them to seek supplies and markets farther afield. In particular it deprived them of salt, a vital commodity required in great quantities by the Dutch themselves for their fishing industry, and all over Europe for the preservation of meat. Most of the salt used in northern Europe in the late six-teenth century came from the south coast of Portugal and was carried in Dutch ships. Their normal supply reduced, the Dutch salt merchants turned first to the Cape Verde Islands and then to the Caribbean, where they discovered and began to exploit the great salt deposits of Araya, near Cumaná in Venezuela. The Araya salt-pan is an enclosed lagoon, about eight miles long, separated from the sea by a narrow strip of beach, and sur-rounded by a vast encrustation of salt left by evaporation. It is one of the hottest and most desolate places in the world; but Dutch skippers anchored there for weeks at a time, and employed their own crews in the work of breaking out and loading great lumps of the rock-hard salt. This point was noted, in the argu-ments used by William Usselinx, the famous proponent of West Indian settlement, to prove that white men could do hard manual work in tropical conditions. The salt ships were large, anything from 200 to 600 tons, and numerous; according to the governor of Cumaná they appeared off the coast of his province regularly at the rate of about ten a month between 1600 and 1605. Natur-ally, these ships did not come out in ballast, but brought European goods, which they sold along the Main and in the islands; and in addition to salt the Dutch took back tobacco from Guiana and Venezuela and hides from Hispaniola. Araya became the centre of a system of illicit trade, enlivened by occasional raiding, more serious than anything the Spanish Caribbean had yet known. The pearl fishery of Cumaná was virtually closed by Dutch interference; and the islands became almost a Dutch commercial preserve. In 1605 seventeen foreign ships, mostly Dutch, were reported in the Bay of Gonaïves. The Dutch themselves admitted that their hide trade to Hispaniola employed twenty ships annually. The Spaniards could still retaliate; the armada sent out under Luis Fajardo in 1605, with orders to surprise the Dutch at Araya, achieved a notable success, captured twelve ships, and for several years closed the trade. The governors of Venezuela achieved a number of successes, also, in catching and hanging smugglers. But the measures taken by the Spanish authorities to curb smuggling were destructive rather than creative, and damaged the interests of the colonists as much as those of the Dutch. Typical of such measures were the prohibition of tobacco-growing in Venezuela, to prevent sales to the Dutch; the proposal, made by the engineer Antoneli, to let in the sea and inundate the Araya lagoon; and the desperate decision, taken in 1605, to depopulate the north-west coast of Hispaniola. This last decision was enforced. The Spanish settlers of Puerto Plata, Monte Christi and Yaguana were ordered to leave their homes and move to the south coast, nearer to Santo Domingo and governmental control. Military force was needed to move them. Many fled to Cuba or turned pirate. Their cattle ran wild; and the vacuum so caused was filled by the buccaneers and later by the French.

The importance and the vulnerability of the West Indies, as emphasised by these events, naturally tempted the Dutch, as they tempted the English, to put forward open claims to navigate, trade and settle. The English claim that 'prescription without possession availeth nothing' was a reiteration of the doctrine of Grotius, and the persistent English approach to the West Indies as the 'apple of the eye' of the King of Spain, whence he derived his revenue which was his 'nervus belli', found an echo in the original plans for the Dutch West India Company. The proposals put forward by William Usselinx, the Calvinist refugee from Antwerp, at intervals from 1592 to 1621, had precisely the same objects as those of the English: the setting up of Protestant colonies which should be at once bases for raiding and smuggling, and sources of supply of ships' provisions and tropical 'staples'. In addition to the always valuable dyestuffs — indigo, fustic, logwood — there was a new and rapidly growing demand throughout Europe for tobacco. It was more satisfactory to buy such things by regular agreement from groups of European settlers than to rely upon getting supplies, uncertain in quantity and quality, from the Indians; and from the point of view of government, settlements might serve a double purpose, by providing a 'vent' for the unemployed, for paupers, vagrants, felons, and all manner of unwanted folk.

The first experiments in colonisation were made after the Treaty of London and in areas where they could be regarded, by a slight stretch, as compatible with peace with Spain — Virginia, Bermuda (by the accident of shipwreck) and Guiana — the 'wild coast' running between the Spanish possessions on the Orinoco and the Portuguese possessions on the Amazon. Such matters as fertile soil and healthy climate were largely guesswork in the seventeenth century. The Guiana coast — swampy, hot and fever-ridden — was to prove a singularly unsuitable place for inexperienced settlers, despite the legend of 'golden Manoa'; but Raleigh, the propagator of the legend, had been there in 1595, Keymis in 1596, the Dutch in 1598, and all had reported hopefully. In 1604 Charles Leigh attempted to plant a colony on the Wiapoco. The survivors were taken off, with Dutch help, two years later. Other equally unsuccessful ventures followed: Harcourt's attempt (1609–13), Raleigh's (1617–18), Roger North's (1619–21). In these enterprises English, Dutch and sometimes French adventurers worked in fairly close co-operation against the common enemy, Spain. Only the Dutch succeeded in making permanent settlements, on the Essequibo in 1616 and on the Berbice in 1624; but the English failures had important indirect results, for they led to the first establishments in the Lesser Antilles. In 1605 emigrants intended for Leigh's Wiapoco colony were landed on St. Lucia, where they were killed by the Caribs. In 1609 a similar group made an abortive attempt to settle in Grenada. Finally, in 1622, Thomas Warner, who had taken part in North's Guiana venture, but despaired of its success, on his return passage to England landed on St. Christopher, in what came to be called the Leeward group. Liking the look of the island, he went on to obtain patronage and capital in England, and returned in 1624 to begin the first permanent English settlement in the West Indies.

About this time a series of events occurred in Europe which

was to alter the whole aspect of affairs in the Caribbean. In the United Provinces, Maurice of Nassau and the Orange party triumphed politically over the republicans. The Grand Pensionary, Oldenbarnevelt, champion of republican oligarchy and the East India interest, was executed in 1619. The Twelve Years' Truce expired in 1621. The Dutch girded themselves for renewed war with Spain, and the West India Company, which Usselinx had urged upon his countrymen for years, received its formal charter. Here at last was an organisation capable of challenging Spain in the West Indies — no mere temporary association of partners in smuggling or raiding, but a great permanent joint-stock corporation with at least a nominal capital of over seven million guilders. The company was not, however, the colonising concern originally proposed by Usselinx; it was to make its profits by war against Spain and Portugal. Plunder, conquest and commerce were its aims. It was to maintain its own fleet of warships, to be supplemented by the Estates General when formal war should be declared. It was to have the right to settle, build, administer and defend; and to hold a monopoly of trade on the coasts of West Africa and the Americas. This early recognition of the essential and complementary relation between Africa and the West Indies was highly significant for the future. Dutch slavers already possessed a 'factory' at Gorée and there is reason to believe that slave merchants were prominent in urging the foundation of the company. Certainly, throughout the company's history the purveying of slaves to Spanish, Portuguese, and, later, French and English settlements was a prominent and lucrative part of its sphere of interest.

The attack which the West India Company delivered against Spanish shipping — even though much of its energy was diverted to Brazil — was heavier and more sustained than anything which had gone before. It strained the overtaxed resources of Spain almost to breaking point, and enabled other groups of foreigners to settle unoccupied Caribbean islands without serious danger of Spanish interference. Behind the organised fleets of the Dutch company, moreover, there still operated a swarm of private Dutch merchants, more or less tolerated interlopers in the company's official preserve, picking up cargoes wherever they could find them, often in places too insignificant to be worth the company's attention. These enterprising poachers

were ready to help settlers of any nationality with capital and
with technical skill, to supply them with slaves and manufactured
goods on long credit, and to buy their crops as soon as they had
crops to sell. Every new colony in the West Indies meant more
cargoes for Dutch shipping, as well as a blow against Spain.
Dutch naval and economic strength sheltered and encouraged
the infant Antillean settlements of France and England. From
envy of the Dutch, and eventual rivalry with them, English and
French governments learned a theory of mercantile imperialism
which was to influence their colonial policies for two hundred
years.

The directors of the West India Company — against Usselinx's
advice — chose as the first object of their aggression the Portuguese sugar-planting area on the north-east coast of Brazil. They
proposed also to capture the Portuguese slaving stations of São
Jorge de Mina and São Paulo de Luanda in West Africa, without
which the Brazil plantations were unworkable. We are not here
directly concerned with the story of how the Dutch between
1624 and 1654 won and lost a great empire in the 'bulge' of
Brazil, except in so far as that story affected the West Indies.
Bahía, the principal city, in Usselinx's words, was 'not a cat to be
taken without gloves'. The company's forces took the place in
1624, but lost it again in the following year. They did not renew
the offensive in Brazil until 1630, and then against Recife, not
Bahía. It was in the intervening five years that their naval commanders sought to recoup their losses in Brazil by raiding in the
West Indies. In this they were overwhelmingly successful.
Successive Dutch fleets carried out sweeps in the Caribbean
which practically drove the local Spanish shipping from the sea;
and in 1628 Piet Heyn, ablest and most celebrated of the company's admirals, in command of a fleet of thirty-one sail, surprised
and intercepted the homeward-bound *flota* off Mantanzas Bay,
and captured the whole sailing almost without firing a shot.
This triumph, achieved for the first time and not to be repeated
for thirty years, yielded booty worth fifteen million guilders;
enough to pay a dividend of 50 per cent to the company's
shareholders, and to finance the renewed offensive in Brazil. It
ruined Spanish credit in Europe. In the West Indies it paralysed
for a time both communications and defence. It was followed
by several years of systematic pillaging by smaller fleets. By

320 330

Occidentalis Americæ partis,
vel earum Regionum quas Chri-
ſtophorus Columbus primù detexit.
Tabula Chorographicæ multorum
Auctorum ſcriptis, præſertim verò ex
Hieronymi Benzoni (qui totis XIIII
annis eas Provincias diligenter
perlustravit)
Historia,
conflata & in æri incisa a
Theodoro de Bry Leod.
ANNO M D XCIIII.

MAR DEL NORT

Circulus Cancri

MAYA

Tierra de S. Spirito

fue maior

Sed iste Navigatio a obtinuit Columbus,
Anaolam appellavit.

Anegada

Porto rico

Anguilla

S. Benedict

In hanc Insulam prima Navigatione ap-
pulit Columbus Desideratam nominavit,
et in Christiam nomine memorà Crucem
sirent.

BORICHEN
S. German
S. Ioanna

Vargines

Antigua

Estazia

S. Crux

Saba

Marigalenti

LA S. IOANIS DE PORTV DIVITE

S. Lucia
Cubuchera

S. Dominica

INC

Charpaten

Xiralanea

Acoa

Guadalup

S. Vincens

Mons Serrat

Marianta Domica

Barodos

Cubucheira

S. Tapatan
Val Duolor are

Diatin

Larosa

Granada

Matinen

P. di. S. B.

S. Iacques
HISPANIA
NOVA

Patsaquar

Fortaga

Maracapana
Carinco

NICARAG

CVMANA
Tavaris

Rio dolce

Cubuchere

Golfo de

CVBAGVA

P. de galea

In istam Insulam delatus est tertia Navigatione
Columbus, cui nomen indidit ab Columbusquar,
Topama, quinta pars Regi cedit.

Monte espico

Camari

Puria

Incon

R. Dolce

Puntabainno

Amapari

R. Ferde

Auapari

R. Salado

P. de S. Vincente Pinço

AVREA
REG CARIBANA

320 Circulus Aequinoctialis 325 Aldea de arpol cedos 330

1630, except for the armed *flotas* — which by a miracle of determination continued their sailings — and for insignificant small craft, there was no Spanish shipping worth mention in the area. The trade of the islands and Tierra Firme was almost all in the hands of the Dutch and their allies. Spain still possessed the power to make occasional effective counter-attacks, as the story of Old Providence was to show, and she could still hold her settled colonies; but she could no longer dispossess other powers or prevent their acquisition of the islands which she had neglected to occupy.

The Dutch, though they were well aware that raiding would not pay indefinitely, did not avail themselves to any great extent of the opportunities for settlement in the West Indies. They seized between 1630 and 1640 Curaçao, Saba, St. Martin and St. Eustatius, all of which were confirmed to them by the Treaty of Münster in 1648. These small crumbs of land were of value chiefly as trading and smuggling depots, though Curaçao had valuable salt-pans, a matter of importance to the Dutch, since the Spaniards had succeeded in making Araya uncomfortable for the salt shippers. The island had only a handful of Spanish residents and was taken by a surprise attack with hardly a shot fired. It has been the centre of Dutch power in the West Indies ever since, and today is enormously prosperous both as a free port and as a refinery centre for Venezuelan oil. The main efforts of the Dutch, however, were concentrated once again after 1630 upon Brazil. Meanwhile the accession of Charles I to the English throne, and of Richelieu to power in France, released a direct hostility to Spain which had recently been restrained. This hostility now took the form of colonisation as well as that of illicit trade. It was the English and the French who followed up the Dutch successes, by establishing themselves permanently in the outer islands.

The opening of opportunities for settlement in the West Indies coincided with the great movement of emigration which was beginning to people the Atlantic coast of North America with Englishmen. Many reasons have been adduced for this seventeenth-century migration of Englishmen overseas, ranging from the growth of enclosure to the ecclesiastical policy of Laud; but the essential element in the situation was the conviction that in England there were more men than jobs or land, while in the

New World there were more jobs and land than men.   The organisers of new colonies at that time could always find men ready to try their luck.   Government approved, or did not oppose, the growth of settlements which could serve as dumping-grounds for felons, paupers or schismatics, and which might produce 'naval stores' or other useful commodities.   England, in short, undertook colonies of settlement rather than of trade or exploration; and this was as true of the West Indies, in the early days, as of Massachusetts or Virginia.

Thomas Warner, having secured the necessary financial backing in London, returned to St. Kitts in 1624 with forty or fifty companions to begin effective settlement.   Shortly after his arrival a French party under d'Esnambuc also landed with the same design.   The two groups, very sensibly in view of the danger of Carib raids, agreed to settle side by side, the French taking the northern and southern extremities, the English the centre — or rather the middle coastal strips, for the centre of the island is steep and uncultivable mountain.   The English had much the better of this bargain, and there was frequent bickering over boundaries.   Both groups of colonists were dispersed by a savage Spanish attack in 1629, but soon returned.   Very shortly after the settlement of St. Kitts, in 1624, John Powell, returning home from Brazil, landed in Barbados, which was then quite uninhabited and forested to the water's edge.   Struck by the beauty and apparent fertility of the place, he took possession in the name of King James.   On arrival in England he persuaded Sir William Courteen, a London merchant with Dutch connections, to back the settlement of the island.   All these settlements took root and led to further expansion.   St. Croix in the Virgin Islands was jointly occupied by English and Dutch in 1625; Nevis was settled from St. Kitts in 1628, Antigua and Montserrat in 1632.   There was an attempt to settle Tobago in 1625, and a settlement in St. Lucia from 1638 to 1641, when the Caribs again drove the settlers away.   The French were behind the English in all this activity, for their urge to colonise was less spontaneous and depended more upon governmental encouragement.   It was not until 1635 that Richelieu's hands were sufficiently free to allow him to intervene effectively in the West Indies.   The establishment of the Compagnie des Isles d'Amérique and the settlement of Martinique and Guadeloupe date from that year. Both these islands, unlike Barbados, were inhabited by warlike Caribs. Their development in the early days was much slower than that of Barbados and St. Kitts.

The organisers of all these settlements quickly took steps to secure royal authority for their ventures, both in order to have clear titles to land, and to exercise official discipline over the settlers. For the French at St. Kitts the problem was relatively simple, because they had as yet no competitors among their own countrymen. Even so, d'Esnambuc procured from Richelieu a formal privilege, which, incidentally, included Barbados in its terms, though he never tried to put it into effect there. The English settlements were planted by a number of competing groups of investors, and in an atmosphere of bad geography and bad faith they all scrambled for patents and patronage in London. Warner and his friends secured the support of the Earl of Carlisle, an influential and able peer whose extravagance, excessive even in that extravagant age, led him to clutch at any opportunity of keeping his creditors quiet. Courteen's patron was the Earl of Pembroke. Both noblemen secured patents which included Barbados. The reckless ease with which such irreconcilable patents were granted bedevilled the early history of English colonisation, and is in itself an indication of the slight importance then attached by government to the whole affair. To quote Macpherson in *The Trade's Increase*, 'The West Indian islands, before they fell into the planting of sugar canes, were in those early times thought of little worth, otherwise the grants would not have been so readily made.' Eventually Carlisle, after a series of complex intrigues, got himself made Lord Proprietor of the Caribbee Islands, including St. Kitts, Nevis and Barbados. He confirmed Warner as his governor of St. Kitts, but imposed his own nominee, the ruffian Hawley, upon Barbados. Pembroke's patent was set aside; Courteen lost the large sums which he had invested, and many of his adherents lost their plantations in the disorders which followed.

The patent to Carlisle was the application to America of a form of grant long obsolete in England — a quasi-feudal grant of territory and jurisdiction to a prominent nobleman. The proprietor nominated the governor and other officials, and drew his revenue from rents and customs. Obviously a peer could obtain grants of this kind from the Stuart kings more easily than

E

a group of merchants; and it was perhaps thought more appropriate that settlements in exposed positions should be made by feudal grant in the old tradition of knight-service rather than by trading companies. In fact the management of the concern was in the hands of a syndicate of London merchants, who were Carlisle's creditors and who sought to exploit his influence at Court in this way in the hope of securing something by way of repayment. Carlisle himself, having obtained the patent, took little interest in anything except his dues; and, as in most English colonies, the settlers exercised a considerable degree of self-government from the start. The grant, however, led to constant quarrelling among the heirs of the earl and the lessees of his rights, and their disputes were reflected in the bitter factions within the islands: Courteens against Carlisles, and, later, Royalists against Roundheads. St. Kitts, under the able and energetic Warner, held aloof from these squabbles, but Barbados was not brought to order until the arrival there, in 1650, of Francis, Lord Willoughby of Parham, as lessee of the Carlisle grant and also as governor-in-chief of the Caribbee Islands by virtue of a commission from the exiled Charles II. Willoughby was a moderate Royalist of great ability and deep conviction. 'I have never served my King', he wrote, on hearing of the battle of Worcester, 'in Expectation so much of his Prosperous Condicion as of my Dutye'; and his duty he conceived to be to keep Barbados for the time being out of English politics, especially as the Commonwealth government seemed determined to quarrel with the Dutch and to exclude Dutch ships from the islands. From the point of view of the islanders, whatever their politics, Willoughby's policy was obvious commonsense, and even at that early date the members of the Barbados Assembly were prepared to cavil at the orders of a parliament in which, as they said, they were not represented. The Commonwealth government, however, could not allow Royalist colonies to exist in virtual independence, and perhaps to serve as bases for Prince Rupert's fleet; so in 1652 a fleet under Sir George Ayscue appeared off Barbados and compelled Willoughby to submit to superior force. When Prince Rupert arrived in the area he could get no help from anyone except the French. Throughout the Commonwealth and Protectorate the proprietary patent was in abeyance. Governors, and a few other officials, came out from England;

but they could not carry out their instructions and exclude all Royalists from office, because there were not enough Commonwealth men to run the government. Willoughby went to the Wild Coast and there founded a new colony in Surinam, which was ceded to the Dutch at the Treaty of Breda in 1667. He returned to Barbados after the Restoration, first as successor to the Carlisle rights, and subsequently (with due compensation for loss of the Propriety) as governor of the Caribbee Islands by Crown appointment. He spent the rest of his life consolidating and seeking to extend British occupation of the islands. He died in 1666 in an expedition against Martinique. He was one of the greatest and most devoted of early West Indians, holding it 'better . . . I and as many of our name as ever was borne should be suncke and perish, than those islands lost'.

Economically and socially Barbados — and indeed all the recently settled islands — must have presented difficult problems to a conscientious governor. The first record of a visit to the island is that of Sir Henry Colt in 1631, who described the slovenly management of the plantations, the rough and inefficient method of clearing by firing the bush — 'Your ground and plantation shows what you are, they lye like ye ruines of some village lately burned' — and the incessant quarrelling of the planters. At that time there were about 4,000 people in the island. They were engaged partly in producing crops for their own subsistence, chiefly maize, and partly in growing tobacco for sale in Europe. Cotton was the only other crop of importance. At the time of the first settlements, tobacco was in great demand in Europe. The expansion of production in Virginia and Carolina had not yet forced down the price. It was grown mostly by small free-holders, farming from five to thirty acres, and employing the labour of indented servants, men who bound themselves to serve for a period of from three to seven years in return for having their passages paid, and in expectation of a grant of land at the expiry of their indenture. The situation of these men during their indentures was an unenviable one. They received no wage, but were supposed to be housed, fed and clothed by their masters. The quality of housing, in an island newly settled and only partly cleared, may be imagined. Food was mostly maize meal and the lowest grade of salt fish imported from North America. The master's rights to his servants' 'time' was absolute. If, for example, a free man married an indented woman, he was obliged to compensate her master by serving out the unexpired portion of her indenture. Indentures were transferable, so that indented servants could, in effect, be bought and sold. In a society where the magistrates were almost all planters, servants were naturally much at the mercy of their masters. There was no lack of emigrants, however. The miserable condition of a landless labourer in England, and the lure of free land in the West Indies, combined to supply a powerful incentive. By 1640 the population of Barbados was well over 30,000, which meant about 200 to the square mile — heavy overcrowding, by seventeenth-century standards. That of St. Kitts and Nevis at the same time was about 20,000. White population in all these islands reached its peak in the middle of the sixteen-forties. Thereafter it declined rapidly, and has never since recovered.

Both French and English islands from their beginning fell into the sphere of Dutch commercial activity. Only the Dutch possessed the necessary shipping to serve the needs of the area. In commerce, especially in seaborne commerce, the Dutch in the seventeenth century were the masters and teachers of Europe, not unnaturally, since trade was the whole life and livelihood of their state. Their capital was more fluid than the English or French, their business methods more up-to-date, their ships better designed for cheap and easy handling. They were the first Europeans to experiment with methods of sheathing ships' hulls against marine borers — a matter of vital importance in the tropics. Even when a choice offered — which was seldom — the planters preferred to ship their crops in Dutch ships, because the Dutchmen offered European goods at lower prices, longer credit and cheaper freight rates. It was said, too, that they understood the problems of stowage better and took greater care of their cargoes. They were directly interested in the prosperity of the islands with which they traded; and when tobacco became a drug upon the European market it was the Dutch who put the West Indians in the way of growing sugar instead. Amsterdam was a great city of warehouses from which all Europe was supplied with tropical and colonial products; and much of the profit to be derived from the colonial settlements of all European nations found its way into Dutch pockets.

Up to the middle of the seventeenth century governments, proprietors and planting companies accepted this situation philosophically, having neither the shipping nor the experience to compete with the Dutch. The first government to react against the Dutch monopoly was the Commonwealth government in England, and that partly for immediate political reasons. Barbados and Antigua, by their adherence to Charles II, gave the London merchants a pretext for attacking Dutch trade with those islands, under colour of a kind of disciplinary blockade. Pressure from the City secured in 1650 an act prohibiting all trade with the recalcitrant colonies 'because of their rebellion against the Commonwealth and Government of England'. The Barbadians under Willoughby refused obedience and maintained their Dutch commercial contacts. It was this, as much as West Indian royalism, which moved government to send Ayscue and his fleet to drive Willoughby out; but meanwhile it became clear that the real purpose of government was not merely to starve rebellious colonists into submission, but to replace Dutch shipping by English throughout the English colonies, as a permanent policy. The Navigation Ordinance of 1651 prohibited the import of colonial products into England, except in English ships; and confined the import of European goods into English colonies to English ships or ships of the country where the goods originated. When the representatives of the Dutch government tried, by negotiation, to get the ordinance suspended, they were reminded that English traders had 'been always strictly forbidden trade in all plantations . . . belonging to the people of the United Provinces'; and were told that 'as for their trading to any of the English plantations, it is forbidden by the late increase of the navigation of this nation, from which we think not fit to recede'.

The boast was premature. English shipping to the West Indies had not in fact developed sufficiently to supplant the Dutch, and the islanders continued to trade in defiance of their government. Nevertheless, the intention of government was plain. The ordinance of 1651 was an act of economic war against the Dutch, and in 1652 it led to real war. The Protestant alliance of eighty years' standing had broken up and a new Caribbean rivalry had emerged. The English government, and its mercantile advisers, now openly sought to weaken the Dutch, and to supplant them by imitating their methods. In peace and in war, Dutch competition, Dutch influence, and Dutch example largely determined the nature of English colonial policy, as it came to be formulated in the second half of the seventeenth century. In this policy there were four main elements: the assertion of the sovereignty of the metropolitan government; the fostering of staple crops for shipment to the United Kingdom and subsequent sale in the markets of Europe; the direction of trade into English ships bound for English ports; and the concentration of this system on the West Indies. The old colonies of settlement, based upon a balanced subsistence economy, nonconformist for both economic and constitutional reasons, lost favour. A plantation system based upon some kind of cheap forced labour came to be preferred. The production of tobacco, cotton, dyestuffs, and later sugar; the need for shipping; the demand for food and timber from the mainland, for food, manufactured goods, and, later, slaves from England—all made the West Indies the colonies *par excellence* of the old colonial system.

In the minds of Cromwell and the restless, rancorous Protestant gentry who supported him, the new rivalry with Holland did not efface the old rivalry with Spain. It remains to notice two English operations against actual Spanish territory in the Caribbean. One, the settlement of Providence, was a failure. The other, the capture of Jamaica, was a lasting success. Both owed something to Dutch inspiration. Both were intended to establish bases for trade and privateering as well as — perhaps rather than — colonies of settlement.

The Puritans, who were the chief Spaniard-haters in England, for both religious and commercial reasons, were also conspicuous colonisers. A company formed by prominent Puritans, including the Earl of Warwick and John Pym, was incorporated in 1629 to settle Santa Catalina, or Providence Island, off the coast of Nicaragua. The island was peopled by settlers from England and from Bermuda, and in the early years both its planting and its seafaring activities showed some promise. By 1632 local agreements had been made with Dutch traders, who undertook to buy the first year's crop. The directors in England complained, but were gradually persuaded — since there was no alternative — to accept the Dutch as their dealers. In 1638 they sought and obtained formal permission for the arrangement. The settlers soon discovered, however, that it was easier to pay for Dutch goods with Spanish loot, and came to prefer raiding to planting as a source of profit, especially after 1631, when the company extended operations to Tortuga, off the north coast of Hispaniola. Tortuga was frankly a base for commerce raiding and little else. In settling colonies of this kind so near the Spanish coasts the company had attempted more than it could perform. The party at Tortuga was massacred by the Spaniards in 1635. In 1639 a Dutch offer to purchase Providence from the company was unwisely turned down. In 1641 a Spanish fleet recaptured the island and expelled the settlers; and the Providence Company came to an end. Tortuga became again, as it had been before the company's day, a rendezvous for wandering buccaneers. It fell eventually into the hands of the French, and later became the base for the French conquest of Saint-Domingue.

The capture of Jamaica differed from all previous English acquisitions, in that it was a formal naval and military operation, organised and paid for by government. The accession of Cromwell to supreme power in 1653 permitted the return to a policy, almost traditional among the conservative-radical gentry of England, of open aggression against Spain in America. The famous 'Western design' in many ways resembled Drake's plan of 1585 for gaining control of the sea-ways of the West Indies. It displayed the same combination of cupidity, religious fervour, and national vanity. It was more ambitious, in that it contemplated permanent acquisitions of territory, to be settled as colonies by English planters, whereas Drake had only proposed to garrison one or two strategic harbours. It was more foolhardy. Drake had possessed accurate local knowledge and had commanded an efficient, well-disciplined force; but Cromwell's project was entrusted to an ill-led, ill-armed mob, and its planning was largely based on inaccurate and prejudiced intelligence. Thomas Gage, the renegade Dominican and author of *The English-American*, was a popular advocate and a violent partisan. The contempt for the enemy which marked all stages of the operation was due largely to his information and advice. Finally, neither Admiral Penn nor General Venables was a Drake.

About 2,500 men, drafted from different units, were hurried on board at Portsmouth at the end of 1654. Five weeks later the expedition reached Barbados, where it assured its own unpopularity by seizing eleven Dutch ships in Carlisle Bay. For weeks it lay at Barbados, 'eating up the island'. The commanders requisitioned food and arms which the colony could ill spare; they seized money from the excise revenue; they recruited 4,000 men — not only freemen volunteers, but (quite illegally) indented servants. Venables assumed temporary command of the island militia, and used the opportunity to oust Royalist officers. The Barbadians protested in vain. They were being punished by Cromwell for their earlier contumacy. They saw 4,000 of their labourers taken from the island, and the safety of the island itself endangered, to help an English government which most of the planters disliked, in an endeavour to establish a colony which might eventually prove to be the ruin of Barbados. Nor were the commanding officers much better satisfied. Their recruits, according to Venables, were the scum of the colony, men 'so loose as not to be kept under discipline, and so cowardly as not to be made to fight'. It was a sad commentary upon the quality of indented servants, and the effect of indented labour in the tropics upon the character and physique of English emigrants. About 1,200 men of slightly better quality were recruited in the Leeward Islands; but it was a mutinous, unwarlike mob which disembarked in Hispaniola in April 1655 in order to launch an overland attack on Santo Domingo. A serious tactical blunder was made, in landing too far from the town — over thirty miles — without giving any thought to the question of water supply for the march. The result of the attempt was a total rout at the hands of a much smaller force of Spanish regular cavalry, assisted by bands of local cattle-hunters. The attackers were saved from massacre only by the landing of a party of sailors to cover their flight back to the ships.

The capture of Jamaica was an afterthought, an attempt to retrieve the expedition from total disgrace; it was, however, a brilliant inspiration. Carew Reynell described Jamaica, with shrewd foresight, as the key of the Indies, equally apt for trade or for an attack on the Main, 'lying in the very belly of all commerce'. Jamaica, moreover, was a relatively easy prize.

Since 1536 the 'marquisate' of Jamaica had been an appanage
of the descendants of Columbus, as hereditary Admirals of the
Indies, but they had done nothing to develop the island. Its
Spanish population numbered only about 1,500, and they were
poor and ill-armed, living mostly by keeping or hunting cattle.
The island had been held to ransom, only twelve years before,
by the privateer William Jackson with but a few hundred men.
When Venables' men landed in Hunt's Bay and marched on
Spanish Town, they met with little resistance and soon both
Penn and Venables were able to return to England, to face an
angry Cromwell, leaving their juniors to conduct 'mopping-up'
operations and to begin the work of settlement. The Spanish
governor, Cristóbal Isasi, held out in the hills on the north side
with a small band of Spaniards and loyal slaves, harassing the
English in the south by frequent raids, and receiving occasional
reinforcements and supplies from Cuba. The Cubans could do
very little, however; a serious epidemic had recently decimated
their population, and made it difficult for them to man their own
defences. There was no hope of help from Spain; Blake's victory
over the Spanish fleet at Santa Cruz in 1657 had made the
despatch of a relief expedition impossible. Even so, it was not
until 1660 that Isasi gave up the struggle and left the island, and
not until 1670 that his government acquiesced in its loss. To
this day Don Christopher's Cove, the little inlet in St. Ann
where Isasi received his few supplies from Cuba, preserves the
name of that brave and resourceful *guerrillero*. The few hundred
slaves who had fled to the hills with their Spanish masters
remained in the fastnesses of the Cockpit country and formed
the nucleus of the redoubtable maroons.

Cromwell, though disappointed, resolved from the first to keep
Jamaica, and went to war with Spain rather than give it up. A
very important position had been gained, and no time was lost
in drawing English attention to the fact. At first, settlement was
slow and difficult. Officers and men of the conquering army
received grants of land to plant and settle, chiefly in the fertile,
well-watered bottom lands of the Rio Minho valley; but many
of them died and few succeeded. Despite government propaganda, despite low taxation and the promise of virgin land,
there was no such wave of migration towards Jamaica as there
had been towards Barbados and the Leewards in the 'thirties.

Jamaica never became a true colony of settlement. Its eventual prosperity — for it was to become immensely prosperous — was based from its beginnings on buccaneering, trade, and slave-grown sugar. At the same time sugar and slavery were invading the other English and French islands; and the profound social revolution which attended their introduction must next be considered.

CHAPTER V

THE SUGAR REVOLUTION

THE FIRST TWENTY YEARS of West Indian settlement had been, for the French and the English, a period of greater activity than achievement, especially by comparison with the much larger and more solid development of the mainland colonies. Tobacco and indented labour were unsound bases for an island economy, as the West Indians discovered when tobacco prices dropped. All contemporary witnesses agreed that Barbados and Leeward Island tobacco was of poor quality and could not compete with Virginian. Nor did anatto or ginger provide adequate substitutes, for the demand for them was relatively small. Attempts to grow indigo in St. Kitts were failures, though some was grown in Barbados. Cotton — as de Poincy explained, writing from Saint-Christophe in 1639 to the directors of his company — required too much land. In islands where the area of usable land was limited, and where the initial cost of clearing bush was high, the only economic crops were those which gave both a high yield per acre and a high price. Sugar was the obvious choice; unlike tobacco, it could be grown only in the tropics. It could be grown by unskilled labour, for long periods on the same ground, without exhausting the soil. The demand for sugar in Europe was growing steadily and seemed insatiable. Sugar-cane, however, by reason of its perishable nature, must be milled and made into sugar almost immediately upon cutting. The planter must be a manufacturer too; or must at least have easy access to a factory. The manufacture of sugar demanded skill, technical knowledge, and equipment which nobody in England or France possessed. It could not be established in the English or French West Indies without help from outside; and such help could come only from Dutch sources. The Spaniards, who had been growing sugar in Hispaniola and on the mainland coast in relatively small quantities for a hundred and twenty years, had never officially recognised the existence of foreign colonies in the Caribbean. The Portuguese, with their much more extensive plantations in Brazil, were fully occupied after 1640 in the struggle to evict the Dutch from Pernambuco, and certainly had no motive for selling the secrets of the trade to foreign West Indians. The Dutch, however, had a powerful motive for doing so. As the universal dealers and carriers of the West Indies, it was to their advantage to encourage the production of any West Indian crop which could be sold in Europe. They had acquired in Brazil the necessary knowledge and experience. They could supply the equipment from Europe, and were prepared to lend the necessary capital. Dutchmen were the first founders of the sugar industry of the French and British West Indies.

The first canes to be planted in Barbados, according to most contemporary accounts, were brought from Brazil by one Pieter Brower in 1637. For several years the only use of the cane was to make a sweet drink for immediate use. Attempts at sugar manufacture began in 1642, backed by Dutch merchants who supplied rollers, coppers and other equipment on credit against the first crop. Ligon's *History of Barbados* gives the following almost contemporary account — the earliest account we have:

'At the time we landed on this Island, which was in the beginning of *September, 1647*, we were informed, partly by those Planters we found there, and partly by our own observations, that the great work of Sugar-making, was but newly practised by the inhabitants there. Some of the most industrious men, having gotten Plants from *Fernambock*, a place in *Brasill*, and made tryall of them at the *Barbadoes*; and finding them to grow, they planted more and more, as they grew and multiplyed on the place, till they had such a considerable number, as they were worth the while to set up a very small *Ingenio*, and so make tryall what Sugar could be made upon that soyl. But, the secrets of the work being not well understood, the Sugars they made were very inconsiderable, and little worth, for two or three years. But . . . by new directions from *Brasill*, sometimes by strangers, and now and then by their own people, who . . . were content sometimes to make a voyage thither. . . . And so returning with more Plants, and better Knowledge, they went on upon fresh hopes, but still short, of what they should be more skilful in: for, at our arrivall there, we found them ignorant in three main points, that much conduced to the work; *viz.* The manner of Planting, the time of Gathering, and the right placing of their Coppers in their Furnaces; [i.e. to conserve fuel and to prevent the flames reaching and setting fire to the boiling syrup] as also, the true way of covering their Rollers, with plates or bars of Iron: All which being rightly done, advance much in the performance of the main work. At the time of our arrivall there, we found many Sugar-works set up, and at work; but yet the Sugars they made, were but bare Muscavadoes, and few of them Merchantable commodities; so moist, and full of molosses, and so ill cur'd, as they were hardly worth the bringing home for *England.* But about the time I left the Island, which was in 1650, they were much better'd; for then they had the skill to know when the Canes were ripe, which was not, till they were fifteen months old; and before they gathered them at twelve, which was a main disadvantage to the making good Sugar; for, the liquor wanting of the sweetnesse it ought to have, caused the Sugars to be lean, and unfit to keep. Besides, they were grown greater proficients, both in boyling and curing them, and had learnt the knowledge of making them white, . . . but not so excellent as those they make in *Brasill*, nor is theyr any likelyhood they can ever make such: . . .'

A more optimistic anonymous account describes the situation in its political context:

' . . . the Dutch beginning to lose their footing in Brazil [they were finally expelled in 1654] many came also from those parts, who taught the English the Art of making sugar, and having at that time [i.e. before 1650] free trade with all people at amity with England . . . their sugar yielded a good price, and they were plentifully supplied with all necessities of life and planting at very cheap rates, and had long credit given them by the Dutch, which together with their being governed by themselves, was the beginning and main cause of their prosperity, and grew and increased very much year by year in the production of their manufacture. . . .'

In the French islands the story was similar except that there the industry was started by Dutch immigrants from Brazil who actually settled in the islands. The Company of the Isles of America made a contract as early as 1639 with one Trezel, who was to establish and manage a plantation of 3,000 acres and a mill in Martinique. Trezel failed, and so did several successors. The first successful factory was started — still with Dutch help — in Guadeloupe by the governor, Houel, in 1647. The following year the company became bankrupt, and the various islands were sold to individual proprietors. Saint-Christophe was acquired, presumably as an investment, by the Knights of Malta, who appointed de Poincy as their governor. Guadeloupe was purchased by Houel. Sugar production spread more slowly than in the English islands, largely owing to lack of labour. It is significant of the greater prosperity of France at this time that in order to attract indented servants (*engagés*) the French planters had to offer better terms than the English. *Engagés* were rarely bound for more than three years, and often less. On the other hand, French manufacturing methods were more ambitious; for the proprietors, with the help of Dutch immigrants from Brazil, embarked in the 'sixties upon the operation of sugar refineries. The English islands produced chiefly muscavado — wet brown sugar — and only a little 'clayed' or 'plantation white'. The hold of Dutch merchants was even closer in the French islands than in the English. No attempt was made to break it until Colbert, from 1665 onwards, abolished the Proprieties and reorganised the French colonies in America on strictly mercantilist principles — which involved, at least temporarily, the closing of the refineries.

In the Spanish West Indies sugar was one product among several, and not the most important. In the French and English islands it became after about 1650 the only product of importance. The growth of this monoculture was much more than the spread of a profitable crop and a new industry. It was a revolution which changed the whole racial composition and social structure of the islands. Sugar was a rich man's crop. Considerable capital was needed to set up a factory; and a plantation, to run economically, had to be big enough to keep the factory supplied constantly with canes throughout the crop season. Once established, however, sugar plantations and factories soon became immensely profitable — far more so than, for instance, tobacco plantations. Successful sugar planters bought up the holdings of failing tobacco farmers. Barbados, which had supported a large population of small proprietors, became in a decade or so a land of relatively large estates; and the profits to be made from sugar encouraged clearing, so that by 1660 almost the whole usable area of the island was cleared and in use. A pitiful emigration of dispossessed small-holders left Barbados to try their luck in the mainland colonies, in Jamaica, in Surinam, Martinique, Guadeloupe, or (for the wilder sort) among the buccaneers. Many of these wanderers failed to find a resting place, and died in the search. As early as 1652 Colonel Modyford (later Sir Thomas, and governor of Jamaica) had written: 'This island of Barbados cannot last in a height of trade three years longer, the wood being almost already all spent, and therefore in prudence a place must presently be thought upon, where this great people may find sustenance and employment.' Fifteen years later a report from Barbados stated that the island contained 'not above 700 considerable proprietors, . . . 12,000 good men formerly proprietors have gone off, wormed out of their small settlements by their more suttle and greedy neighbours.'

The size and complexity of the estates acquired in Barbados by 'suttle and greedy' planters, even in the early days of the industry, is indicated by Ligon, whose detailed *History* was published in 1657. He described a plantation, in which Modyford bought a half-interest in 1648, as containing '500 acres of land, with a faire Dwelling-House and *Ingenio* [presumably turned by cattle] in a room 400 feet square, a boyling house, filling house, cisternes and still house, with a curing house 100 feet long and 40 feet broad, with stables and smith's forge and room to lay provisions of Corne and Bonavist. Houses for Negroes and Indian Slaves, with 96 Negroes and 3 Indian women with their children, 28 Christians, 45 cattle for work, 8 milch cows, a dozen horses and mares and 11 *Assinigoes*. . . . In this plantation of 500 acres, there was employed for sugar something more than 200 acres, about 80 acres for pasture, 120 for wood, 20 for Tobacco, 5 for Ginger, as many for Cotton Wool, 70 acres for provisions, viz. corne, potatoes, Plantaines, Cassavie and Bonavist; some few acres of which were for fruit, viz. Pines, Plantaines, Millions, Bonanas, Goaves, Water Millions,

Oranges and Limons'. Modyford paid £7,000 for his half-share. Eight years earlier the whole estate had been worth only £400.

Establishments of this type required a large and well-disciplined labour force, which the old practice of indenture could not adequately supply. Free land had been the essence of the indenture system. The landless labourer left England in the hope of becoming — if he lived long enough — a small proprietor. It was in that expectation that he signed his contract, went overseas, endured the years of hard work, the tropical climate, the poor food and housing, the arbitrary whims of a strange master. But when no land remained to grant; when small proprietors could not make ends meet, and sold or deserted their holdings; and when there was no ready sale for any crop but sugar, then no incentive remained, and the supply of volunteer indented labour dwindled and ceased. Only compulsion in one form or another could meet the need. Every conceivable method of propaganda was employed to recruit labour in Europe, especially in North Germany, where the Thirty Years War had left thousands homeless, ready with the credulity of utter misery to go to the West Indies or anywhere that offered a ray of hope. Crimping became a regular trade, in England and in continental ports. More legally, but no less brutally, the English penal system was adapted to West Indian needs. The Civil War produced a crop of Royalist prisoners who were shipped out, seething with bitterness, to Barbados. Irish rapparees spared in the massacre of Drogheda went the same way, to be 'derided by the negroes as white slaves'. Transportation became a regular punishment for vagrants, for political prisoners, and for many convicted felons. Magistrates in Bristol with West Indian connections were bribed — so it was said — to give transportation sentences. Jeffreys as Lord Chief Justice had hard things to say about magistrates who 'for a pint of sack . . . will bind people servants to the Indies'; but Jeffreys himself sent to a like fate hundreds of the Somerset yokels who followed Monmouth. The effect of all this was to create a class of poor white labourers, miserable, desperate and despised; men — to quote Josiah Child — 'such as, had there been no English Foreign Plantation in the World, could probably never have lived at home to do service for their country but must have come to be hanged or starved, or dyed untimely of some of those miserable Diseases, that proceed from Want and Vice'. They were treated accordingly, often enough. Transported — 'barbadoed' — persons were, in effect, slaves; but as their enslavement was limited to the term of their sentence they were less valuable than true slaves, and often, therefore, worse cared for. 'I have seen such cruelty there done to servants', says Ligon, 'as I do not think one Christian could have done to another.'

None of the methods of persuasion or compulsion employed in Europe produced labourers in sufficient numbers to meet West Indian demands, and eventually, as the Spaniards and Portuguese had done before them, the French and English planters found a solution of their labour problem in the purchase of slaves from outside Europe, mostly from that apparently inexhaustible reservoir of humanity, West Africa. The Dutch, in the late sixteen-thirties, had seized most of the Portuguese slave barracoons in West Africa, as the necessary complement of their Brazilian empire. They had slaves to sell and were anxious to extend the trade in the West Indies. Whether the inability of white labour to hold its own in plantation agriculture was the cause or the effect of increasing dependence on black labour is doubtful; but certainly as sugar-planting spread, so the number of white labourers declined and the number of slaves increased. Barbados had a few hundred negroes in 1640; by 1645 there were over 6,000 negroes and about 40,000 whites; in 1685, 46,000 negroes and 20,000 whites, bond and free; twenty years later the number of Africans was about the same but the European population was down to 12,000. In the Leeward Islands the change began a decade or so later, but, once begun, was more rapid and more nearly complete than in Barbados. The systematic settlement of Jamaica began in 1664, upon the arrival of Sir Thomas Modyford as governor. Emigrants from Barbados formed a substantial proportion of the settlers, sugar was the main crop, and estates were large almost from the very beginning, some over 5,000 acres and very few under 150. In 1673 the population was 7,700 white and 9,500 black. The white population remained almost constant for fifty years, but the number of negro slaves in the same period rose to 74,000. In the French islands the process of change, in the early years, was slower. The white population of proprietors and *engagés*, though small,

F

proved very tenacious. Even at the end of the seventeenth century, except in Saint-Domingue, most properties were still small, employing an average of less than a dozen slaves each. An official count in 1687 gave a total for all the islands of 18,000 whites and 27,000 slaves. Of the slaves, 16,000 were in Martinique and 7,000 in Saint-Domingue. By 1701 the total number of slaves had increased to 44,000, while the white population remained stationary, or increased very slightly, in most islands; Martinique was not robbed of whites to settle Saint-Domingue as Barbados and Nevis were to settle Jamaica. After the turn of the century properties increased rapidly in size and the number of slaves went up by leaps and bounds. Martinique alone had 21,000 by 1710, and in Saint-Domingue the increase was more dramatic still. By the early eighteenth century, then, Africans formed in most of the British and French islands the great majority of the population. The Europeans had become a small garrison among the slaves.

It is difficult to form, from contemporary accounts, any clear idea of the nature of this great body of people brought against their will from Africa. Most West Indian writers concerned themselves only with the economic aspects of slavery, with the cost of slaves, their efficient management, their capacity for work. The few accounts which treat of slaves as persons usually only mention details of customs or appearance which struck the authors as quaint or interesting. Of the African homeland of their slaves the West Indians knew and cared little. Even the slavers visited West Africa only as traders, enjoying limited and revocable privileges granted to them by the local rulers. Their knowledge did not extend beyond the coast; and the coast on which they operated was long and varied, with a deep and populous hinterland. The markets which chiefly supplied the West Indies lay on the great middle stretches of the coast — Sierra Leone, the Grain Coast (Liberia), the Ivory, Gold and Slave Coasts, the Oil Rivers of the Niger Delta, Cameroon, Gaboon and Loango. Naturally people from this great area spoke many languages and exhibited many variations of culture and custom; but they also shared many traits in common. Their languages belonged to one or the other of two great families — Sudanic and Bantu. The principal tribes in the heart of the slaving area were the Fanti-Ashanti peoples of the Gold Coast, the Dahomeans, the Yoruba of western Nigeria and the Bini of southern Nigeria. All these peoples were composites of many smaller groups, welded through a long process of conquest into more or less homogeneous kingdoms ruled by powerful, stable, and often ruthless dynasties. All were essentially agricultural: but they possessed also a considerable range of handcraft industries, and wide trade connections. They had cities of considerable size, elaborate markets for the exchange of goods, a recognised means of exchange — cowrie shells — and crude but efficient systems of taxation. Slavery had long existed throughout the region. Prisoners taken in inter-tribal war were commonly enslaved, and wars were undertaken deliberately for the purpose. Slaves might also be recruited by kidnapping or by purchase. All the rulers of the area kept large numbers of slaves. In Dahomey a plantation system existed, resembling the régime which the slaves were to encounter in the New World. Apart from work in field or household, slaves were valuable for sacrifice and as export goods, with which the rulers and their sub-chiefs could purchase guns, gunpowder, hardware and European cloth, from the deep-sea slavers who supplied the New World market.

Arrived in the New World, the Africans displayed the variety of their origins, and most West Indian accounts of plantation life give lists of types of slaves, with the characteristics ascribed to them: Senegalese, Coromantees, Whydahs, Nagoes, Pawpaws, Eboes, Mocoes, Congoes, Angolas, Mandingoes, and so on. The names are imprecise and sometimes misleading; many of them refer merely to ports of shipment. Beneath the variety of origin and language, and the real or supposed differences of character, the newcomers showed underlying similarities of behaviour. As might be expected of fighting peoples, they reacted against their enslavement and exile with a bitter and active resentment, very different from the sullen apathy of the Amerindian. The first serious servile mutiny in Barbados occurred in 1649; and throughout the history of New World slavery, mutiny, or the danger of mutiny, was a constant feature of plantation life. There was no lack of leaders for such designs, for the recruitment of slaves by war or kidnapping did not discriminate on grounds of social status, and chiefs and shamans reached the New World with the rest. Overt risings, it is true, could usually be prevented, or punished, by stern repression, but individuals could and did express their resentment in other ways: by suicide, by infanticide, or by running away — especially in islands such as Jamaica where mountains and forests offered shelter to fugitive groups. Apart from these desperate acts, resentment found regular expression in calculated idleness, giving the owner the bare minimum of labour necessary to escape the whip; in wilful carelessness and destructiveness in handling the owner's property, whether tools, fences, buildings or stock; and in feigned stupidity. On the other hand, the natural resilience, physical strength, and imitative capacity of the African enabled him to adapt himself to adverse conditions and to acquire, given the opportunity, such European habits and skills as seemed to him desirable. Eventually negroes and mulattoes worked out, in the West Indies, a way of living which was not that of any single African group from which slaves were drawn, nor a composite of African folk-ways, but a character-istically West Indian amalgam. The process was slow; for plantation life discouraged inventiveness, and the purely African element was constantly reinforced, for a hundred and fifty or two hundred years, by fresh importation.

The character and habits of the European community, no less than those of the negroes, were modified and shaped by the growth of plantation slavery. The planters, or at least the more successful among them, soon came to form a small close-grained oligarchy in the islands. Living as they did, surrounded by men of another colour, concentrated on getting rich quick in strange surroundings and in a trying climate, they naturally appear acquisitive, quarrelsome, often ruthless; but they must have been men of enterprise and courage. They, together with a handful of lawyers, doctors and merchants, ran the politics of the islands. Below them in the social and economic scale were the various grades of plantation employees — overseers, 'book-keepers' or foremen, and the skilled tradesmen, carpenters, masons, smiths and the like, who, with the help of slaves, maintained the buildings and estates. Farther down the scale came the considerable but dwindling body of poor whites. The poor white labourers on the estates in the seventeenth century worked alongside the slaves, lived in similar circumstances, and interbred with them; but towards the end of the century in most of the English colonies the legislatures, alarmed at the growing disproportion between Europeans and Africans and the shortage of free men to serve in the militias, began to pass Acts designed to improve the condition of white servants and to leave avenues of employment open to them. The amount and kind of punishment inflicted on them was limited; it was forbidden in many islands to train slaves in skilled trades; and 'Deficiency Acts' required planters to employ fixed proportions of white servants under pain of fine. These measures, distinguishing as they did between white, as such, and black, as such, emphasised the division of society according to colour rather than, as formerly, according to legal and economic status; and naturally the poor whites clung fiercely to the theory of social superiority which the Acts implied. Legislation, however, had very little effect in attracting fresh indented labour; and as for the Deficiency laws, prosperous planters often preferred to pay the fines. They no longer had much use for indented servants.

The small garrison of white planters believed, with reason, that its safety depended upon maintaining rigorous discipline among the slaves; hence the severe penalties imposed for servile indiscipline, by Acts of the island legislatures in the British islands, and by metropolitan legislation in the French. Typical of such penalties were flogging, for threatening a white person; the loss of a hand, for striking a white person; the loss of an ear for theft; or for repeated thefts, hanging. The punishments for mutiny were savage in the extreme, including, in some places, burning alive. In addition, the internal discipline of plantations, though it naturally varied greatly according to the disposition of owner or overseer, was necessarily also severe, and the whip, wielded by privileged slaves or 'drivers', was often in evidence in the fields. The French colonies possessed a general code of slave law, the *Code Noir*, based on information collected by Colbert, and promulgated by Louis XIV in 1685. This celebrated and detailed code reflected in its every clause the haunting fear of servile mutiny, and the determination of government to prevent insurrections being provoked by the irresponsibility of owners. It made clear the legal status of slaves, whose ownership and sale was to be regulated by 'nos ordonnances et les coûtumes pour la saisie des choses mobilières'. It limited plantation punishments and forbade 'Traitemens barbares des maîtres envers leurs esclaves'. It prescribed minimum conditions of feeding and housing, in order to 'assurer la conservation des esclaves, et le . . . repos des peuples qui sont fatigués et même la plupart ruinés par le vol et le pillage qu'ils souffrent des esclaves qui, ne recevant pas de nourriture des patrons, en cherchent partout et n'en peuvent trouver'. Though it prescribed very severe penalties for the criminal offences of slaves, it affirmed their right to formal trial, and granted them a number of important civil rights, especially in the matter of marriage. The separation of families was prohibited; and the rules concerning manumission were relatively liberal. The Spanish laws of the Indies contained similar provisions, and on the whole the slaves seem to have been better treated in the Spanish dependencies than elsewhere. In practice, however, the plantation slave everywhere was very much at the mercy of his owner, and his hope of good treatment depended largely upon the owner's reluctance to damage valuable property.

Bryan Edwards, that cultivated planter-philosopher whom only the eighteenth century could have produced, quotes Burke's remark that 'Where slavery is established in any part of the world, those who are free are by far the most proud and jealous of their freedom'. Certainly the sugar revolution did nothing to weaken the attachment of the British West Indians to the representative institutions and the legal guarantees of personal liberty which they had brought with them from England. Each island had its assembly, elected by the freeholding planters, with the right to vote taxes and make laws not repugnant to the laws of England. It is true that the determined and skilful attempts of the later Stuart administrations, to tighten and centralise control over the colonies, affected the assemblies' powers to some extent. Barbados and the Leeward Islands were obliged, in 1663, to accept the imposition of a permanent 4½ per cent export duty as the price of the resumption by the Crown of the Carlisle grant; and this revenue, which lasted until 1838, was not always used entirely for the benefit of the islands. From the Restoration onwards, moreover, government was able to insist on colonial laws being sent home for confirmation, and the power of disallowance was freely used. The home government also appointed the senior colonial officials; governors were appointed by commissions under the Great Seal, and they nominated the members of their councils, which were the local policy-making bodies; other officials, colonial secretaries, provost-marshals, and so on, were appointed in England by letters-patent; a mode of appointment which, like many other arbitrary practices, originated under the Commonwealth but was widely extended at the Restoration. The habits of representative government, however, were too deeply ingrained to be easily changed. The permanent revenues granted in Barbados, the Leeward Islands, and, later, Jamaica were quite inadequate for the needs of administration, so that assemblies always held a powerful weapon in their ability to withhold supply; governors chose their councillors from among leading local planters, having no alternative; patent officers commonly served by deputy, and the deputies were usually local people, so that the king's administration lay largely in West Indian hands. In practice it was extremely difficult for governors to enforce unpopular legislation in the teeth of local public opinion, and governors such as Dutton in Barbados, who took an unduly high tone with their assemblies, were often rewarded by recall and disgrace. So strong was the self-governing tradition that even a newly conquered colony, Jamaica, was able to secure the grant of representative institutions, similar to those of Barbados, within a few years of the conquest, and to defend them, between 1676 and 1680, against the encroachments of a Restoration government whose policy was avowedly one of centralisation and control — 'there being nothing' (in the words of the Assembly) 'that invites people more to settle and remove their family and flock to this remote part of the world than the assurance they have always had of being governed in such a manner that none of their rights should be lost, so long as they are within the dominions of the Kingdom of England'.

No such traditional obstacles to centralised administration existed in the French islands. In 1664 Colbert arranged for the resumption of the Proprieties which had been created after the collapse of the Company of the Isles of America, and entrusted the administration of all the French possessions in America and West Africa to a new company, controlled and partly financed by government, known as the Compagnie des Indes Occidentales. This mammoth corporation obviously owed many of its characteristics to Dutch example. It was better designed for plunder and territorial aggression than for trade or administration, and its monopoly was bitterly resented by the colonists. The company, collapsing under its own weight, became bankrupt and was wound up in 1674 — the same year which saw the end of the Dutch company. The Crown assumed direct control, and the islands thereafter were governed by the curious dual administration characteristic of all the French colonies for the next hundred years and more. The supreme command in the area was entrusted to an officer whose chief duties were indicated in his title — 'Lieutenant-général, commandant des armées de terre et de mer, et gouverneur-général des îles du Vent pour le roi'. Under the governor-general stood the military governors of the several islands, whose seniority — Martinique, Guadeloupe, Saint-Christophe, Marie-Galante — was laid down by royal instruction in 1667. The authority of each governor was supported, or balanced, by that of a civil administrator, an *intendant*, who was primarily responsible for justice, economic regulation, and finance. Each governor, also, was assisted by a *conseil souverain*, which advised him in matters of policy, though its primary function was that of a court of appeal. The *intendants* were presidents *ex officio* of these bodies, but the other council members, in most cases ten in number, were nominated by the governors. A majority of them were usually *officiers d'épée*; the French government, unlike the Spanish, had no particular predilection for professional lawyers in colonial government. Just as the assemblies in the British islands aped the prerogatives and pretentions of the House of Commons, so the *conseils souverains* claimed rights analogous to those exercised by the *parlements* in France; in particular the right to register, or refuse to register, ministerial decrees emanating from France. Such claims were never recognised or encouraged by the Crown. Repeated and emphatic instructions, addressed to governors, laid down that the *conseils* were to confine themselves to their judicial duties and to offer advice only when asked for it. The *conseils*, composed of prominent local people, wielded a formidable local influence, and could make things difficult for governors they disliked. In this they resembled the British West Indian assemblies; but in no other way. They neither voted money nor made laws. Legislation and taxation were both by royal decree. The governors had wide powers in their own right, notably in matters of defence; they might, for instance, require the use of privately owned slaves for building fortifications and other public works. The planters complained constantly to the king about abuses of this power, but seldom got any satisfaction. The governors of the English islands, accustomed to wheedling money from factious assemblies, must often have envied their French colleagues in this respect. The French system was designed for military ends; despite the small numbers of the island populations, it could be very formidable, as the English West Indians discovered to their cost in the war of 1665–67 when Antigua, Montserrat and Saint Kitts fell into the hands of the French, to be either recaptured, or restored at the Treaty of Breda, in sadly damaged condition.

In the formulation of mercantilist theory, in the enactment of legislation, and in the creation of a colonial trade system, the English held a slight lead over the French. The Acts of Trade under the restored Stuarts had strengthened and reduced to a system the tentative enactments of the Commonwealth. The Navigation Act of 1660 provided that no goods should be imported into or exported from any English colony except in English (or colonial) ships; and that 'enumerated' commodities — sugar, tobacco, cotton, indigo, ginger and dye-woods, all West Indian products — should be shipped only to England or to another English colony. The Staple Act of 1663 laid down that all goods, English or foreign, intended for the colonies must be shipped from an English port; the only exception of importance to West Indians was Madeira wine. The Plantations' Duties Act of 1673 laid a substantial export duty on all 'enumerated' commodities shipped from one colony to another; its purpose was to discourage illicit sales to foreigners under colour of inter-colonial trade. In return for the restrictions placed upon colonial producers by these measures, the home government offered a protected market for sugar and other West Indian products, and naval protection. A special official — the Clerk to the Naval Office — was appointed in each colony to enforce the Acts; and offences against them were punishable by the Courts of Vice-Admiralty, set up in the colonies by the consolidating Navigation Act of 1696.

The West Indian colonies were ideally adapted to the economic concept of empire embodied in these enactments. For mercantile theorists the ideal colony was one where a small number of

English planters supervised a large non-English labour force in producing tropical commodities. To complete the mercantilist scheme, a chartered monopoly was granted in 1660 to the concern which later (in 1672) became known as the Royal African Company, to supply the West Indians with the slaves they needed for the large-scale production of sugar. The company was never a financial success; but its failure to supply slaves in adequate number was more than made up by the activities of English interlopers. The profits of the trade in slaves and sugar justified the legislative care bestowed upon them; despite their repeated protests against restrictions and monopolies, the West Indians themselves grew rich, and the merchants who dealt with them grew richer still. At the end of the seventeenth century the West Indies supplied 9 per cent of English imports, as against 8 per cent from the mainland colonies; they took more of English exports than the mainland (4 per cent as against less than 4 per cent), and they accounted for 7 per cent of the total English trade, as against 6 per cent by the mainland. Their value proved so great and so enduring that even Adam Smith — certainly no friend of colonies in general — had to admit, three-quarters of a century later, that 'The profits of a sugar plantation in any one of our West Indian colonies are generally much greater than those of any other cultivation that is known either in Europe or America'.

In the French West Indies the enactment and, as far as possible, the enforcement of consistently mercantilist legislation began with the appointment of Colbert to ministerial power in 1661. It followed closely the precedents set by the English Acts, and like them was initially directed against the Dutch middlemen. The Compagnie des Indes Occidentales held, from 1664, a monopoly of all trade, including the slave trade, with the French West Indies. The monopoly ended with the company in 1674, but a long series of decrees thereafter forbade foreign ships to visit the islands, and a succession of companies held monopolies of the slave trade, beginning with the Compagnie d'Afrique chartered in 1679. All these ventures ran into financial difficulties and became the target of bitter attack by the colonists (as did the English company which they resembled; but the French for a long time were unable to fill the gap by 'interloping', and French planters often bought from Dutch and English slavers). The whole body of provisions which comprised the 'pacte colonial' were embodied in a decree of 1698, which laid down severe penalties: confiscation of ship and cargo for the foreign smuggler; and fine, imprisonment, or galley sentence for French colonists who engaged in contraband trade with foreigners. Enforcement was entrusted to the governors of the several islands. No special officers were appointed, and on the whole the French were considerably less successful than the English in keeping foreign smugglers and slavers away from their West Indian colonies. Their merchant marine was not adequate for operating an efficient monopoly and English interlopers as well as Dutch poached upon their preserves. Not until the eighteenth century, when the French islands began to exceed the English in productivity, and French shipping became more nearly equal to its task, was an effective yet flexible system of regulation introduced. In Colbert's own day the peculiarly rigid mercantilism which he introduced rested on blanket prohibitions, and on the use of force.

Widely though they differed in constitutional habits and administrative methods, the French and English Caribbean empires resembled one another closely in their social structure, with its brittle and quarrelsome planting oligarchies and its mass of recently imported mutinous negro slaves. They were even more alike in their economic character and policy. Both had profited by Dutch precept and example; in both the sugar revolution had been fostered by Dutch trade and Dutch capital; both, when they felt themselves to be strong enough, had turned upon the Dutch and sought to exclude them. The policy of exclusion had, in large measure, succeeded, and Dutch trade declined. The Dutch West India Company's Caribbean business had suffered a major reverse in 1654, when at the Treaty of Westminster its slaving stations in Angola and the Congo Delta were restored to Portugal, and the English obtained the right to trade there. In 1664 the English seized also the Dutch barracoons at Gorée and Cape Coast Castle. Gorée was soon recaptured; but in 1677 it was again taken, this time by the French, who kept it. In addition, the wars with England and France severely damaged the company's shipping. In 1674 the company went bankrupt. Individual Dutch traders still did much business in the Caribbean, but decreasingly in the French and English islands. Two rival groups of settlers, two sets of mercantile monopolists, and two metropolitan governments, French and English, confronted one another in the Outer Antilles. Both governments appreciated the immense value of the sugar industry; both understood the importance of the slave trade and the complementary connection between the West Indies and West Africa. Each was resolutely determined to monopolise the trade of its own colonies; and each looked with envious eyes on the trade and the territorial possessions of the other. The mutual tolerance which had permitted, for instance, the original partition of St. Christopher, was giving way to mutual fear and jealousy. As early as 1667 Père du Tertre in his *Histoire Générale des Antilles* had listed the 'Raisons qui prouvent qu'il est impossible que les deux Nations Françoise et Angloise puissent vivre en paix'. The rivals were preparing for the vast and costly game of beggar-my-neighbour which was to be the history of the sugar islands throughout the eighteenth century.

CHAPTER VI

THE BUCCANEERS

THE TREATY OF BREDA, which ended the Second Dutch War in 1667, laid down a territorial division in the eastern Caribbean which was to endure without major change for half a century. The Dutch kept Willoughby's old settlement of Surinam; the French kept Tobago; St. Christopher was divided as before; and all other conquests were restored. The lines of future Anglo-French rivalry were clearly laid. Wars in plenty, it is true, lay ahead. In the Third Dutch War (1672–78), in which England joined with France in an attack on the commercial ascendancy of the Dutch, and in King William's War (1689–97), in which the alliances were reversed, war in Europe was reflected by fighting in the West Indies. The governors of settled islands, in particular Barbados and Martinique, led armed expeditions against neighbouring islands and made many temporary annexations. St. Eustatius — that scrub-covered rock in the Leeward Islands which Dutch genius made the richest free port in the Americas — was bandied about like a shuttle-cock; it changed hands ten times between 1664 and 1674. But usually the peace treaties restored the *status quo ante bellum*; and at least the wars were official wars, formally declared. The peace between wars was real peace, not a mere exchange of piracy for privateering. Intelligent and public-spirited governors like Willoughby, Stapleton, and Codrington, realising that the uncertain support of gangs of desperadoes could give no lasting assurances of safety in peace or war, gave no countenance to pirates within their governments.

Farther west, in the Greater Antilles and the sea surrounding them, no such convention yet existed. The long privateering war against Spain had sown dragons' teeth among the islands. For generations this continuous, irregular warfare had been a source of wealth to the bold or the lucky. In Jamaica, in western Hispaniola, in Tortuga, in the Bay Islands, there were whole communities of the men, commonly called buccaneers, with whom raiding was a habit, not easily or willingly discarded. To the buccaneers a treaty of peace meant merely a change from public employment to private enterprise; for the 'sweet trade' was their livelihood.

The word *boucan* means the process of curing strips of meat by smoking over a slow fire; and the *boucaniers* were originally men who lived by hunting and by selling hides and smoked meat to passing ships. All the islands of the Greater Antilles supported great herds of wild — or rather feral — pigs and horned cattle, the descendants of escapes from Spanish farms and ranches, which multiplied and throve upon the virgin savannahs. The pursuit of these ownerless beasts offered a rough but not un-attractive living to masterless men — marooned or shipwrecked sailors, deserters, escaped felons, runaway indented servants, and all such as disliked organised society; and many of them varied hunting with robbery by land or by sea. Spanish settlements and shipping, being nearest to hand, naturally suffered most. The Spanish governors did their best to round up these wild people living in the unsettled areas of the islands. In Hispaniola mobile lancer squadrons — 'cinquantaines' — were employed against them from about 1640, and attempts were made to starve them into surrender by killing out or driving away the herds on which they depended. The only result was to drive the buccaneers to further piracy, and to turn their antipathy to government in general into a vindictive hatred of Spanish government. By the middle of the century they had come to form dangerous outlaw bands, accustomed to hardship, well armed and (for so long as they chose to obey) well led. Like most wild and lawless communities, they possessed conventions of their own and were rigid in their adherence to the 'custom of the coast'. The best description of their ways is that of the indulgent du Tertre, who had dealings with them, and knew them well enough to say Mass occasionally on board their ships; for many of them retained vestiges of their religious allegiance. Political allegiance they had none, except on occasion as bloodthirsty and unreliable mercenaries. The presence of such bands in the heart of the Spanish Caribbean was a perpetual temptation to aggressive colonial governors, French or English, and a perpetual menace to trade and peaceful settlement.

The buccaneers included in their ranks desperadoes of many nations, or of none; but most of them were either English or French. The idea of employing them as auxiliaries for commerce raiding in time of war seems to have occurred first to a Frenchman, de Poincy, governor of Saint-Christophe on behalf of the Knights of Malta. De Poincy had had difficulty in controlling quarrels between his Catholic and Protestant settlers, and solved the problem in 1639 by sending the leading Huguenots away on an expedition to settle the island of Tortuga as a French outpost. Tortuga had become an international haunt of buccaneers since the massacre of the Providence Company's settlers in 1635; but there had been quarrels there between French and English freebooters. The Huguenot leader, Le Vasseur, managed to get himself accepted as governor by the French among the buccaneers, and soon elbowed out the English. Le Vasseur was a competent military engineer, trained in the hard school of the siege of La Rochelle. He made himself virtually independent of de Poincy, systematically fortified Tortuga, and established himself there as a semi-official governor and robber leader. The island became the most notorious of the pirate strongholds from which attacks were launched against the Spaniards, and to which the resulting booty was carried for division.

Le Vasseur was a leader of unusual skill. After his death — he was assassinated in 1653 — the Spaniards defeated his successor and captured the island, driving the buccaneers back into the forests of northern Hispaniola; but the Spanish garrison, stationed at Tortuga in 1654, was withdrawn in 1655 to help in the defence of Santo Domingo against Penn and Venables, and the buccaneers came drifting back. D'Oyley, when governor of Jamaica, tried to attach the island stronghold to his government, but the French element was too strong, and he gave up the attempt. Instead, the English buccaneers, outnumbered in Tortuga, began more and more to make their headquarters at Port Royal.

To leave Tortuga and the Hispaniola forest camps and establish themselves openly in an English Crown colony the buccaneers needed at least the tacit approval of the governor. The attitude of the government of Jamaica depended, at any moment, upon its relations with Spain and with the surrounding colonies. There were two alternative policies. One was the old

Commonwealth (and late Elizabethan) policy of continuous informal war against the Spanish colonies, encouraging the buccaneers to raid where they could and to bring their spoils to Jamaica. The other policy was to make Jamaica a commercial centre, selling slaves and manufactured goods to the Spaniards, by agreement if possible, or, failing agreement, by smuggling. Obviously the two policies could not be combined, because the second required the establishment of an understanding with the neighbouring Spaniards, and so necessarily involved calling off the buccaneers. Both the home government and the government of Jamaica wavered between these two policies for twenty years or more. During the initial fighting in Jamaica the buccaneers were welcomed and encouraged. Charles II, however, on his accession, attempted (while retaining Jamaica) to secure a trade with the Spanish Indies by agreement. In accordance with this policy Sir Thomas Modyford, an old Barbadian, was appointed in 1664 governor of Jamaica, bringing with him about a thousand Barbadian farmers who decided to settle in Jamaica. He did his best, at first, to convince his Spanish colleagues of his will and his ability to suppress the buccaneers, but without much success; for if he succeeded in driving them from Port Royal they merely transferred to Tortuga. By the end of 1664 Charles had become persuaded that his hopes of accommodation with Spain were unlikely to be fulfilled. At the same time he was confronted with war against the Dutch, and the possibility, which in 1666 became a fact, of having to fight Dutch and French together. The buccaneers were almost the only fighting men available in the West Indies. In order to enlist their help Modyford, in 1665, was authorised to grant commissions of 'reprisal' to buccaneer captains. The plunder they might secure from the Spaniards was to be their payment for their services in the war. Once again there was to be 'no peace beyond the Line'. Since the home government could not easily afford the expense of regular naval and military forces, it hoped to defend Jamaica, Barbados, and the other West Indian colonies by means of planter militias, using the buccaneers as a striking force by sea.

The main drawback to this plan of using the buccaneers as mercenaries, paid by plunder, was that they would only willingly serve where plunder was to be had — against the Spaniards, with whom England was technically at peace. The events of the

Dutch wars showed how unreliable they were against Dutch or French. They proved useless against Saint-Christophe; they flatly refused to attack Curaçao; and although they took St. Eustatius in 1666, that island was seized by the French very shortly afterwards, and restored to the Dutch at the Treaty of Breda. It was not the efforts of the buccaneers, but the belated arrival of a small naval squadron under Berry, which enabled the Barbadians to take the offensive in 1667 and recapture Antigua and Montserrat. Against the Spaniards, on the other hand, under colour of 'reprisals' for real or fancied injuries, the Port Royal buccaneers maintained a campaign as brilliant as it was brutal. The success of their first big raid in Central America, where they penetrated far up the San Juan river and sacked the undefended town of Granada, upset the balance of Modyford's plans; but he, having no other force at his disposal, was obliged to truckle to success and welcome them back to Port Royal. Probably his disapproval was half-hearted; and from most of the inhabitants of Jamaica the buccaneers could count on an enthusiastic welcome. In 1665–66 under Mansfield (himself a Hollander) they raided the coasts of Cuba, temporarily re-captured Old Providence, and raked over the ruins of Granada for whatever might be left.

After this first Cuba raid Mansfield disappeared, and the leadership at Port Royal fell upon a greater and luckier ruffian, Henry Morgan, whose career provides an epitome of this period of West Indian history. He had come out as an indented servant to Barbados, but ran away to join the buccaneers and became prominent among them while still in his twenties; he exploited his position as a leader of mercenaries, acquired wealth and land, was knighted, became lieutenant-governor of Jamaica, and was found by Hans Sloane living there in 1688 in dropsical middle-age, surrounded by doctors (including Sloane), peevishly dis-regarding their advice and drinking himself to death. He was at the height of his fame in the 'sixties and early 'seventies. In 1668 Modyford commissioned him, first to carry out a reconnaissance in Cuba, where he suspected that an expedition against Jamaica was fitting out, and then to make a diversionary attack on Puerto Bello, with a force of 400 English buccaneers. Puerto Bello was fortified and had a garrison of some 300 men: but Morgan took the place by the kind of surprise attack at which he excelled,

G

advancing up creeks and through swamp and forest by night.
The garrison, after surrender, were locked up in the fort,
which was then blown up by firing the magazine. It was at
Puerto Bello that Morgan first acquired his unexampled reputation for pillage and torture of prisoners. His men brought
back 250,000 pieces of eight, besides goods and munitions, to
Port Royal, where — according to the unctuous Esquemeling,
who probably sailed with them — 'they passed here some time
in all sorts of vices and debauchery, according to their common
manner of doing, spending with huge prodigality what others
had gained with no small labour and toil'.

The raid on Puerto Bello established Morgan's reputation as
a bold, skilful and lucky leader, and in the following year, 1669,
he openly fitted out in Port Royal a fleet of ten sail with nearly
a thousand men, for an attack on Cartagena, the centre of Spanish
naval power in the southern Caribbean. At the last moment,
however, Morgan decided that Cartagena was too strong for him
— the buccaneers in general were not at their best in attacking
formal fortifications — and sailed for Maracaibo instead. Maracaibo had been thoroughly sacked and looted the year before, by
a force from Tortuga under the savage L'Ollonais, and the
familiar routine of burning and torture produced only a small
ransom; but on his way out from the lagoon Morgan encountered
three Spanish men-of-war, carrying silver from Puerto Bello,
which had been ordered to intercept him. All three were
captured, and burned or beached, so that Morgan returned to
Port Royal with enough loot to satisfy his men, to keep the
governor quiet, and to fit out yet another expedition in 1670.
This was Morgan's last and biggest enterprise. Commissioned
by Modyford in reprisal for a small Spanish raid on Jamaica, he
sailed for the Main, with some 1,500 men, including about 500
Frenchmen from Tortuga, sacked Santa Marta and Río de la
Hacha, paid Puerto Bello another devastating visit, and then,
in December 1670, marched his men across the Isthmus, to
attack Panama. The march took nine days. The citizen militia
of Panama resisted to the best of their strength, which was not
large; it was on this occasion that the Spaniards attempted the
curious, but hopeless, expedient of stampeding herds of wild
cattle in the hope of breaking the enemy's ranks. But Panama
was doomed. Most of the inhabitants — those who failed to

escape in the forest — were killed or tortured to death; the city was utterly destroyed by fire, and was never rebuilt upon its old site.

Panama was the climax of Morgan's bloodthirsty career, and the events of this last raid naturally invite comparison between his achievements and those of Drake a hundred years before. There was little enough similarity between the two men — the chivalrous, narrowly pious and patriotic naval officer, leading a sternly disciplined force against an empire at the height of its vigour and defended by admirals of genius; and the elected leader of bands of cut-throats, organising the pillage of almost undefended towns of the same empire in a period of hesitation and decline. Drake, moreover, brought his fleets from England, four thousand miles away; Morgan had a convenient base for his operations, in the midst of the enemy's possessions. Nevertheless, in his boldness, in his brilliant tactical skill, especially in combined operations, and in his leadership, Morgan was in the tradition of Drake. He covered most of Drake's ground, and the forces which he led were of the same order of size. The buccaneers of the seventeenth century were the debased and brutalised successors of the Protestant corsairs of the sixteenth.

Morgan got a formal vote of thanks from the Council of Jamaica in May 1671; but during his year of absence events had taken place in Europe which put an end to the use of buccaneers as an important instrument of English policy. The long negotiations between England and Spain, for a formal treaty of peace which should include America, concluded in 1670 with the Treaty of Madrid, which bound both parties to abstain from pillage and to revoke all letters of marque and reprisal. More significant still, by this treaty Spain for the first time acknowledged officially the presence of the English in the Caribbean: 'The Most Serene King of Great Britain, his heirs and successors, shall have, hold and possess for ever, with full right of sovereignty, ownership and possession, all the lands, regions, islands, colonies and dominions, situated in the West Indies or in any part of America, that the said King of Great Britain and his subjects at present hold and possess. . . .'

The logical outcome of all this was the recall of Modyford, and his replacement by a governor who could be trusted at least to try to enforce the new policy; but for years Jamaica remained an open haunt of the ruffians whom he had protected. Modyford himself went to England and was lodged in the Tower, for appearance' sake, though he was soon released, and never brought to trial or deprived of his share of the buccaneers' loot. He died in Jamaica. His monument in Spanish Town Cathedral describes him as 'the best and longest Governor, the most considerable planter, the ablest and most upright judge, the island ever engaged'. His successor, Sir Thomas Lynch, made strenuous attempts to carry out the new policy, as lieutenant-governor, though with no armed force at his disposal he could not move very effectively against the buccaneers. Morgan was still swaggering about Port Royal, in possession of the gains of ten years of rapine; and under two of Lynch's successors, Vaughan and Carlisle, he was employed as lieutenant-governor, on the dubious principle of setting a thief to catch a thief. In 1677 six English buccaneering ships sacked Santa Marta, and neither Vaughan nor Morgan could lay them by the heels. Coxon, an old associate of Morgan, in 1678 raided the ports of the Gulf of Honduras, and loaded up his ships with cochineal, indigo and cacao. When he put into Port Royal, Morgan allowed him to refit there before sailing to Rhode Island to sell his loot — for the New England ports were the best market then for stolen cargoes. This same Coxon, in association with another pirate named Sawkins, actually crossed the Isthmus in 1680, seized some Spanish ships, and plundered a series of small harbours all down the Pacific coast, returning home by way of Cape Horn. This outrage occurred during the negotiations for the Treaty of Windsor between Spain and England. Every West Indian governor was alert to punish the perpetrators of it, and some of Coxon's men were caught and hanged. Even Morgan turned policeman in earnest; but it was not until 1685 that a small frigate squadron was sent to Jamaica for the purpose of hunting down pirates, and that buccaneers in considerable numbers came to 'swing and sun-dry' at Port Royal or Execution Dock. By that time Lynch had returned to the West Indies for his second period of office, and even in Jamaica public opinion had turned against the buccaneers. Both the West Indian interest in England and the merchants in the West Indies were determined to 'force a trade' with the Spanish colonies, by smuggling if need be, using Jamaica as a base and *entrepôt*. For this they needed real and not merely formal peace. As if to mark the end of an age, both Morgan himself and Albemarle, the last governor who countenanced the old ruffian, died in 1688; and old Port Royal, wicked, opulent and shabby, paid the price of its sins — so the pious believed — and disappeared beneath the sea in the great earthquake of 1692.

All this time Tortuga had remained wide open; for the French were not greatly interested in the prospects of local trade with the Spanish colonies, and still saw advantages to be gained from backing the buccaneers. The activities of the Tortuga *flibustiers* had one important indirect result, the establishment of Saint-Domingue, the western part of the great island of Hispaniola, as a French plantation. After the evacuation of the small Spanish settlements in 1605, the area for many years was inhabited chiefly by cattle-hunting buccaneers. The fortification of Tortuga in French hands gave them a supporting base to which they could retire by sea whenever the Spanish authorities tried to hunt them out; and similarly when French discipline at Tortuga became irksome they could disappear into the Hispaniola forest to resume their butcher's business. Not only in Tortuga, but in Hispaniola also, buccaneer harbours grew up, at Petit-Goave, Léogane and Port-de-Paix. The conscious organisation of these nests of pirates into a colony began with the appointment of d'Ogéron as governor of Tortuga for the Compagnie des Indes in 1665. D'Ogéron already knew the West Indies well; he had been a planter in Martinique and Jamaica, a salt trader in the Caicos, and at times a buccaneer. The orders which the company gave him, to use Tortuga as a base to cover settlement in Hispaniola, probably originated in his own suggestions, and he carried them out with conviction and great ability, settling families on the land, often at his own expense; encouraging the cultivation of maize, tobacco and cacao, and organising their sale, often to the buccaneers; and even arranging for prostitutes to be rounded up in France and transported, in order to encourage the buccaneers to settle in domestic surroundings. With the buccaneers themselves he maintained friendly relations; he succeeded in making himself indispensable to them, both as the official approver of their raids and as an efficient, though grasping, middleman. Any successful West Indian governor at that time had to become a receiver of stolen goods if he wished, as both Modyford and d'Ogéron did, to keep on good terms with the buccaneers and employ them as mercenaries. With great skill d'Ogéron separated his government by gradual degrees into two distinct communities: a comparatively respectable settlement in Saint-Domingue, where the spread of planting drove away the wild cattle and the development of trade discouraged piracy; and a strongly held base in Tortuga under his own control, where he hoped to discipline and militarise the 1,500 or 2,000 buccaneers who frequented the place.

The Tortuga buccaneers took a prominent part in the Caribbean fighting during the Third Dutch War from 1672 to 1678, which brought the Dutch West India Company to bankruptcy and ruin in 1674, and enabled the French to enforce a commercial monopoly in their own West Indian colonies. Like the English buccaneers, however, the French preferred raiding the Spanish Main to fighting the Dutch; and like the English, they balked at the task of attacking Curaçao. The major French successes of the war were in Europe. At the Treaties of Nijmegen in 1678 Louis XIV hoped, on the basis of European victories, to secure from Spain a recognition of his possession of Saint-Domingue. Had he succeeded in this he might well have decided to follow England's example and suppress the buccaneers. The Spanish government, however, refused to compromise on Saint-Domingue. At the same time Louis XIV was advised by D'Estrées that Spain was so weak that with a little additional pressure she would be compelled to grant France a share of the supposed 'riches of the Indies'. Accordingly the *flibustiers* were reprieved, maintained as a striking force, and backed by a strong fleet under D'Estrées. The years from 1678 to 1685 were the years of their greatest success and most savage reputation. During those years many of Morgan's old associates, preferring a pirate's life with a chance of the gallows to planting or standing up to their knees in water hauling logwood, left Jamaica for Tortuga and Saint Domingue to sail with van Horn, de Graaf, de Grammont or the Marquis de Maintenon. The Jamaica Assembly found it necessary to pass an Act forbidding British subjects to serve in foreign ships; but Morgan, in Jamaica, privately invested in some of the *flibustiers*' enterprises, many of which, for daring and cruelty, equalled his own. De Grammont established himself for six months in 1678 at a base near Maracaibo, whence he systematically raided the coastal settlements of Venezuela. The wretched settlers, indeed, had grown so accustomed to raiding that a hasty retirement to the woods, followed by ransom negotiations, was the automatic reaction to the appearance of a strange sail. De Maintenon robbed and almost destroyed the Margarita pearl fishery and pillaged the small Spanish settlements which were then the only habitations of white men in Trinidad. He invested the proceeds of these raids in sugar, and became the owner of the biggest plantation and factory in Martinique. The most successful and daring of all the French enterprises, however, was led by the two Hollanders, van Horn and de Graaf, with de Grammont as van Horn's lieutenant. This party in 1683 took and sacked the hitherto untouched port of San Juan de Ulúa, Vera Cruz. Their fleet was surprised in harbour, just as Hawkins had been a hundred years before, by the arrival of the *flota* from Spain; but times had changed. The *flota* was now a small fleet, only fourteen sail, and the captain-general dared not attack, but stood off and on outside the harbour while the buccaneers loaded their ships with money, goods and slaves, and sailed away to a nearby cay to divide the spoil. There the leaders fell to fighting over the division, and van Horn died of his wounds; but de Graaf and de Grammont survived to make another large-scale raid, against Yucatán in 1685, in which the city of Campeche was reduced to ashes.

These seven years, 1678 to 1685, were, ironically but characteristically, years of official peace, except for the brief war between Spain and France from December 1683 to July 1684, begun partly as the result of the Vera Cruz episode and terminated by the Truce of Ratisbon. Throughout the period the depredations of the buccaneers, though chiefly aimed against Spanish settlements, spared no ship which looked a likely prize. They were costly and embarrassing auxiliaries; and eventually the French government, like the English ten years before, was compelled by repeated protests to take measures against what had become a major international plague. Political circumstances pointed the same way. Common fear of France had begun to range England and the United Provinces on the side of Spain, both in Europe and in the Caribbean; and although neither did anything to help Spain in 1683, both were vigorous in their protests against the buccaneers. Moreover the possibility now lay before Louis XIV of acquiring the whole of the Spanish Indies by inheritance from the sickly idiot king Charles II; or else of imposing a successor who would grant the French a privileged position in the American trade. This was a more attractive prospect than mere casual plunder or piecemeal conquest. Already the Dutch, at the Treaty of The Hague in 1673, and the English, at the Treaty of Windsor in 1680, had made with Spain mutual and permanent promises to cease raiding. Only France still stuck to the convention of 'no peace beyond the Line'. At the Truce of Ratisbon France, too, abandoned the old convention, with its savage implications, and agreed that 'All hostilities shall cease on both sides, both by land and by sea and other waters, in all Kingdoms, countries, provinces, territories and dominions . . . within Europe and without, both on this side of and beyond the Line. . . .' As a guarantee of peace the truce was no more effective than any other of the numerous treaties of the period; but it marked the official end of buccaneering.

The actual end naturally took some time to achieve. The first governor with definite orders to put down buccaneering was de Cussy, appointed to Saint-Domingue in 1684. He could think of no better way of doing it than buying the leaders. De Grammont died at sea before his new royal commission could take effect, but de Graaf was successfully bribed into the royal service, as Morgan had been, and like Morgan played a part in the suppression of his former comrades. He lived to be one of the founders of the new French colony of Louisiana in the early eighteenth century. The final disbandment of the *flibustiers*, however, and the creation of lasting order and prosperity in Saint-Domingue was the work of an abler governor than de Cussy and a better sea commander than de Graaf. Jean-Baptiste du Casse began his seafaring career in the employment of the Compagnie de Sénégal, following up D'Estrées' capture of Gorée in 1677 by establishing his company's factory there. He first went to the West Indies, as a slaver, in 1680. From slaving he took to privateering, achieved a great local reputation, and in 1691 was appointed governor of Saint-Domingue. By that time William III was firmly established on the throne of England and most of Europe was allied against France in the war which bears his name. Du Casse's part in the war, besides the defence of Saint-Domingue, included two considerable offensive operations. The first was an invasion of Jamaica in 1694, which did great damage to crops, mills and dwellings and which was called off, apparently in the full tide of success, for reasons which have never been fully explained. The second was the successful and immensely lucrative capture of Cartagena, in 1697, in which du Casse and a force of buccaneers served alongside a formal naval squadron under de Pointis. In this engagement the buccaneers, for the first time, were paid the same exiguous share of the prize-money as naval seamen. They protested, and thanks to du Casse their protests were upheld; but once paid off they were disbanded and never employed again. Some became planters and some pirates, but under the rule of du Casse and his successors, with naval force in the area, they ceased to influence policy and were never again a serious menace.

As for du Casse, his ability found recognition in France; he became an admiral, served with great distinction the Kings of France and Spain in the war of the Spanish Succession, and ended his days as a Knight of the Orders of St. Louis and of the Golden Fleece — the last a distinction usually reserved for princes. His most enduring memorial, however, was Saint-Domingue, which by the Treaty of Ryswyck in 1697 was at last formally ceded to France. Du Casse gave it a firm and efficient administration, replaced piracy by peaceful trade, cattle-hunting by planting. He compelled the remaining buccaneers in Tortuga to evacuate the island and settle in Saint-Domingue. Saint-Domingue became for France a bigger and richer Jamaica. Like Jamaica, it developed as a land of large sugar plantations worked by slaves. In the eighteenth century it came to be regarded as the most valuable tropical possession of its size in the world.

With the Peace of Ryswyck, then, the age of the buccaneers came to an end. At no other time in Western history can a few thousand desperadoes have created a reign of terror over so vast an area, or have exercised so great and so continuous an influence upon the policy of civilised states. Their toll had been a terrible one. During the six years of Morgan's ascendancy, from 1655 to 1661, they had sacked eighteen cities, four towns, and nearly forty villages: Cumaná once, Cumanagote twice, Maracaibo and Gibraltar in Venezuela twice, Río de la Hacha five times, Santa

Marta three times, Tolú eight times, Puerto Bello once, Chagre twice, Panama once, Santa Catalina twice, Granada in Nicaragua twice, Campeche three times, Santiago de Cuba once, and other towns and villages in Cuba and Hispaniola for thirty leagues inland innumerable times; and this fearful tale of outrage does not include the English expeditions made after 1670, nor the still more wholesale depredations of the French. The development of the Greater Antilles as productive settlements was impossible while the buccaneers continued to receive support. Their suppression, delayed by political and strategic needs, was economically essential to merchant and planter alike. It did not, of course, mean an end to fighting; for in the eighteenth century the Caribbean was one of the essential theatres of a maritime war that lasted, with comparatively brief intervals, from the days of du Casse to those of Nelson. But eighteenth-century wars were fought by disciplined forces under responsible leaders, not by gangs of ruffians for private profit, at the expense of individuals. It was a sign of the growing importance of the West Indies in the economy and in the estimation of the Western world, that the age of the buccaneers should be followed by the age of the admirals.

CHAPTER VII

THE SLAVE TRADE AND THE *ASIENTOS*

THE SLAVE TRADE WAS the indispensable handmaid of the sugar industry. As sugar expanded at the expense of tobacco, and as the flow of European indented labour to the West Indies slowed to a trickle, the problem of organising a regular and reliable supply of slaves became a major preoccupation of governments. If supply failed, even for only a year or two, sugar production suffered; for slaves in those days were short-lived. Apart from ill-treatment, many negroes died in epidemics of unfamiliar diseases, or as the result of drinking raw spirits stolen from the distilleries. From the owners' point of view, replacement was more economical than rearing slave children. More and more negroes were constantly required, and the difficult, dangerous, and speculative business of importing them across four thousand miles of ocean became a trade second only in importance to that in sugar itself.

Naturally, in a mercantilist world which regarded monopoly as an essential measure of defence, and commercial competition as a mild form of war, the slave trade gave rise to incessant international dispute; and in the West Indies dispute was sharpened and complicated by the disproportion between territorial possessions and maritime strength. Of the five peoples most prominent in Caribbean trade, four — Portuguese, Dutch, English, French — acquired slaving bases in West Africa and engaged actively in the trade; but the Spaniards, while possessing by far the biggest and most populous colonial empire, never secured a firm foothold on the slave coasts and never (at least until the nineteenth century) appeared as serious competitors in the trade. They were always customers, never, or very rarely, suppliers. The policy of each of the other four powers, therefore, was to establish a monopoly of the supply of slaves to their own colonies; to sell a surplus to foreign colonies wherever possible; and above all to secure a share — or, better still, a monopoly if possible — in the supply of slaves to the Spanish colonies. In fact the Spaniards in the West Indies did not need, and could not afford to buy, very large numbers of slaves in the seventeenth century; the great days of Cuban sugar were still to come; but an exaggerated notion of the importance of the Spanish empire as a source of wealth and as a market for goods and slaves was prevalent throughout northern Europe, and persisted until the nineteenth century. It was the mercantilised version of the legend of Eldorado — a coveted prize, equally elusive, and no less a cause of misunderstanding and war.

In the sixteenth century Spanish America had depended chiefly upon the Portuguese for its supply of slaves. By means of fictions before 1580, openly thereafter, Portuguese slavers had shipped cargoes under individual licence from Seville, or else had smuggled slaves into the Indies. In 1595 the Spanish government, accepting the inevitable, had consented to the first of a long series of slave *Asientos*. This was an agreement for farming out the slave trade, or the greater part of it, to a contractor who was to organise the whole business, maintaining his own stations in Spain, in Africa, and in the Indies. He was to take over from the government the task of selling licences to sub-contractors, remitting the licence fees to the Crown. He and his sub-contractors might ship slaves directly from Africa to America, making their own arrangements for convoy and escort if necessary. From 1595 to 1640 Spanish America got most of its slaves from Lisbon slavers under agreements of this kind. From the sixteen-twenties, however, the effects of Dutch competition and hostility began to make themselves felt, both in West Africa and in the Caribbean; Portuguese contractors found it increasingly difficult to obtain and deliver cargoes, and were compelled to raise their prices. Finally in 1640 Portugal revolted successfully against Spanish rule and the *Asiento* broke down. From 1640 to the end of the seventeenth century the slave trade to the Spanish Indies was mainly contraband in Dutch hands. With the slave trade went an equally lucrative illicit trade in the main products of Spanish America — sugar, tobacco, cacao, cochineal, hides and silver. The Spanish trade monopoly, never very complete in practice, during this period broke down almost entirely.

In the sixteen-forties, when Dutch commercial ascendancy was at its height, sugar was introduced into Barbados and the Leeward Islands, and the English planters also began to buy slaves from Dutch traders; but this practice soon attracted adverse comment in England. It was contrary to mercantile policy to buy so valuable a commodity from foreigners, and the Navigation Acts made it illegal for Dutch ships to trade to English colonies. An alternative method of supply had to be found. An open trade would be dangerous in face of the inevitable hostility of the Dutch, firmly entrenched on the African coast. The English Crown had not the resources to undertake the building of forts and the provision of armed ships, so a company had to be formed for the purpose, and in 1663 Charles II granted a charter to the Company of Royal Adventurers of England trading into Africa. This group was the immediate successor of a company formed three years before for trading in ivory, dyewoods and gold. The 1663 charter changed it into a slaving concern. It was the direct predecessor of the larger and more powerful association incorporated in 1672 as the Royal Africa Company. Several members of the royal family were shareholders in this enterprise, which was to supply the English sugar colonies with 3,000 slaves a year at an average price of £17, or one ton of sugar, per slave. The purchase price in Africa at that time was about £3.

Through its many financial and constitutional vicissitudes the company drove a thriving trade, but nevertheless was perpetually on the verge of bankruptcy. There were three main reasons for this — the same difficulties which afflicted most of the great trading companies. One was the constant interruption of commerce by war — in this case the Dutch wars, which involved the company in serious losses of forts and ships and soon compelled it to put up its price to £25 or £35 per slave. Another was the invasion of the company's monopoly by interlopers. This was extremely difficult to prevent, because the company, like most such concerns, could not carry the stipulated number of slaves in its own ships, but made use of sub-contractors, who operated at their own risk but under licence from the company. It was easy for other slavers, who had paid no licence fee and had no connection with the company, to take advantage of the arrangements made with the slave-dealing chiefs, and then to undersell the company in the West Indies. Thirdly, the company — again like all such concerns — was cheated by its own agents, who bought slaves on their own account, transported them at their employers' expense, and sold them privately at the other end. A limited right to shipping space for private use was a normal perquisite for captains and other officers, but the limits were constantly exceeded. The practice increased the usual overcrowding still further, and contributed to the very high mortality on passage. The losses fell, of course, on the company: the negroes who died were always the company's slaves.

The company could increase its profits by selling some of its slaves at an enhanced price to the Spanish colonies; but Spanish-American ports were legally closed to English shipping. One solution of this difficulty was to make the Spaniards come to Jamaica or Barbados, buy their slaves there and take them away in their own ships; but that was contrary to the Navigation Act. The company had recourse, therefore, to one of the powers of the royal prerogative which was beginning to be a subject of constitutional dispute — the power to grant dispensations from statutes in particular cases. In 1663 Charles II granted a dispensation from the Navigation Act, to allow Spanish ships to visit English West Indian harbours for the purpose of buying slaves. The company sold a number of slaves to Spaniards in this way in Barbados; but the innovation raised a storm of protest among the English West Indian planters. They wanted all the available slaves for their own plantations. They feared that the competition of Spanish buyers would raise the price, and that the slaves sold to the Spaniards would be employed in producing sugar, which would compete with their own sugar in the European market. They carried on a bitter propaganda campaign against the Royal Africa Company's monopoly, clamoured constantly for a free trade in slaves, and continued to buy slaves from interlopers whenever they could. By 1698 this incessant propaganda had its effect, and an Act of Parliament in that year threw open the whole African trade to all British subjects, the company receiving a duty on imports into Africa, and on certain exports (not including slaves) to enable it to maintain its forts for the protection of all traders.

English official policy towards the slave trade faced a fundamental dilemma. Was the trade merely a means to an end, to supply the English colonies with slaves in order to increase and cheapen their production of sugar? Or was it to be an end in itself, to supply slaves to any market, English or foreign, where a demand existed? In the late seventeenth century the government on the whole supported the claims of the slavers against those of the planters, where they conflicted. It appeared, however, that the only hope of pleasing everybody lay in securing a separate contract for the supply of slaves to Spanish America. The Spaniards, for their part, were well aware that the *Asiento*, if revived at all, would have to go to a foreign company; but it was now regarded as so valuable a concession that its grant acquired all the characteristics of an international treaty, and would inevitably be used as an instrument of Spanish foreign policy. Charles II and William III both failed to secure the *Asiento* for their subjects; it was Louis XIV who succeeded.

The French, during the second half of the seventeenth century, had begun to take a close interest in the West African coast, particularly in Senegal, where French slavers, sailing mostly from Nantes, had almost ousted the Dutch by the end of the century. The French had a trade plan very similar to that of the English: a monopoly, operated by chartered companies, of the supply of slaves both to their own islands and to the Spanish possessions in the Caribbean. Political circumstances favoured their design. A union between the French and Spanish crowns, or at least a Bourbon prince on the Spanish throne, seemed at the end of the century to be a likely development; and no more suitable contractor for the *Asiento* could be found. An *Asiento* was accordingly concluded with the French Guinea Company in 1702. Naturally this arrangement did not suit the English or the Dutch; and while, no doubt, the principal concern of the English in the war of the Spanish Succession was to keep Louis XIV and his relatives off the throne of Spain, the Netherlands and the Indies, at least a subsidiary motive was to prevent the French Guinea Company from keeping the slave *Asiento*.

The war was fought in Europe; operations in the Caribbean were mostly of a defensive kind, though they were important enough to demand the services of eminent naval officers. Châteaurenault was despatched to Martinique with a strong fleet before hostilities began, and it was to counter the resulting threat to the British islands that Benbow was sent out in 1702.

Ill-supported by his captains — two of whom were condemned to death for cowardice — he stood the French off from Jamaica and died of his wounds at Port Royal. In the same year the French part of St. Kitts was occupied, to be retained by England at the Treaty of Utrecht. On the other hand, English commerce and settlements suffered severely at the hands of French and Spanish privateers. The Bahamas colony was wiped out in 1703, St. Kitts and Nevis were savagely raided in 1706 and Montserrat in 1712. The only serious attempts at retaliation were Wager's successful attack on the galleons at Cartagena, and an abortive raid on Guadeloupe. Although Great Britain had twenty-four warships in the Caribbean by 1707, they were not enough to protect trade. It was successful fighting in Europe which eventually enabled the English, at the Treaty of Utrecht in 1713, to extract from France and Spain the objects for which they had been fighting: a firm assurance that the Netherlands and Spanish America should not fall under French domination; and the transfer of the slave *Asiento*, together with certain other trading rights in Spanish America, to an English concern, the South Sea Company, floated expressly for the purpose.

Only exhaustion and defeat could have induced the Spanish government to consent to these concessions. The Spanish Crown still claimed a general lordship over all the Americas, except in those few places where it had expressly acknowledged the rights of others. This claim, in many parts of the Caribbean, was a mere pretence. On the mainland, in provinces un-questionably recognised as Spanish, great tracts of mountain and forest had never been occupied or even explored. Unsub-dued and often hostile Indian tribes lived upon the Isthmus of Panama itself, within striking distance of the main treasure route from Peru to Spain, and of Puerto Bello, where the greatest trade fair in the Americas was held. Small bands of English settlers lived in scattered camps at Belize in Honduras, and at Black River. These Baymen, as they were called, made a hard living by cutting and selling logwood for the dyeing industry. They received intermittent support from the government of Jamaica, and though well within Spanish territory they could not be dislodged. Among the islands, Jamaica, Curaçao and Saint-Domingue had been lost to Spain's rivals years before. Most of the Lesser Antilles, including some of the best sugar-producing lands in the New World, never occupied by Spaniards, had been settled by English, French, Dutch and Danes, and were to be throughout the eighteenth century the scene of a new international rivalry in which the claims of Spain were hardly even considered. But Spanish claims were not thereby abated; for Spanish statesmen, what Spain had not expressly granted was still hers by right.

Similarly in commerce: if the Spanish government could not prevent foreign settlement in the islands, still less could it prevent the foreign settlers trading with its own colonial subjects. But Spain still insisted, in the face of facts, upon an exclusive monopoly of trade, and in the attempts to enforce that monopoly found it necessary to claim a general right of regulating seaborne traffic in the Caribbean, of defining the courses to be followed by *bona fide* traders between other European countries and their respective colonies, and of stopping and searching foreign ships which deviated from those courses.

Such being still the official policy of Spain in the Caribbean, Spanish statesmen were bound to grudge the concessions which they had been bullied into making at the Treaty of Utrecht. The French even more bitterly resented seeing a privileged position, which they had secured by negotiation, taken from them as a result of war. The South Sea Company now had its foot in the door, as it were, while all other foreign traders had to smuggle their goods through the back windows. Sooner or later the privileges of the company were certain to be challenged, and the British government would inevitably be drawn into the resulting conflict.

In actual fact, the English, for all their aggressiveness, had made a bad bargain. The peace settlement had assigned the *Asiento* for the supply of slaves to the company for thirty years, together with land and facilities at Spanish ports for the 'refreshment' of slaves. In addition, the company secured the novel privilege of sending a shipload of general merchandise to Spanish America every year. These concessions — though impressive enough on paper to send the price of shares soaring — were much less than had been hoped for, and the opportunities of profit which they offered were limited. The size of the annual ship was restricted, and the King of Spain was to have a quarter share in the cargo and 5 per cent of the profit on the rest. The

H

cargo was to be sold at the Puerto Bello fair, and not before the arrival of the galleons. The company could not select the place and the time for selling at the best prices, as the smugglers could, so that its profits from this source were necessarily moderate. As for the *Asiento*, it obliged the company to supply only slaves of a certain quality; the company's cargoes, therefore, could always be undersold by smugglers who shipped inferior slaves of a quality which the Spanish colonists could afford not only to buy but to pay for.

If the company's opportunities for profit were limited, its opportunities for causing trouble in the Caribbean were very great. The company undertook, in return for its slaving monopoly, to refrain from illicit trade. Admittedly this promise could be broken — was certain to be broken, either by the company itself or by its agents trading privately; and admittedly no undertaking given by the company could effectively bind interlopers. But the company, because of its official concession, its large stocks, and its expensive establishments in America, was vulnerable to Spanish resentment. The directors knew that any irregularity committed by an English ship, or any reprisals taken by English interests against Spanish depredations, might be punished by confiscation of the company's property. For this reason they often dissuaded their government and the local naval commanders from taking proper action to defend English West Indian shipping. The interests of unprivileged traders were sacrificed to those of the company; and the company incurred thereby a double unpopularity. The private traders of Jamaica hated it because of its obvious intention of superseding them in a trade which was an essential part of the economic life of the English islands. The islanders imported great quantities of food and timber, largely from North America; and since the North Americans preferred to buy their sugar and molasses from the French, who sold it cheaper, the imports of the English islands had to be paid for in money. To obtain the necessary bullion the English islands were especially obliged to develop their smuggling trade with Spanish America. The illicit cutting of logwood in Campeche and the Bay of Honduras was in part an answer — a quite inadequate answer — to this problem of the drain of money from the West Indies. But the company carried goods from England direct to Puerto Bello, and sought to suppress the local irregular trade. The English planters also hated the company, on the grounds that it raised the price of slaves, and exported the best slaves to the Spanish colonies, leaving only the weaklings for the English islands. The company was supposed to buy its slaves from the Royal Africa Company, but it could never obtain enough from that source. It was compelled to buy many of them in Jamaica in order to fulfil its contract; but this argument did not mollify the planters, or the private traders, or their Whig supporters in England.

For the Spanish government the arrangements made with the South Sea Company were a new and unwelcome departure from normal trade policy. Only good faith and cordial relations could make such a concession work smoothly, and these were almost always lacking. Two outbreaks of war interrupted the trade, in 1718 and 1727. The Bubble crisis in 1720 brought discredit as well as interruption. Even in normal times sailings were irregular. The Spaniards suspected that the *Asiento* and the annual ship, instead of being accepted as substitutes for the old illicit trade, were used as a cover for smuggling. The company's slave sloops from Jamaica carried other goods besides slaves, and the annual ship often sailed accompanied by provision ships which also carried contraband. The Spaniards alleged, too, that the annual ship, while discharging its cargo off Puerto Bello, was sometimes re-loaded by night from Jamaica. So the Spanish government made endless difficulties over the grant of *cédulas* for the annual ships, and in fact only eight voyages took place in the whole life of the concession. The company constantly complained that it made little profit by the annual ships and none by the *Asiento*; the King of Spain on his part suspected that the company concealed its profits in order to defraud him of his share. The company's steady refusal to produce its accounts for inspection lent some colour to this suspicion. Long before the expiry of the agreed thirty years the Spanish government wearied of the whole concession, and would have terminated it had agreement been possible on the question of compensation.

The position of the local Spanish authorities was difficult. The colonial shipping of three or four foreign nations plied in the Caribbean, carrying lawful trade with their own colonies and unlawful trade with those of Spain. Law-abiding French traders, under orders from their government, usually gave bond not to engage in smuggling. The Dutch, on the other hand, went armed for an avowedly illicit trade; they were at least known for smugglers on sight. English colonial ships were far more numerous than either, but the English government would never accept the suggestion that their shipping should give bond as the French did. English shipping in the Caribbean included the South Sea Company's ships and slave sloops carrying a lawful, or ostensibly lawful, trade with Spanish America; ships engaged in normal traffic to England, North America or the islands; and smugglers to Latin-American ports. In order to distinguish between fair traders and smugglers the Spaniards claimed and exercised a right to stop and search foreign ships anywhere in the western hemisphere.

The enforcement of the Spanish trade monopoly was entrusted at this time to *guarda-costas*, fitted out in Spanish or colonial ports and carrying commissions from the local governors. These ships were manned by ruffians trained in the long war against the buccaneers. They were fitted out privately, and received their remuneration from the sale of the prizes they brought in. They cruised in the regular routes of colonial trade, stopping every English ship they met, and searching for 'contraband'. The *guarda-costas* and the Spanish courts accepted the presence in a foreign ship of any Spanish colonial product — indigo, cocoa, logwood, or Spanish money — as evidence of unlawful trade. This was flimsy evidence indeed, for Jamaica produced indigo and logwood in small quantities, and had produced cocoa; and Spanish money was the commonest means of exchange throughout the West Indies. Moreover a ship might be seized and condemned merely because its position at the time of encounter was — in the opinion of a Spanish court — off the direct course to a lawful destination. Colonial governors received a share of prize-money; no doubt there was much collusion between them and the captains of the *guarda-costas*. Ships approaching or leaving Jamaica had to pass close to the coasts of Florida, Cuba or Hispaniola, and many peaceful traders suffered unjust seizure and condemnation. The official process of appeal was long, expensive and usually fruitless; and even the intervention of the British ambassador at Madrid often failed to obtain redress.

As a result of these depredations, a long list of financial claims, and a mounting wave of national indignation, piled up in England against Spain. The West India merchants clamoured for redress and the Opposition supported them in Parliament. The South Sea Company demanded compensation for property which had been seized in the brief wars of 1718 and 1727, and the government supported its claim. Against the bill, admittedly, had to be set the sums owed to the King of Spain by the company — slave duties, share of trading profits (if any) and so forth — but the company never allowed these to be ascertained, and estimates varied widely. Besides these financial disagreements, and the perennial dispute over free navigation, there was the problem of the logwood cutters in Honduras, and a boundary dispute between Florida and Georgia. None of these disputes need have led to war; but war was made inevitable by the truculence and clamour of the 'trading part of the nation' in England, and in particular by the intransigence of the South Sea Company.

In March 1738 Captain Jenkins appeared in London with his famous tale of woe. The House of Commons promptly resolved that 'it was the undoubted right of British subjects to sail their ships in any part of the seas of America'. Letters of reprisal were offered to English merchants — an absurdly old-fashioned gesture — and Admiral Haddock was sent on a minatory cruise in the Mediterranean. Walpole — still patiently working for peace — produced with the Spanish ambassador a draft agreement, which was accepted in Madrid and actually ratified in January 1739 as the Convention of El Pardo. By its terms Spain was to pay £95,000 — the estimated excess of Spanish over English depredations; but the South Sea Company refused to co-operate, because the convention did not expressly recognise its rights of navigation, nor guarantee a renewal of its *Asiento*. The Opposition in England were by this time clamouring against any concession or agreement. Newcastle, impressed as always by popular clamour, and frightened by fresh reports of a Franco-Spanish family pact, kept Haddock cruising off the Spanish coast, despite the convention; and the Spanish government retorted in May 1739 by suspending the *Asiento*. The £95,000 was never paid, and in October 1739 war was declared between England and Spain.

Before tracing the course of the 'war of Jenkins' ear' — the first major European war to be fought expressly for West Indian ends — it will be convenient to consider in more detail the unsavoury trade which was the original subject of the dispute. Most contemporary accounts of the slave trade and of life on board English or French slavers refer to the years immediately preceding the abolition of the trade, and many of them are hotly partisan on one side or the other. Exact information for the first half of the eighteenth century is hard to come by. In general, as the century progressed, the volume of trade increased. In the last twelve months of lawful trade over 40,000 slaves were carried in English ships (the French trade throughout the century was about half of the English). The average size of ships engaged in the trade also increased; and health conditions improved, partly through legislation, partly through improved knowledge and enlightened self-interest; it was not uncommon, in the last years of the trade, for captains to boast of bringing ships in without loss of a single seaman or a single slave. Even so, the conditions of the trade in 1800 or so make grim reading; half a century earlier they were undoubtedly worse. Apart from these progressive palliations of misery, the general lines of the trade remained fairly constant throughout the century.

Both in France and in England the slave trade shared with the fisheries the reputation of being a valuable 'nursery of seamen'. Slavers had to carry large crews — usually about twelve men to a hundred tons in ships of three hundred tons and over, as against about seven to a hundred tons in other branches of the West Indies trade. The ratio was naturally higher in smaller ships. The biggest in the trade, with a capacity for four or five hundred slaves, had crews of sixty or seventy. These numbers were needed not only to work the ship and stand guard over the slaves but also to fight the ship in case of trouble off the coast, or with Barbary or Caribbean pirates. Slavers went well armed. An armament of twenty or thirty 'long nines', with bow and quarterdeck carronades, was not uncommon. A slaver's crew needed unusually capable petty officers and tradesmen — not only gunners, gunner's mates and quartermasters, but carpenters, coopers, sailmakers, cooks and the rest. The special responsibilities of these men may be judged from examples: a slaver during the 'middle passage' would have to carry a barricoe of water for every person on board; several hundred barricoes at least. If the cooper was incompetent everybody on board might die in mid-Atlantic. The carpenter, similarly, was responsible not only for ordinary structural repairs but for the maintenance of several hundred leg-irons, neck-rings and pairs of manacles; and woe betide officers and crew if the slaves slipped their shackles while the ship lay off the Coast. Even the cook had an unusual task, in catering for several hundred slaves in addition to the ship's company. The senior officers, also — the captain in particular — needed a high degree of professional competence as seamen, and had to be specialised merchants, diplomats, and on occasion fighting men as well. They were well paid, by comparison with most other trades, both in salary and in opportunities for private trade. They were not necessarily, or even usually, the brutal sadists of abolitionist propaganda; they did not suffer any social stigma by reason of their trade in the eighteenth century — certainly they were not regarded as monsters. On the contrary, like merchant officers in other trades, they took a normal pride in delivering their special type of cargo in as good condition as possible. The standing orders of most slaving firms forbade officers and seamen to strike or ill-treat slaves. A very few slaving trips, however, robbed a man of any sense of the humanity of the slaves he carried; for him they were so many cattle, to be treated with no more and no less consideration than other animals of commercial value.

Employment in slavers was not only exacting; it was obviously unpleasant, and often dangerous and nerve-racking. Apart from the ever-present danger of insurrection, ships lay off-shore for weeks on end in hot and unhealthy estuaries. An outbreak of infectious disease, in the packed conditions of the middle passage, could carry off the greater part of company and cargo; hence, the insistent regulations about scrubbing decks, sprinkling with vinegar, and so forth. Even the regular rate of mortality among the crews of slavers was very high, 20 or 25 per cent on average, and this in an age when health at sea in general was improving and the incidence of diseases such as scurvy was being rapidly reduced. It is significant that the death rate among the crews was usually about the same as that among the slaves themselves. In a more tender-hearted age the trade would have been called a grave of seamen rather than a nursery. The high rates of pay sufficed to attract competent officers and tradesmen; but ordinary seamen in slavers were not particularly well paid by comparison with other trades, and seamen — though certainly not squeamish — seem on the whole to have avoided slavers when they could get other berths. The frequency with which the item 'crimpage' occurs in slaving accounts indicates the methods to which slavers often had to resort in order to make up their complement of seamen.

Slavers made long passages. The triangular voyage was usually at least twelve months. A ship would sail from its home port in England or France with a cargo of 'trade goods' — woollen or cotton cloth in bright colours, firearms and other weapons, tools, pots and pans, and trinkets. The run down to the Coast might take two, three, even four months. Arrived off the Coast, negotiations began, usually through resident middle-men, most of whom were Portuguese half-castes, for slaving the ship. Slaves might be picked up in small lots here and there; or more commonly assembled in hulks, or in barracoons ashore. All this trading might take many weeks. Meanwhile, 'trade goods' were landed in payment, water barricoes filled ashore, and temporary decks constructed by the ship's carpenters. On these extra decks the slaves were to travel, lying prone all night and most of the day, for there was no room to stand upright, except during periods of exercise on deck. As soon as a cargo was assembled the slaves were hurried on board, and the ship set sail without delay, carronades trained inboard and gunner's mates standing by with lighted matches until the Coast was out of sight. Once at sea, the danger of mutiny was less, and slaves could be allowed on deck for exercise, though always under strict guard. Arrived in the islands, after a middle passage in which speed was the best safeguard against mortality, the process was reversed; the slaves might be sold on board, if the demand for them was urgent, but usually they were landed, 'refreshed' for a short period ashore on fresh provisions, doctored in various ways to improve their health and appearance, and then sold at auction, usually in small lots, by the agent of the slaving firm, to factors or local planters. Planters were bad payers, and many of the transactions involved credit. Unless there was a great shortage of slaves, the planter usually had the advantage in these transactions, because the slaver was in a hurry to dispose of his perishable cargo and get under way again. Payment might be in local currency — sometimes at an arbitrary rate of exchange fixed to the purchaser's advantage — or in bills if the purchaser's credit was good; but more commonly it was in produce, and there again prices were a fruitful source of disagreement.

The process of sale or barter might take many weeks. For the ship's company this was a period of rest and release from strain, for once a slave was sold his new owner was responsible for him. Ship's discipline relaxed; many seamen deserted in the West Indies, and others had to be signed on, usually at rates of pay far higher than those ruling in Europe — a frequent cause of dispute. Some worn-out ships also remained in the islands, being adjudged unequal to the homeward passage. The French, but not usually the English, enforced a system of inspection to determine seaworthiness at this stage. Eventually, sales made, crew rounded up and formalities done, the ship's people dismantled the slave decks and loaded in the return cargo, usually sugar, for the last lap — and usually quickest and least eventful part — of the voyage: passage back to Europe.

The pattern of the 'triangular voyage' was never neat and consistent, and in the later eighteenth century it changed considerably. The commitments of planters to their factors increasingly obliged them to ship their sugars in the factors' ships. For this reason, and also because they could not time their sailings to coincide with harvests, slavers found increasing difficulty in getting return cargoes, and often returned to Europe in ballast. This in turn encouraged differentiation of design between slavers, built for speed, with high 'tween-decks, and sugar freighters, built for capacity, with deep holds. In the period we are considering, however — the first half of the eighteenth century — this specialisation had hardly begun and slavers still usually carried sugar back to Europe. The ships then engaged in the trade were of all sizes from fifty to over five hundred tons, and of all designs and rigs. Seaworthiness and stout construction were more important than speed, for the triangular voyage was as exacting for the ships as for the men. Relatively few ships survived more than about ten years in the trade, which meant perhaps half a dozen voyages. The chief home ports were London, Bristol and Liverpool in England — London declining relatively in importance and Liverpool gaining rapidly in the course of the eighteenth century — and in France Bayonne, Bordeaux, La Rochelle, Dunkerque, and above all Nantes. In all these ports slaving firms were prominent in the local merchant communities, for the trade created markets for half a dozen connected trades. Slaving required good capital backing. A firm normally operated at least three ships: one outward, one homeward, and one refitting; the cost of fitting out a ship and freighting it for the trade was high, the wage bill was heavy, and heavy dues had to be paid to the old monopolist companies — the Royal Africa Company in England (down to 1730 when its dues were replaced by a parliamentary subsidy charged upon the duties), and in France the Compagnie des Indes, as reorganised after the fall of Law. These bodies no longer traded extensively, but performed services of defence on the Coast and exacted licence fees from other traders. Reserve capital was needed, also, to meet the possibilities of total loss of ship or cargo through the hazards of the sea, or mutiny, or epidemic. But for the merchant with adequate capital, given capable captains and reasonable luck, the trade was enormously profitable; for each voyage brought three distinct profits, and a ship very rarely needed to make a passage in ballast. Investors, economic pamphleteers, and politicians in France and England thought nothing of the miseries of the trade because they never saw them. Only the factors on the Coast, and the slaving ships' companies, saw the brutalities of the round-up at the barracoons and the close-packed horror of the middle passage; and they were men hardened to such sights, and paid to ply their trade. The ordinary man in Europe saw only the returns, and his point of view may be summarised in the words of an anonymous and typical English pamphlet of 1749:

'The most approved Judges of the Commercial Interests of these Kingdoms have ever been of the opinion that our West-India and African Trades are the most nationally beneficial of any we carry on. It is also allowed on all Hands, that the trade to Africa is the Branch which renders our American Colonies and Plantations so advantageous to Great Britain: that Traffic only affording our Planters a constant supply of Negro Servants for the Culture of their Lands in the Produce of Sugars, Tobacco, Rice, Rum, Cotton, Fustick, Pimento,

and all other our Plantation Produce: so that the extensive
Employment of our Shipping in, to, and from America, the
great Brood of Seamen consequent thereupon, and the daily
Bread of the most considerable Part of our British Manufactures, are owing primarily to the Labour of Negroes; who,
as they were the first happy instruments of raising our Plantations: so their Labour only can support and preserve them,
and render them still more and more profitable to their Mother-
Kingdom. The Negroe-Trade therefore, and the natural
consequences resulting from it, may be justly esteemed an
inexhaustible Fund of Wealth and Naval Power to this Nation.'

This was the view of the trade held by most people in England
— and, *mutatis mutandis*, throughout western Europe — who
thought about trade at all. Nobody of importance — except
Walpole, worldly-wise and weary — seemed to think it strange
that England should enter enthusiastically upon a major war to
retain and increase its share in so rich an enterprise.

CHAPTER VIII

COMMERCE AND WAR
1739–63

BOTH MINISTRY AND PEOPLE in England, when they embarked in 1739 on a war for trade in the West Indies, must have been willing to fight France as well as Spain. France, besides being connected with Spain by dynastic ties, had long been England's chief rival for the trade of Spanish America; and in the mood of greedy and truculent imperialism in which the English entered the war, they were eager also to make permanent conquests of Spanish territory, which would certainly have led to war with France. The great preparations made in 1740 for the departure of Lord Cathcart's expedition against Spanish America in fact prompted Fleury to send out a fleet under d'Antin, which might well have involved France in war; but d'Antin lay so long at Saint-Domingue awaiting reinforcements and trying vainly to arrange a junction with the Spanish fleet, that his men fell sick, his stores ran out, and he was obliged to return to France without accomplishing anything. For three years the French did no more to support Spain. Fleury had no desire for war and no particular love for the Spain of Elizabeth Farnese. France and England kept the peace at sea, more or less, until 1744.

The war between England and Spain hung fire. Vernon's initial success in capturing Puerto Bello and destroying its fortifications was not repeated. He was obliged to spend part of 1740 looking for d'Antin's fleet. The great force sent out under Ogle and Cathcart to join him suffered from ambiguous orders and divided counsel. Havana was deemed too strong to be taken. Cartagena, where the galleons lay, was chosen as the first object, but the combined naval and military attacks on Cartagena, and afterwards on Santiago de Cuba, were both failures. On the other hand, the English took many prizes and dislocated the normal lawful trade of Spanish America. Only one treasure fleet reached Spain, and no galleons or *flotas* sailed during the war. The Puerto Bello galleons were never again restored. The trade had to be carried either by single 'register-ships' — which, though faster and cheaper than the convoys, were often taken — or by foreign smugglers. The smugglers throve by the war, as their governments intended they should; and the English government explicitly ordered Admiral Vernon to do all he could to protect and convoy English trade with the enemy's colonies.

The war between England and France in the West Indies, which broke out openly in 1744, was a very different affair. It was governed not by desire to acquire new territories or new trades but by the bitter rivalry between two existing sets of sugar colonies. The French Caribbean islands — larger in area and with soil less exhausted — were competing more and more successfully with the English islands in the production of cheap sugar and in trade with Europe and English North America. Since England could not control the supply of sugar, none of the peaceful methods known to mercantilist economists could avail against this growing competition. The Molasses Act, which had been passed in 1733 at the instigation of the West India interest in England to stop French West Indian trade with English North America, proved difficult to enforce, and naturally irritated the North Americans, whose interests it attacked. Fiscal concessions, such as the removal of sugar from the 'enumerated' list in 1739 to permit direct export to Europe, were of little help to the English planters, because they did not remove the basic cause of difficulty — high production costs. Depression in the English West Indies affected too many English interests to be tolerated; and in that time of truculent trade rivalry, if peaceful measures would not serve, war was welcomed as a possible solution of commercial problems.

War offered the English an opportunity to cripple French sugar production, since they could not defeat it in open competition. Planters on both sides disliked the acquisition of fresh sugar-producing territory; they feared that increased production would lower prices within their protected markets. Each side hoped not to acquire and exploit the enemy's colonies but to destroy and depopulate them; to burn the canes, to wreck the machinery, and, above all, to carry off the slaves, who were the most necessary, most valuable, and most mobile part of the planters' capital.

Failing the destruction of the enemy's colonies, the next-best thing was to cut off their trade, starve them of provisions and slaves, and prevent them from selling their sugar. In this war naval activity was, in practice, almost confined to this second type of operation. By 1744 the energies of both combatants were taxed elsewhere, in Europe and North America. Forces were not available for major operations in the West Indies, and the fighting there was little more than a rehearsal for the much sterner struggle which was to break out in 1756.

As a rehearsal, the war had lessons to offer. It revealed the disadvantage which the French suffered through having no naval bases in the West Indies. Fleets for particular operations were sent out direct from France. This policy ensured that ships arrived in the West Indies fresh from dockyard and in good repair, and sometimes gave them the advantage of surprise; but it had also serious disadvantages. Having no repair facilities, fleets had to time their sailings so as to arrive after the hurricane season, and leave to go back to France before the hurricane season of the following year. This meant that their time away from France was at most about ten months. Usually it was less, because wooden warships could only carry stores and provisions for about six months. A fleet could not easily be victualled on the station, for the West Indian islands did not then — and do not now — produce any considerable surplus of food. Warships were sometimes sent out *en flûte*; that is, with the lower tier of guns struck down and the space on the gun deck filled with provisions. Some extra stores could be brought out in this way; but it was dangerous for a ship to throw away half of its firepower if there was any likelihood of its having to fight on the way out. Also, when the fleet arrived it had to put in to harbour to land the extra stores and remount the guns. This was a long and heavy job and had to be done with the help of slaves requisitioned from unwilling planters. Apart from this question of stores, some time might have to be spent in harbour on arrival, in order to establish contact with the military governors and obtain up-to-date intelligence; and a very few days in a West Indian harbour sufficed for men fresh from France to fall ill of yellow fever or malaria, sometimes in such numbers that the fleet could not put to sea. It became axiomatic in French naval circles, therefore, that a force sent to the West Indies must engage the enemy at once or not at all. Over and over again French fleets came out, and returned having accomplished little or nothing.

The English system, first worked out and applied in the seventeen-forties, was quite different. The West India interest in England was already powerful politically; it insisted on squadrons of warships permanently stationed in the West Indies. There were two naval dockyards: one at Port Royal in Jamaica, the other at English Harbour in Antigua. Today, the Port Royal yard has disappeared and that at English Harbour is a ramshackle, though still fascinating, relic; but in many tricks of speech and manner people in Antigua and Jamaica to this day show the influence of these naval bases, of close contact with ships and sailors through several generations in the hey-day of wooden warships. The West Indian dockyards were not very large or very efficient, but they could effect ordinary repairs; and during the hurricane season ships could either go into dock for refit or could be sent off cruising for prizes in the southern Caribbean, out of harm's way. Food and other stores could be kept in bulk at the dockyards and replenished by convoys from North America. The crews, being on the station for two or three years, had time to fall ill and get well again, though of course a certain proportion always died on first arrival. The station system was expensive and wasteful because it entailed keeping ships hanging about the West Indies for long periods doing nothing, and also because the ships deteriorated and became foul under tropical conditions much faster than at home. The system did not remove the need for major expeditions, because the squadrons were necessarily small; and whenever a fleet of any size broke out from France reinforcements from England had to be sent hurrying after it. Sometimes the reinforcements arrived too late; but in general, for protecting trade and for attacking or defending small and ill-armed islands, small squadrons all the time were better than big fleets occasionally. The English could count on retaining the initiative at sea in the Caribbean for the greater part of every year. The superiority of the English system was eventually recognised by the French themselves, who, somewhat belatedly, established a naval base for the Windward Islands at Martinique in 1784.

The main weakness of the English position was colonial indiscipline. The dependence of the French islands upon North

America for grain and timber and upon Ireland for beef should have given the English an important tactical advantage; but in war as in peace the shippers of New England continued to trade with the enemy, either directly or through the neutral Dutch harbours in Curaçao or St. Eustatius. The privateers which sailed from Martinique to prey upon English shipping were often stored with North American provisions; meanwhile the English islands went short, and sometimes had to be supplied with food from England. It was largely the profit-seeking of the New Englanders which prevented the British navy from achieving its object: the commercial isolation of France in the Caribbean. The British imperial structure, like the Spanish, though for different reasons, creaked ominously under the stress of war.

The Treaty of Aix-la-Chapelle, which ended the war in 1748, settled no important question between France and England in the West Indies. No territories changed hands. Four disputed islands in the Windward group — Dominica, St. Lucia, St. Vincent and Tobago — were declared 'neutral', and both parties agreed to evacuate them; but even had the colonial governments honestly wished to carry out this agreement, it would have been difficult to round up the unorganised groups of squatters, mostly French, who drifted in from the older colonies. The islands remained an English grievance and a bone of contention for the next war; in this respect, as in others, the treaty between England and France was only a truce. The commercial treaty of 1750, which supplemented the general European settlement and wound up the maritime quarrel between England and Spain, was similarly inconclusive. It contained no reference to the freedom of navigation in whose name the war had begun. The irritating problem of the Honduras log-wood camps, which had expanded considerably during the war, with the encouragement of Trelawny, the governor of Jamaica, remained unsolved. The South Sea Company had almost ceased to present a problem; it no longer traded; its last 'annual ship' had sailed in 1733, and its slave trade ended in 1739. Under the treaty it received £100,000 in return for the surrender of all claims under the *Asiento*. Thus the English gave up the long attempt to force or persuade the Spaniards to allow direct trade to their colonies, while the Spaniards took a leaf out of the English (and French) book and themselves organised new joint-stock companies to handle certain colonial trades. The trade of Cuba, for instance, was from 1740 to 1760 officially a monopoly in the hands of the Compañía de Comercio de la Habana, which undertook in exchange to build warships and suppress smuggling. Illicit local trade between the English and Spanish islands went on, but it remained as illicit as ever, and could no longer be hidden by the *Asiento*. During the second half of the century the Spanish government proved increasingly willing to reorganise its trade system, and increasingly able to protect its monopoly. What the English lost by the process, the French gained. They had stuck steadily to the lawful channel of trade, consigning goods for Spanish America through Spanish merchants at Cadiz; and the greater part of this trade was in their hands by 1750. Meanwhile their commercial competition in the West Indies and their strategic pressure in North America steadily increased.

Slaving and smuggling to Spanish America, however, were for most West Indians profitable side-lines. The sugar trade was what mattered most, and for British sugar planters the war seemed to have served its purpose. The years from 1748 to 1756 were their golden age. Prices remained reasonably steady and fairly high — the average was 33s. 8d., which was 50 per cent higher than that for the decade before the war, and high enough to allow efficient planters a net return of 7 to 10 per cent. Production was increasing steadily — it trebled between 1700 and 1760 — but so was the capacity of the English market, which now absorbed the whole product of the British West Indies, and demanded more. Grocers and refiners in England, indeed, were beginning to murmur at the high prices of British West Indian sugar, and to ask for leave, failing an increase in British production, to import foreign sugar; but no-one in authority in mercantilist England paid much attention to such unorthodox proposals. Jamaica, with its large area of virgin land, was the chief beneficiary of this steady expansion of a protected market; the economy of Barbados and the Leeward Islands was propped up rather than expanded; but for all the British islands, war was the guarantee of their prosperity. War had incidental disadvantages — privateering losses, high freight and insurance rates, and so forth, which offset war-time rises in the price of sugar. But war crippled the commerce of the productive French islands; it raised national anti-French feeling;

I

it caused people in England to shelve the economic question of the merits of British dependence on British-grown sugar. War, or the constant possibility of war, in the middle eighteenth century was to the advantage of the British West Indies; and no one in England doubted that the West Indies were worth fighting for.

The Seven Years War began, not in the West Indies, but in Europe and North America, and in the mind of one leading statesman at least — Pitt — there was no doubt that the major purpose of war in the Americas was to safeguard English North America by seizing Canada. Nevertheless, the West Indies were again a centre of heavy fighting, and the forces employed there were far larger than in the previous war; far larger, incidentally, than those used in the simultaneous struggle in India. Great expeditions were sent out on both sides, and their commanders now had orders to annex the enemy's sugar colonies, not merely to pillage them. This change of policy, though supported by the West India interest in London, had its origin in European events. At the outset of the war England had lost Minorca to the French. The capture of this important naval base affected the West Indies directly, by releasing units of the French Mediterranean fleet for service in the Caribbean. Subsequently the English took from the French Cape Breton Island with its great fortress, Louisbourg. Each side considered the possession of both places essential, and each hoped to recover its loss without surrendering its gain. Both therefore set about making other conquests to serve as ransoms at the peace. For this purpose they naturally picked on the valuable and very vulnerable islands of the West Indies. It was to secure a bargaining counter, to avoid surrendering Cape Breton Island for Minorca, that Pitt was moved to attack Martinique; though later in the war, when victory exceeded even his expectation, he began to favour the retention of some at least of England's West Indian gains for their own sake.

The change of policy was favoured even by the West Indians. The presence of full-scale naval war in the Caribbean reminded them of their small numbers and of their weakness against an enemy fleet or a slave mutiny, and forced upon them a more strategic, a less purely commercial appreciation of their position. The planters of Barbados and Antigua, weary of constant alarms, began to realise that their properties would be safer if Martinique, Guadeloupe and the neutral islands were in English hands, at least for the duration of the war. If it were decided at the peace to keep any islands captured from the French, then the dangers of the admission of their sugars to the English market would have to be faced; but even that danger might be avoided by evicting the French inhabitants and by forbidding their English successors to plant sugar. By such arguments as these even the sluggish island militias were stirred to a military activity less purely defensive than usual; and local hostilities ranging from slave raids to plans for outright conquest were endlessly discussed in the first two years of the war.

Ultimately, however, most of the serious fighting was done not by militia-men or by privateers but by the line-of-battle fleets of the contending powers. In 1757 the French launched an ingenious plan of co-ordination by three naval squadrons off North Africa, the West Indies and North America, which damaged English trade considerably and put Jamaica in fear of invasion for some weeks; but the necessity of going to the relief of Louisbourg prevented any of the French admirals from achieving much in the Caribbean. After 1757 the French gave up the attempt to maintain a constant relief of squadrons in West Indian waters. Theoretically the best English naval defence of the West Indies was therefore a thorough blockade of the Channel and Atlantic ports. The English West Indians, however, would never accept this reasoning. They liked to have warships in sight, in their harbours or cruising off-shore. The Jamaicans would not even agree that a squadron off Antigua, up to windward and near the route from Europe, was an adequate defence of their island. They clung to their station squadrons, and clamoured for battle fleets to be sent to the Caribbean.

Late in 1758 Pitt, now possessing in Louisbourg the key to Canada and confident of success in Europe, launched two attacks, one direct and one indirect, against the French West Indies. The indirect attack was against the French stations in West Africa, and culminated in the capture of Gorée by Keppel. This comparatively minor operation achieved economic results out of all proportion to the cost of the force employed. It crippled the French slave trade and seriously hampered the working of the sugar plantations in the French West Indies.

Meanwhile a series of English naval victories in the Mediterranean and the Bay of Biscay destroyed or delayed the French fleets intended for America, and created favourable opportunities for England in the Caribbean. The combined naval and military force under Moore and Barrington sent to attack the French West Indies found Martinique too strong for it, but seized, in the spring of 1759, the wealthy island of Guadeloupe; a French fleet under Admiral Bompar arriving just too late to raise the siege. The planters of Guadeloupe were allowed to capitulate on very favourable terms. They were to be neutral between France and England while the war lasted; their goods were to be admitted to English markets; their slaves exempted from *corvée*; they retained French law under English military occupation and were fully protected in possession of their property. English planters, indeed, were forbidden to settle, and nothing was done to alter the French character of the colony. After the initial damage of the fighting had been repaired, the island began to enjoy a new prosperity, for English and American merchants rushed in to supply the food, the timber and the slaves for which it starved. Feckless planters escaped from their debts to French *commissionaires* and were allowed to run up new debts to English factors from Antigua. Best of all, they found at last a safe European and North American market for their sugar. The planters of Guadeloupe were envied alike by their compatriots in Martinique and by their English rivals. This was precisely the kind of conquest most disliked by the English planters; it struck directly at their profits without giving them any permanent promise of security. The flooding of the London market with Guadeloupe sugars was one reason for the drop in sugar prices in 1760, and explains the bitter complaints of the West India interest against the terms of the capitulation.

During the second half of 1759 and through 1760 no major operations were undertaken in the Caribbean, chiefly because the attention of both belligerents was concentrated on events in Europe and North America. In 1761 there followed a period of abortive and insincere haggling over peace, in which Choiseul played for time by demanding terms which England would not accept, in the expectation that Spain would be brought in on the side of France. Apart from its dynastic connection with France, Spain had a number of serious grievances against

England. Some of these concerned the West Indies directly; in particular, the question of the logwood camps. The Treaty of Aix-la-Chapelle had provided for a mutual restoration of conquests; but the English government did not regard the camps as a conquest, and had taken no steps to evacuate them. The governors of Jamaica, indeed, had continued to support the logwood cutters after the end of the war, and the Belize settlement now numbered some five hundred people, with a rudimentary system of government of their own. Further south, on the Mosquito Shore of Nicaragua, English agents continued to intrigue with the Indians against Spanish government, and in 1749 Trelawny even appointed a resident superintendent there. The local Spaniards tried every method, from peaceful penetration by missionaries to armed expeditions, to win over the Indians and to evict the Baymen from their settlements. The Spanish government was prepared to offer supplies of logwood on reasonable terms in return for the evacuation of the camps; but this the English would not accept, being naturally unwilling to depend upon a Spanish monopoly. In 1753 an armed attack, believed to have been ordered by Ensenada in Madrid, was launched against Belize, and the Baymen were temporarily driven away to Black River. They soon returned, and rebuilt their settlement with the help of soldiers from Jamaica; and English indignation over the attack helped to bring about Ensenada's fall from office. The dispute continued to disturb Anglo-Spanish relations, even after the appointment of the anglophile Wall as Foreign Minister.

After the outbreak of the Seven Years War other disputes emerged. The Treaty of Commerce of 1750 had never been executed to Spanish satisfaction. In peace the English had done little to restrain their smugglers; in war they showed the arrogant disregard of the rights of neutral shipping which belligerent naval powers commonly display. The Admiralty either could not or would not control the activities of privateers. Spanish merchant shipping was repeatedly molested, even in Spanish territorial waters. The situation grew worse when the hard-pressed French threw open the trade of their starving Caribbean colonies to neutrals, for under the 'rule of the war of 1756' any Spanish ship suspected of having touched at a French colonial port was liable to seizure. Worse still, as the tide of war turned in favour of England and against France, it seemed clear that Pitt intended, if he could, to seize all the French possessions in North America and the Caribbean, including the neutral islands in the Windward group, to which Spain made some shadowy claim. If England and France made peace upon such conditions, Spain would be left to negotiate alone with an England all-powerful in the West Indies. It was in these circumstances that the Spanish government agreed to the Family Compact of 1761, which bound Spain to declare war before May 1762 if peace had not been made between France and England. Peace was not made, and the English government anticipated events by declaring war on Spain in January.

The entry of Spain into the war brought no relief to France in the Caribbean. In the same month that war was declared Rodney, fresh from England with a powerful fleet, took Martinique. Again a strong French squadron, this time under Blénac, was hurried out from France. Its departure was delayed, however, by repeated interceptions of necessary stores on their way coastwise to Brest, and it reached the West Indies too late to save Martinique. Blénac's arrival off Saint-Domingue in March 1762 caused the usual panic in Jamaica; but Rodney, with his great fleet up to windward, was able to detach a squadron large enough to deter Blénac from attacking Jamaica, and Blénac's expedition soon found itself blockaded harmlessly at Cap Français. It might indeed have been destroyed before it got there, but for the short-sighted cowardice of the governor and council of Jamaica, who insisted on most of the available naval strength remaining in Kingston harbour to protect them.

To the annoyance of the English planting interest, the inhabitants of Martinique were granted a capitulation similar to that of Guadeloupe; though since nobody expected Martinique to be kept at the peace, its capitulation was less likely to be of permanent importance. The neutral islands were less fortunate, no doubt because Rodney thought that his government might wish to retain them. Dominica had surrendered to a North American force in June 1761; Tobago was for all practical purposes British already; and Rodney reduced St. Lucia, St. Vincent and Grenada to submission shortly after the capture of Martinique. Of all the French possessions in the West Indies only Saint-Domingue remained.

Meanwhile Spain, far from helping to save the French colonies, began to lose her own. The English government at once prepared an attack on Havana; and profiting by former experience, the Admiralty planned the operation in detail and avoided the uncertainties and delays which had beset Cathcart's expedition in 1740. The chief difficulty was the presence in the West Indies of Blénac's fleet, which, having failed either to save Martinique or to join with the Spaniards to attack Jamaica, might at least have been expected to go to the help of Havana; especially since Rodney, always ready to subordinate considerations of strategy to those of prize-money, had sent many of his ships away cruising off the Main, and now had none to spare. But Blénac, short of victuals and with half his men sick, allowed himself to be bottled up at Cap Français while the force commanded by Pocock and Albemarle sailed through the islands, picked up more ships and men from Jamaica, and proceeded undisturbed to reduce Havana. Havana had been thought by the Spaniards to be impregnable. Its fall in August 1762 made a great stir; the captors destroyed a considerable Spanish naval force and collected great sums in prize-money, while the English politicians, when they heard of it, were encouraged to raise their peace terms still higher. Two other misfortunes befell Spain in the same year. An English fleet sailing from the East Indies captured Manila; and an invasion of Portugal, intended by Charles III as a diversion, proved an unexpected failure. Lisbon was never in serious danger, and the English, though they abandoned the war in Germany, did not allow themselves to be diverted from Havana. In October 1762 Charles III capitulated. The French had been pressing him for some months to make peace. After the fall of Havana Choiseul had to admit that France and Spain together were no match for England at sea. France could no longer face the strain of unsuccessful war, and in Europe her ally Austria was also at last ready for peace.

The English ministers were almost as eager for peace as Choiseul, though for somewhat different reasons. George III was anxious to be rid of responsibility in Germany. Pitt, who would have fought till he deprived the Bourbons of every colony they possessed, had given place to the timorous and inexperienced Bute. Many English politicians felt nervous about the tremendous ascendancy achieved in the colonial field, and feared a future combination of all the other colonial powers against England. The North American colonists were becoming restive; with Canada subdued, they saw no need of further fighting, and such enthusiasm as they had shown for West Indian conquests had evaporated. They intended, after all, to go on trading to the French West Indian islands, whether those islands became British or remained French. For all these reasons, the Treaty of Paris was concluded in haste and embodied the concessions and compromises which haste entailed.

The numerous and valuable conquests made in the late stages of the war proved an embarrassment to English ministers in their attempts to hasten the peace settlement. Something must be sacrificed to have peace; but something beyond the original objects of the war must be kept to satisfy popular clamour. The principal object of the war had been to safeguard the North American colonies, and to achieve this end there was little doubt that Canada, or part of it at least, would have to be retained; on the other hand, the trade and revenue of Canada were small, and the public reasonably expected the acquisitions at the peace to pay part of the cost of the war. The French West Indian islands would bring in an immediate revenue. They could more easily be settled with Englishmen than the vast spaces of Canada; and West Indian planters habitually returned to England to spend their money, while most settlers in North America stuck to their farms and businesses and kept their money, if they had any, in the colonies. These were plausible reasons for preferring West Indian to North American acquisitions. Guadeloupe in particular was a tempting prize. The slave traders naturally pressed for its retention. Exporting merchants in England pointed out the need for developing more sugar land, since the British islands were not producing enough sugar to allow for re-export to the Continent. Even the English West India interest was partly converted to a policy of annexation, for the planters and their advocates had learned what dangerous neighbours Martinique and Guadeloupe could be, particularly as privateering bases. Many people in England thought that Guadeloupe should be kept, even in preference to Canada, and the question of Guadeloupe against Canada was made the subject of much acrimonious debate.

It is unlikely that the British government paid much serious attention to this debate so long as Guadeloupe alone was in question; but the conquest of Martinique in 1762 raised the problem of choosing between Canada on the one hand and all the French West Indies except Saint-Domingue on the other. Rodney attached great strategic importance to Martinique. If, as seemed likely, the French would not make peace without Martinique, then England might keep Guadeloupe in payment. Bute, however, apparently thought that France would not yield any settled colony, and decided in the end on a compromise. He agreed to restore both Martinique and Guadeloupe, and, as a necessary adjunct, the French slaving stations in West Africa; but he demanded the cession of Grenada, all the neutral islands and the whole continent of North America east of the Mississippi. These were all almost empty territories, open to English enterprise, and containing few Frenchmen to make trouble for government. With the cession of territory was to be included the right of navigating the Mississippi itself. In the final peace terms all these demands were agreed, except that France insisted on retaining St. Lucia, on the ground that the island was essential to the defence of Martinique — a very good reason, as Pitt complained, for England to keep it; but the French had their way.

Bute's very moderate proposals were as good as the French could hope for, but they ignored the claim of Spain to be considered. Spain had been dragged into war in the interests of France, had suffered serious losses, and was now being urged to make a hasty peace, also in the interests of France. Charles III resented the prospect of Englishmen in the Gulf of Mexico, firmly established in Florida, running their smuggling trade under cover of the Mississippi navigation, intercepting the Mexican *flotas* with greater ease than before. Choiseul was obliged to recognise the force of the Spanish arguments, and decided eventually to buy Spanish acquiescence by ceding Louisiana to Spain.

The old disputes between Spain and England were settled without much difficulty. The logwood settlements in Honduras received for the first time a precarious recognition. Spain agreed to tolerate the presence of the cutters and to respect their property; England agreed not to fortify the camps. Neither the boundaries of the settlements nor the rights of the cutters were defined, and the exact position of the English in Honduras continued to be disputed for the next twenty years. Finally, England restored Cuba to Spain and obtained Florida in exchange; and Spain renewed the treaties of commerce with England which were in force when the war began.

From the English point of view Bute's willingness to make colonial concessions in order — as he thought — to hasten a lasting peace was wasted, for a lasting peace with France was scarcely possible at that time. The long conflict of England, France and Spain in the Americas was by no means ended. Choiseul, far from being contented with England's moderation, began planning and organising for revenge almost as soon as the treaty was signed. Bute's desire for peace merely led him to accept terms less favourable than those he might have obtained; and Pitt, for all his factious ill-temper, was right in saying so. In the West Indies the concessions made were remarkable. Cuba commanded much of the American trade of Spain, Martinique much of the West Indian trade of France, and all these islands were also in close though illicit commercial contact with British North America — a contact which might have flourished the more if it had become open and lawful. There were good reasons, both strategic and economic, for England to retain some of these West Indian conquests; yet all were cheerfully restored, with little to show for their capture. No doubt the risk of prolonging a 'bloody and expensive war' had to be considered, and probably the English peace-makers assumed that English predominance at sea would always assure the mastery of the Caribbean, without the retention of the French and Spanish bases. Yet Pitt's forebodings were to be realised in his own lifetime. The English naval command of the Caribbean, so glibly postulated in the seventeen-sixties, was to prove insufficient in the seventeen-seventies and -eighties to prevent the French from capturing many islands in the Leeward and Windward groups and threatening the safety of the whole of the British West Indies. The great superiority achieved by England in the Caribbean during the Seven Years War — and the last opportunity to unite the greater part of the West Indies under one flag — was thrown away at the peace, in return for continental gains, which, though immense, were some of them very short-lived.

Parry and Sherlock : West Indies : Macmillan

CHAPTER IX

REORGANISATION, REBELLION AND WAR
1763–83

THE HOUSE OF BOURBON was not crushed, as Pitt had hoped, by the Seven Years War. Its members were firmly seated on the thrones of France and Spain, united by the family compact, guided for the most part by men whose ruling passions were hatred of Great Britain, desire for revenge, and longing to regain what had been lost in the colonies and at sea. Choiseul at once set about rebuilding naval and military strength, a task in which he achieved notable success; and repeatedly urged his Spanish colleague Grimaldi to do the same. For the French, the resumption of war was certain. It awaited only financial recovery and a suitable opportunity; for the conditions of peace, as Pitt repeatedly complained, were not severe enough to prevent France from entering at once upon the task of upsetting them.

In terms of actual territory, Spain had gained a great stretch of the coast of the Gulf of Mexico; she did little to develop this acquisition, and Rodney's comment was that Spain had added another desert to her empire. Of more immediate importance, the Spaniards recovered Cuba, and with interest, for many of the officers of the British and colonial forces who occupied the island acquired a taste for Cuban cigars, the best in the world, and even more for Cuban snuff; their return home was the beginning of the spread of that taste through Northern Europe and North America. The occupation was important in another direction also: in fostering the development of a young but growing sugar industry. Tobacco, the principal Cuban crop, was grown on small properties; the large slave-worked sugar plantation was comparatively rare; but during the British occupation optimistic traders, who thought that England might keep the island, had introduced some 10,000 slaves, all or almost all destined to work on sugar plantations. The influx of slaves continued after the peace, under an *Asiento* granted in 1763 to the Marqués de Casa Enrile and his associates; and many were also introduced by smugglers, English and Spanish. In general the events of 1762 accelerated — if they did not originate — a striking development and a significant change of direction in the economic activity of Cuba. At the same time, however, a more ambitious and flexible strategy of defence, together with the abandonment of the old convoy system, caused a decline in the purely military importance of Havana and a great increase in that of Puerto Rico, far out to windward. In the post-war years the great forts of San Cristóbal and San Felipe del Morro were developed, on plans derived from Vauban, into the most powerful stronghold in all the Americas. Like the Morro at Havana, these works were paid for by *situados* from Mexico.

The French had lost immense tracts of mainland territory and had ceded a few undeveloped islands; but their position in the West Indies remained strong. Martinique, it is true, had suffered heavily both from English maritime pressure during the war and from the commercial speculations of the Jesuits before, but its good harbours, its fertile soil, and its windward position made it a valuable asset, well worth recovering, and it remained the seat of government, and the chief market and shipping station, of the French Windward Islands. Guadeloupe, less important strategically, exceeded Martinique in productivity, and had prospered under four years of British occupation; for during that period it had sold its sugars openly on the London market and had imported some 40,000 slaves through British merchants. Saint-Domingue, relatively untroubled by the war, was now economically much more important than either, and was by a considerable margin the biggest producer of sugar in the West Indies. Finally, the restoration of Gorée assured to the French the all-important supply of slaves, without which the production of sugar under eighteenth-century conditions could not be maintained.

For the French West Indies the Peace of Paris ushered in a golden age. All the energy and trade which had been absorbed by Canada and Louisiana were now directed to the West Indian islands. Their sugar production already exceeded that of the British islands. In 1767, the first year for which sets of comparable figures are available, the French islands exported about

77,000 tons, the British (including the newly ceded islands) about 72,000. The French exports, moreover, included a high proportion — nearly 30,000 tons — of 'clayed' or semi-refined sugar, while the English product was nearly all raw muscavado, the commonest and cheapest form of exportable sugar. In the next three decades both French and English production increased steadily, but the French maintained their lead. On the eve of the Revolution the French islands were exporting about 100,000 tons of sugar annually, the British islands from 85,000 to 90,000. The possibilities of expansion of wealth seemed to some contemporaries to have no limit. 'The labours of the people settled in these islands', wrote the Abbé Raynal, 'are the sole bases of the African trade; they extend the fisheries and culture of North America, afford a good market for the manufactures of Asia, and double, perhaps treble, the activity of all Europe. They may be considered as the principal cause of the rapid motion which now agitates the universe. This ferment must increase, in proportion as cultures, that are so capable of being extended, shall approach nearer to their higher degree of perfection.'

The prosperity of the French islands was due in some measure to their close commercial contact with the British North American colonies; a contact which, even in war-time, proved extremely difficult to break. French sugar was cheaper than English, partly because the French planters still had access to virgin land and were not put to the heavy expense of manuring; partly because the export duties on sugar were lower in the French islands — only 1 per cent and no 'enumeration' duty. Molasses and rum were very much cheaper, because the French preference for brandy, and the heavy protection given to brandy in France, made rum almost unsaleable there, so that French West Indian sugar manufacturers would almost give molasses away to anyone who would come and fetch it. The New Englanders found a ready market in both French and English islands for provisions, chiefly grain and salt fish; for timber, chiefly barrel staves; and for horses. They tended more and more to sell these commodities in the English islands for cash, or bills on London, and to buy sugar and molasses — in defiance of the Molasses Act — chiefly from the French. Some of the vessels engaged in the slave trade followed the same line, turning their triangular trade into a quadrangular one;

and undoubtedly some of the French sugar carried to New England in this way was re-exported to England as British grown.

The British islands had had their golden age in the years between the wars, and most British West Indians in 1763 hoped for a return to what they regarded as normal. Those who had fulminated against the capitulations in Guadeloupe and Martinique could congratulate themselves that those islands had been handed back to France, though not in as devastated a condition as the British planters would have liked. Nevertheless, the more far-sighted planters were justifiably uneasy. The older islands were in bad shape. They still carried a serious economic handicap, in the old 4½ per cent export duty on their produce, which government had never levied in Jamaica and now failed to extract from the ceded islands. Their exhausted land was giving poorer and poorer yields and demanding frequent replanting and generous manuring. These heavy hand-operations in turn necessitated a larger labour force; but indented servants were almost unobtainable and the price of slaves went up and up. For this, the ceded islands were to some extent responsible; they attracted the poorer class of white settler who wished to acquire small holdings, thereby reducing the white population of older colonies; but at the same time they were turning to sugar and demanding slaves for plantation work. The steady expansion of sugar production both in Jamaica and in the ceded islands prevented the price on the London market from rising to cover the increasing cost of production. In the ceded islands, and to some extent in Jamaica, relief could be found by the cultivation of other export crops — coffee (then in high demand in Europe), cacao, cotton; the ceded islands in particular avoided the worst evils of monoculture and absentee ownership. But Barbados and the Leeward Islands were almost entirely, Jamaica largely, dependent upon the export of sugar for their livelihood and all suffered from price fluctuations and high taxation in the years following the war. As an aggravation of misfortune, Jamaica experienced in 1764 a prolonged drought which destroyed both crops and cattle in the northern half of the island.

In these circumstances the British West Indians, as they have always done throughout their history, turned to government for relief. They wanted lower duties on their sugar, cheaper slaves, the prohibition of North American trade with the French islands, and easier facilities for borrowing upon West Indian security; but they found government less automatically willing than formerly to legislate in their interests. The Seven Years War had drawn the attention of English mercantilists to wider economic horizons. Other groups were beginning to make their voices heard. Grocers, refiners and distillers wanted cheap sugar and molasses and did not greatly care whether or not these products were British grown. Slavers wanted a plantation market for their slaves, British or foreign, island or continental, wherever demand was brisk and prices high. Manufacturers of textiles and hardware, in the first enthusiasm of industrial revolution, wanted large, populous and wealthy provinces as markets for their wares, rather than small islands which produced nothing but sugar and bought nothing in large quantity but slaves. Interest was beginning to shift from the West Indies to continental America, North and South; from the Caribbean to the Atlantic as a whole. Ominous things had been said about the West Indies during the debates on the Peace of Paris. Shelburne, defending the restoration of Guadeloupe, had remarked that 'wherever sugar grows population decreases' and that 'our sugar isles weaken and depopulate our Mother Country'. It was the discovery that they were no longer the pampered favourites of government which made the English West Indian planters, factors and merchants band together for the defence of a privileged position which they felt to be threatened. The years following the Peace of Paris saw the rise of the Society of West Indian Merchants and the Society of West Indian Planters and Merchants in London, and a number of similar bodies in the out-ports. The West Indians used all available means, public and private, commercial and political, to urge their views upon government, and organised one of the most compact and powerful parliamentary lobbies England has ever known.

Wealthy, persuasive and determined though they were, the West Indians were not by any means uniformly successful in their political approaches. They lost nothing, it is true. The protection which their sugar enjoyed in the English market was not yet assailed. On the other hand, they failed to gain much. Government in those years was endeavouring to reorganise and tighten imperial administration as a whole, to formulate an imperial policy, and to make the empire pay its share of the cost of the war. Reduction of duties was out of the question. Colonial provincialism, suggestions for the benefit of one group of colonies at the expense of others, or at the expense of Great Britain, were out of favour. In dealing with the question of French West Indian trade, for example, government acceded neither to the North American argument for no duty, or only a negligible duty, on foreign molasses; nor to the West Indian plea for the total prohibition of the trade, or a prohibitive duty. More concerned with financial and administrative reorganisation than with strict adherence to mercantile principles, the Sugar Act of 1764 lowered the duty from sixpence to threepence a gallon; and for the first time effective measures were taken to collect the duty.

In some directions, on the other hand, the West India interest won small but useful victories. One minor but significant achievement was the order given to the victualling office in 1775 to contract for West Indian rum instead of French brandy for use in the Navy. Other victories concerned borrowing facilities in the West Indies. An Act of 1773 — passed against strenuous opposition — permitted foreigners to make loans at 5 per cent interest, with the same rights in recovering debts in peace and war as if they had been British subjects. A further Act, designed to induce wealthy Englishmen to invest in the colonies, authorised the lending of money against West Indian real estate at whatever interest charge might prevail where the property lay, even though the charge exceeded the legal English rate (5 per cent at that time). These measures made borrowing a great deal easier, and West Indians were all too ready to avail themselves of such facilities.

One familiar source of British West Indian profit had formerly been the illicit trade between the British islands and Spanish America. This trade had much declined since the war. Choiseul had persuaded the Spanish government to reduce drastically the duties on the direct trade between Cadiz and the Spanish-American ports, a reduction which favoured France indirectly, since most of the goods carried were French. At the same time, easing of internal restrictions had stimulated Spanish colonial trade, and the colonies were more prosperous than they had ever been. Foreign smuggling had been rendered more difficult by a general tightening up of Spanish administration. The rapacious and venal irregulars who had formerly manned the *guarda-costa* service were being replaced by paid men recruited in Spain. The time was not very propitious, therefore, for an attempt to revive the British West Indian trade; but the attempt was made, not indeed by running goods in British ships, but by offering inducements to Spanish ships to trade, within fixed limits, in British West Indian ports.

Free ports already existed in the West Indies. The Dutch islands of St. Eustatius and Curaçao, producing nothing themselves, were prosperous clearing houses for manufactured goods and tropical products, and were used by the shipping of many nations. The French also began, immediately after the war, to develop a free port system, designed in their case to provide sugar estates with plantation supplies. Ports were opened at Martinique and Guadeloupe in 1763, in St. Lucia and at Mole St. Nicholas in Saint-Domingue in 1767. These ports were much frequented by foreign traders, chiefly North American, who exchanged timber, livestock and provisions for molasses, rum and European merchandise; and the trade in general seems to have been a success. The English were not primarily concerned to secure plantation supplies, which they could get readily from their own North American colonies; their object was to earn money to pay for such supplies, by means of an export trade to the Spanish and French colonies. With this end in view they adopted in 1766 a modified form of the free port system already used by the Dutch and the French.

The British Free Ports Act of 1766 was not a departure from mercantilist principles, but in most respects a logical development of them. It opened four ports in Jamaica — Kingston, Lucea, Montego Bay and Savannah-la-Mar, and two in Dominica — Roseau and Prince Rupert's Bay — to foreign shipping. Foreigners might purchase and export slaves, or any British goods legally imported, except naval stores and tobacco. They might pay for these purchases either in coin or in their own colonial produce, subject to certain exceptions. At the Jamaican free ports it was forbidden to import goods which Jamaica itself produced — sugar, coffee, pimento, ginger, molasses and tobacco — and manufactured goods. In Dominica, where trade with the French islands was the object of the

K

measure, sugar, coffee, and the rest, were allowed to be imported. Precautions — which proved ineffective — were taken to prevent the re-export of such commodities to North America. They were to be sold in England as foreign produce, the small quantity of sugar produced in Dominica itself being warehoused separately and sold as British grown. These cumbersome regulations in Dominica proved unworkable. It was absurd, in any case, to try to restrict a fertile island to the rôle of a mere entrepôt. The act had little effect in drawing French sugar into British warehouses — except smuggled French sugar which the Dominica planters marketed as their own.   In Jamaica a considerable amount of export business was done with Cuba, chiefly in slaves, which were sold to the Spanish Asiento Company, and with Puerto Rico; but the arrangement threw upon Spanish traders the risk of seizure by their own *guarda-costas*, and provoked the Spanish authorities to counter-measures, such as procuring copies of the Jamaican customs-house register and prosecuting such of their people as were caught trading. Naturally the Spaniards were wary of such risks. The act revealed that Great Britain would no longer go to war to protect her own subjects in illicit trade; it came too late to arrest the decline in trade with the Spanish colonies and its consequence, the acute shortage of currency.

Sugar prices remained low; the coffee market — chiefly in Germany — crashed disastrously in 1773, largely because of duties and restrictions introduced by the German princes; in 1722 a severe hurricane devastated the Leeward Islands. All in all, the British West Indies were in poor condition to withstand the shock of the war, long hoped for by France and Spain, which finally broke out between Great Britain and the North American colonies in 1776. War against France had long been regarded as a panacea for the economic ills of the British West Indies; but war against North America was a major disaster, which the West India interests in London did their utmost to prevent. Up to the very eve of the war, in 1775, they were still holding meetings and petitioning Parliament to avert the conflict which they saw coming.

The petitions were rejected; and in 1776 the British West Indians had to make up their minds which side they were on. There were many close connections, cultural and sentimental as well as commercial, between the two groups of colonies. Sympathies and loyalties in the West Indies, as indeed in North America, were divided. The American rebels tried hard to persuade the West Indians to join in the revolution, and at first sight there was some force in the arguments they used. The West Indian colonies had constitutions similar to those of the rebellious thirteen; they had representative government, but not responsible government. They had largely the same grievances — taxation without representation, interference with their legislative freedom, an adverse trade balance, the inconveniences and restrictions of the Acts of Trade. Like the North Americans, many West Indians rioted against the Stamp Act. Like North America, the West Indies were taxed to pay part of the cost of imperial defence; but there lay the difference. The North American colonies believed that they did not need the defence for which they were asked to pay. The West Indies did need it, and knew they needed it. The islands were rich and vulnerable; their free population was small and many of their leading landowners lived in England. The Royal Navy was their only sure defence. For all these reasons, as well as from loyalty, the British West Indians refused to join the American rebels; the only colony, other than the thirteen, to send representatives to Congress was Bermuda, where a few enterprising people made a business of stealing munitions from the royal arsenals and selling them to the Americans. In the West Indies proper, people smuggled and grumbled, and hoped that the war would be short.

The West Indians could not stay out of the war, however; France in 1778, Spain in 1779, joined in the fighting with the intention not only of assisting the Revolution in North America but also of seizing or plundering the British possessions in the Caribbean. The West Indians suffered all the dangers and hardships of a major international war. Apart from actual fighting, they were heavily taxed, their trade was interrupted and they were cut off from their main source of food. The price of flour in Barbados rose, in the first year of the war, from between 15s. and 25s. to between 30s. and 37s. 6d. and at times, as in 1780–81, there was a danger of actual starvation. Two major hurricanes and a tidal wave increased the islanders' misery. The slave population of Barbados fell from 68,500 in 1773 to 57,400 in 1783, as a result largely of malnutrition and physical disaster. Jamaica, which grew a larger proportion of its own food and could be more easily supplied from the areas under British control in Georgia and South Carolina, was less hardly hit, but even Jamaica suffered severe distress.

The planters had difficulty not only in obtaining supplies but in getting their sugars away. In the first year of the war the quantity shipped to London fell by nearly half, insurance rates reached 23 per cent and freights rose similarly. Prices rose too, but with such violent fluctuations that planters could have no certainty of covering their costs at any given moment; and in any case there were limits to what grocers and refiners in England would pay. The refineries, indeed, raised again their old demand that when the price of sugar on the London market reached a certain figure importations of foreign prize sugar at a low rate of duty should be allowed. The West India interest in the House of Commons was again strong enough to block this proposal, but it could not prevent the importation, at British rates, of sugar from Dutch Guiana during its occupation by British forces; nor, more serious still, could it prevent doubling of the British rates of duty in the course of the war.

While Jamaica and Barbados thus experienced the commercial strangulation which in former wars had been the lot of Martinique and Guadeloupe, most of the other British islands suffered actual capture. For the first time in a hundred years the French and Spanish navies were able to establish a superiority of forces in the Caribbean for long periods continuously. The French fleet, thanks to Choiseul, was at the peak of its fighting strength; the Spanish fleet, though less efficiently manned, included many new ships of excellent design, built under French influence. The British, with many ships tied down in support of the armies in America, were hard put to it to provide a defence for their own coasts and had no force to spare for a blockade of the French ports. French and Spanish fleets could cross the Atlantic at will and deliver their attacks in North America or the West Indies, as opportunity, the time of year and the state of the weather suggested; operating in the Caribbean, as a rule, in the spring and early summer, on the continental seaboard in the late summer and autumn, returning to the West Indies with the end of the hurricane season and the onset of the North American winter.

The defences of the outer islands went down like ninepins before these repeated blows. The French began with the capture of Dominica in September 1778. To this the British fleet under Byron replied in kind by taking St. Lucia three months later — a considerable victory, won against d'Estaing's fleet as well as the land garrison. St. Lucia became — as Rodney had always predicted — the base from which the British could watch the movements of the French at their centre, Martinique; but even from this point of vantage the British forces were inadequate to prevent the French capturing St. Vincent and Grenada in the early summer of 1779. Spain declared war in June of that year, but the initial operations of the Spanish fleet were directed against England itself, not against the British West Indies. The combined Bourbon fleets were prevented, as usual, from striking a decisive blow in the Caribbean — against Jamaica, for example — by the shortness of the operating season for fleets sent out from Europe each year. The great armament which de Guichen brought out in 1780 achieved little but an indecisive battle against Rodney's fleet off Martinique.

During all this time the comparative weakness of the British at sea had greatly favoured neutral trade; but the habitual high-handedness of the British Navy in dealing with such neutral ships as it caught trading with the enemy as usual exasperated neutral governments. The Dutch were the people most concerned. Their Leeward Island colony of St. Eustatius was a free port, and a vast depot for the supply of munitions to America. In 1780 John Adams visited The Hague and persuaded the Dutch government to recognise North American independence; and the British, in what was almost the only firm and well-judged stroke to the credit of Lord North's cabinet, declared war. Holland was much less dangerous as an open than as a secret enemy, and St. Eustatius was almost undefended. Rodney, in spite of the damage which his ships sustained in the 1780 hurricane, took the place, with hardly a shot fired, early in 1781, and found there over a hundred and fifty sail of contraband traders and a vast stock of goods of all kinds — a greater haul even than Havana twenty years before. The island never recovered from the thorough plunder and devastation to which Rodney subjected it. The three Guianese colonies, Demerara, Essequibo and Berbice, soon followed, and Curaçao might have fallen too, but that Rodney characteristically preferred to lie at St. Eustatius supervising the sale of prizes. He had some justification for making hay while the sun shone; St. Eustatius was recaptured by de Bouillé in November 1781, but by that time most of the loot had been sold or carried away, and Rodney himself was back in England.

Meanwhile Cornwallis had surrendered at Yorktown and the French fleet was thus released for West Indian operations under its ablest commander, de Grasse. Not only St. Eustatius, but Demerara, Essequibo, Berbice and Tobago were recaptured by the French in the course of 1781. The Spaniards, operating from New Orleans, took Pensacola and reconquered Florida, which they had ceded to Great Britain in 1763; and shortly afterwards captured New Providence, the capital of the Bahamas. The Caribbean obviously was to be the final battle-ground of the fleets, with the British islands, so long coveted, the objects of the triumphant Bourbon combination.

St. Kitts fell early in 1782. Its small British garrison was shut up in the fortress of Brimstone Hill by an army of 8,000 men landed by de Bouillé, and Hood's bold and successful action against de Bouillé's ships in Basse-Terre road came too late to affect the issue ashore. The inhabitants did nothing to help the garrison. Their capitulation to the French was un-heroic, but it was prudent common sense; and by it they secured terms very like those granted by the British to Guadeloupe in the previous war. The terms were so favourable, indeed, that men of property, whose plantations had been saved from plunder by the surrender, chiefly feared that their good relations with the French commanders might be endangered by the patriotic indis-cretions of the negroes and the poor whites. In Nevis and Montserrat, which surrendered shortly afterwards, events followed much the same course.

It was at this critical juncture that Rodney returned from England with a fleet which, joined to Hood's squadron, made him approximately equal to de Grasse in strength. He brought de Grasse to action in April 1782 near the Saintes, the small rocky islets between Guadeloupe and Dominica, and in the battle which followed his genius as a tactician more than re-deemed the negligences of which — in pursuit of prize-money — he had been guilty in the past. De Grasse himself and seven of his ships were taken, and his fleet scattered. The attack on Jamaica was put off, and eventually abandoned, for towards the end of the same year the combatants, compelled by their financial exhaustion and their enormous commercial and maritime losses, began to treat for peace. In the Treaty of Versailles Great Britain recovered Grenada, St. Vincent, St. Kitts, Montserrat, Nevis and Dominica. The right to fell logwood in Central America was restored on the former ambiguous and precarious terms. New Providence had already been recaptured. France recovered St. Lucia. The only changes in Caribbean territory were the cession of Florida to Spain and Tobago to France. These were trivial results indeed for years of bitter and destructive fighting; but nobody in France, Spain or England yet appeared to question whether the West Indies were worth the enormous cost of war.

The British West Indies had been the scene of the fiercest and most destructive of the Caribbean land fighting during the war; and the British West Indies were the worst sufferers by the terms of the peace, which recognised the United States as an independent country. The immediate reaction of the West Indians, who had resented the war from the first, was an attempt to ignore its results. Their representatives in London petitioned for a resumption of trade on the old terms. The petition — not unnaturally in the circumstances — was refused. The logical but rigid views expressed in Lord Sheffield's *Observations on the Commerce of the American States* (1783) found favour with Parliament; the more liberal views of Pitt were rejected. The United States were now a foreign power, outside the system of imperial preferential trade. An Act of 1783, subsequent Orders in Council, and a consolidating Act in 1788, together laid down the new policy. They provided that sugar, rum, molasses, coffee and pimento could be exported to the United States on the same terms as to a British colony; timber, livestock, grain, flour and bread could be imported from the United States, but only in British ships; United States meat and fish could not be imported at all. Supplies formerly obtained from the thirteen colonies must now be sought in Canada, Nova Scotia, and Newfoundland, in limited quantity and at a higher price.

Attempts were made from 1784 to persuade government to extend the Free Ports Act to allow American ships to trade to

British West Indian ports on the same terms as Spanish and French colonial ships. The French had taken action on these lines immediately after the war; *arrêts* of 1783 and 1784 had opened still more ports in Saint-Domingue and the French Windward Islands to foreign shipping, and slaves and provisions were being brought in in great quantities by American ships. The British Board of Trade, however, though it studied the French regulations in some detail, refused to entertain so glaring a departure from the principles of the Acts of Trade, and the British West Indians, failing to twist the Free Ports Act to their own purposes, lost interest in the Act. The Free Port trade before the war had been largely in the hands of North Americans settled in the West Indies. After the war it languished despite all the efforts of the British Government to revive it.

The obvious recourse of the British West Indians was smuggling; and once again the Navy made itself unpopular, as Nelson did at Nevis, by attempts to enforce the law. But the price of supplies still went up. White oak staves for hogsheads in 1784 cost four or five times their pre-war price. Rice, formerly imported from the Carolinas, more than doubled in price as a result of the war. Meat and fish from Canada cost 30 to 40 per cent more than pre-war imports from the thirteen colonies. Local food crops in Jamaica were devastated by hurricanes in three successive years, in 1784, 1785 and 1786, and the lieutenant-governor reported the loss of 15,000 slaves as a result of famine. At the same time the duty on sugar, increased to meet the cost of the war, was raised again to 12s. 4d. in 1787, to 15s. per hundred-weight in 1791. No wonder that reports were all of distress, of the burden of mortgages, of estates sold for debt. It is true that the quantity and value of the sugar sent to England was still increasing — it increased by about 30 per cent from 1772 to 1788; but most of the profit was absorbed by the London factors and did not reach the planters. West Indians were becoming acutely aware of the twin dangers of over-dependence on sugar as a cash crop for export and on imported meat and grain for food, and were eagerly seeking ways of escape. In 1791 the Jamaica Assembly resolved that 'Every encouragement is to be given to the cultivation of Yams, Cocos, Maize, Plantains and such products as the Breadfruit, Nutmeg, Cloves, Cinnamon . . . and

Coffee: it being believed that the cultivation of such exotics would, without doubt, in the course of a few years, lessen the dependence of the sugar islands on North America for food and necessaries; and not only supply subsistence for future generations, but, probably, furnish fresh incitements to Industry, new improvements in the Arts, and new subjects of Commerce'. Coconuts, coffee and nutmeg did indeed become valuable crops, taking their places beside the native cacao and pimento; and Barbados and the Leeward Islands, towards the end of the century, achieved an extraordinary expansion of their production and export of cotton, which a newly mechanised industry in England was demanding in vast quantity. At the same time, the British government was sufficiently impressed by the urgency of the food problem to send warships cruising in the East Indies and Pacific to collect plants for introduction into the West Indies. Nevertheless, sugar remained, and remains to this day, the chief crop and the determining factor of West Indian life. The British sugar islands were to enjoy one more reprieve, a brief Indian summer of prosperity and public consideration, before the long bleak neglect of the nineteenth century. This reprieve resulted not from efforts to diversify their economy — useful though such efforts were — but from the destruction of the rival French sugar trade, by the disasters of revolution and resulting war.

CHAPTER X

THE SUGAR ISLANDS ON THE EVE OF REVOLUTION

IN THE SEARCH FOR West Indian prosperity the historian is constantly driven farther and farther back, the object of his search receding as he pursues it. The several islands reached their peaks of prosperity at widely different times. In Barbados, perhaps, the peak may be placed well before the end of the seventeenth century. In Antigua, St. Kitts, Martinique, Guadeloupe, it came later; in Jamaica later still — after the middle of the eighteenth century; and Saint-Domingue was at the height of its wealth and reputation in the two or three decades before the Revolution. Even at these peaks prosperity in the islands concerned was rarely universal. It is extremely difficult to speak in general terms of West Indian prosperity. The symptoms by which prosperity was ordinarily measured — price and volume of exports, custom-house receipts, the incomes received by absentee landlords and dealers in tropical products in Europe, the influence exerted by West India 'lobbies' in European capitals — did not always reflect the real state of affairs in the colonies. The West Indians formed a series of small groups of homesick and often quarrelsome exiles, surrounded by much larger groups of alien and often resentful slaves — also exiles — living in a country and climate which — at that time — were distinctly unhealthy. It was a precarious and artificial society in which prosperity came and went suddenly, with the fluctuations of price and duty, with droughts and hurricanes and the chances of peace and war. Declining prosperity produced bitter wails of complaint and demands for legislative help. Rising prosperity encouraged extravagance and absenteeism; but it produced also more durable results — the architectural distinction of the cities in the Spanish islands; the solid elegance of the 'great houses' in the British; the remarkable production of French and English books about the West Indies, written by people who were born or who resided there; the taste for good horses and horsemanship; and the boundless hospitality of planters who, prosperous though they might appear, were by no means exempt from financial worry, from physical danger, and from the necessity of hard work. All these represented a notable achievement on the part of eighteenth-century West Indian society, considering the flimsy foundations on which that society rested. One has only to read the works of Bryan Edwards or of Charlevoix — intelligent, critical, full of pride in the West Indies — to realise that wealth was not easily acquired, still less easily retained; that planters were not all extravagant, incompetent, brutal, debauched — or absent; that slaves did not necessarily live in constant terror of the whip. One learns also, however, that many of the weaknesses of West Indian society and economy today have their origin in the peculiarities of plantation life, in the hey-day of eighteenth-century prosperity. Of these peculiarities, the most significant were monoculture; slavery; absentee ownership; social emulation; and dependence on the outside world.

In the three centuries since their first discovery the West Indies had produced for export a series of major crops, besides animal products such as bacon and hides. The crops included tobacco, cacao, indigo, ginger, sugar, cotton and coffee. Throughout the eighteenth century in most of the islands sugar was incomparably the most important. In terms of money returns to the acre it was then by far the most valuable of all tropical crops. It attracted the attention of all planters who could obtain suitable land and raise the necessary capital, and in many islands it had driven out all other crops. Tobacco had long disappeared from the British and French islands (not, of course, from the Spanish). Cacao and ginger had always been comparatively minor products, and both lost ground in the eighteenth century; indigo held its own more or less in Martinique, but almost disappeared from the British islands, because a high duty made it unprofitable. Cotton of very good quality was grown in the Leeward Islands, but it was only during the French wars at the end of the century that the West Indians temporarily became the chief suppliers of cotton to England's expanding textile industry. Coffee was important, and gained ground steadily in the second half of the century; but even where, as in Jamaica and Saint-Domingue, sugar and coffee were both grown and exported in large quantity, they were grown in different places, at different altitudes, on different soils. A planter grew either sugar or coffee: he was unlikely to vary or alternate his crops. Certainly there was never any likelihood of coffee supplanting sugar. On the whole it is true to say that most of the West Indian islands depended for their livelihood chiefly on the cultivation, manufacture and export of sugar. To that extent their economy can be called a monoculture.

Reference has already been made to the peculiar characteristics of sugar: the relative ease with which cane could be grown — given fertile soil — on the same ground year after year, by processes admittedly laborious, but needing little skill or care; the breathless haste with which it must be cut as soon as ripe, and carted and milled as soon as cut; the high cost of the equipment required for milling and evaporating; and the considerable skill, organisation and judgement needed in the processes of manufacture. There was an inexorable tenacity about sugar; once a mill and boiling-house had been established, land bought and planted to cane, slaves acquired and trained, there was no breaking the grip of sugar on the place. The preparation was too costly and too specialised to allow of change. The estate must go on producing sugar, or grow up in ruinate. During the eighteenth century the scale of manufacture tended to increase, and with it the intensity and completeness of monoculture. The slow and primitive cattle mills gave place to windmills, which ground much faster; their ruined towers can be seen on every side in the Leeward Islands. Windmills in their turn were replaced, wherever the supply of water allowed, by more powerful and reliable water-mills. In the latter half of the century great ingenuity was exercised in Saint-Domingue and in Jamaica, in designing and fitting huge over-shot wheels which could be turned by comparatively small streams, the water being carried by aqueducts to the point where power was required, and then channelled away to irrigate low-lying fields. The ruins of many fine aqueducts and mills solidly built of cut stone still stand as monuments to the prosperity and energy of the industry at this time. All this improvement in machinery demanded a quicker flow of canes to feed the iron maws of the mills. More land had

A mill yard, printed by Edward Suter
for the Ladies' Society for Promoting Early Education of Negro Children, London, c. 1830

Holeing a cane-piece, c. 1830

to be taken in, more slaves bought and trained; more and more capital was needed and was obtained by mortgages and other forms of borrowing. Patrick Browne, in his *Civil and Natural History of Jamaica* (1756), writing of Jamaica in its most prosperous days, remarked that the planters, 'though rich and in easy circumstances, are seldom out of debt, for the charges attending a sugar settlement are very considerable and their natural propensity to increase their possessions constantly engaging them in new disbursements and contracts'. This was all very well while prices were high and steady; but every monoculture is vulnerable to fluctuations in price. A monoculture which exports the greater part of its product and which operates under a heavy load of capital debt is trebly vulnerable.

The largest part of a planter's capital was sunk in his slaves. The peculiarities of sugar cultivation demanded a large and disciplined force of unskilled labour, available at short notice, capable of being concentrated and driven hard during the seasonal crises of the plantation year. Of these crises, the most important was 'crop' — the period of several months in the spring of every year when the cane was cut and milled and the sugar made. All careful planters agreed on the importance of getting crop over as quickly as possible. During crop all the ordinary work of cultivation ceased; the mill ground incessantly day and night; and there was little rest for man or beast. It was a merry time in some ways, for there was cane to chew, and rum allowed or stolen, there was excitement and activity, and usually at the end of crop some sort of feast — a rustic and often somewhat dangerous Saturnalia; but it was a wearying time also. The work was not particularly skilled: the only manual jobs which called for skill and judgement were those of boiling and of 'striking' — the damping of the fire under the 'tache' or final copper when the syrup was sufficiently evaporated to allow the sugar crystals to form. Some jobs — that of feeding canes into the rollers, for instance — could be done by children. But the work of cutting and carting the cane, ladling the syrup from one boiler to another in the boiling house, and manhandling the heavy casks to the curing house, where they stood for weeks while the molasses dripped away — these were laborious tasks on which every available hand was needed, by shifts, day and night while crop lasted.

The exigencies of crop fixed the size of the labour force, without which an estate could not be worked; and this fact helps to explain the laborious and primitive nature of field operations during the rest of the year. The slaves were there all the time; they could not be paid off, as casual cane-cutting labour is paid off today; they might as well be used. There was very little incentive, therefore, for planters to introduce labour-saving devices or even to conduct their field work by ordinary European standards of efficiency. The biggest operation of the planter's year, next to crop, was the replanting of cane. Cane roots could be left in the ground after cutting, to send up ratoons which could be cut and milled the following year; but ratoons yielded less sugar each year, and after a period of three or four years the roots had to be grubbed up. About a third to a quarter of the land in cane, therefore, must be replanted each year, in rotation. The ground was prepared by the process known as 'holing'; slaves armed with heavy digging hoes dug out holes some four feet square and nine inches deep, into which manure was forked, and cane cuttings planted. As the cane grew it was banked up by hoeing the soil back into the hole. The planting process was extremely and unnecessarily laborious, and could have been done far more quickly and efficiently by the use of ploughs; but a planter had little incentive to buy ploughs and to train plough-men and plough cattle when he could dispose, out of crop, of the labour of a large gang of slaves. The plough was only beginning to make headway in most islands at the end of the eighteenth century.

The rest of the slaves' year was occupied in harrowing, trashing, weeding (this last a job for children) and in the odd jobs of any estate — cutting wood, cleaning drains, patching roads and so on. Some field hands naturally became specialised as carters or as penners in charge of cattle. The negro made a good cowman, except that his slave resentment broke out at times in periods of wilful neglect or acts of needless cruelty. Most plantations had also a certain number of tradesmen among their slaves — carpenters, coopers, masons, and so on; on large properties it was not uncommon to employ a few European workmen, paying them a high wage and requiring them to train slaves in their trades. These European artisans were trouble-some employees, difficult to fit into the social structure of an

Sugar: a cane cutter at work
[*Courtesy of Jamaica Tourist Board*]

Sugar: the buildings of an eighteenth-century mill
[*Photo: Packer, Kingston*]

Sugar: a modern mill
[*Photo: Packer, Kingston*]

estate; but the quality of the masonry and joinery in eighteenth-century mills and estate houses shows that the training they gave was not wasted; that the negro slave was perfectly capable of becoming a skilled craftsman, and was willing to learn if some small incentive could be provided. Money and greater freedom of movement were both incentives towards this end. A skilled slave was a valuable piece of property; the practice of hiring out such slaves by the day or by the job was common, and the slaves had considerable opportunities of earning money for themselves, over what their owners received for their hire. Finally, in addition to field hands and tradesmen, a number of slaves — often an unnecessarily large number — were occupied in the domestic service of great house and overseer; to take a slave off domestic or specialised work and send him (or her) to field labour was usually regarded as a punishment; the reverse process, a promotion.

The lodging, clothing and feeding of these armies of slaves was one of the major problems of the West Indian economy. Slaves usually built their huts themselves, of timber, wattle-and-daub and thatch, mostly grown on the estate (more substantial building would have to be roofed with imported shingles, which were expensive). They wore clothes supplied by their owners — two suits a year was the usual allowance in both French and British islands — and various types of coarse linen cloth — osnaburg, Dutch stripes, Guinée bleue — were manufactured expressly for this market in England and France. As for food, the proprietor of a plantation could import it, or grow it on part of his land, or allow land and time to his slaves to grow it for themselves. In Saint-Domingue and Jamaica, which were the chief sugar-planting areas in the eighteenth century, it was the custom to set aside marginal land, usually in the foothills, as provision grounds. Slaves were able to grow there all their own vegetable requirements — yams, plantains and the like — and to have a surplus for sale at the Sunday markets which were the main social gatherings of the slaves' week. This habit was of great importance for the future, for it prepared the development of the independent peasantry who inhabit the hills of Haiti and Jamaica to this day. In the outer islands mountain land was not usually available in sufficient quantity for provision grounds; planters used part of their land for growing maize and plantains

— planting corn was traditionally the task of the 'second gang' composed of old men, nursing women and older children; but even in Martinique and Guadeloupe considerable amounts of corn, rice and the like had to be imported; and islands such as Antigua, where nearly all the land was either in cane, or cotton, or pasture, imported nearly all their food. Throughout the sugar islands such animal food as the slaves got — chiefly salt fish and an occasional treat of salt beef — came from outside (as of course did the wine, the wheaten flour and other delicacies which European taste demanded). Most plantations throughout the area had to devote at least half or two-thirds of their land to the production of food for slaves, pasture for draught animals, and woodland for fuel and timber; but nevertheless all the islands were dependent to some extent — some almost entirely — on imports of food for their slaves. Interruptions of supply, such as occurred in time of war, always caused distress and sometimes widespread disaster.

Governments in France and England, and in the several islands, were very keenly aware of the danger of starvation in time of war. Both during and after the War of American Independence, strenuous attempts were made to introduce new food plants. Two plants of very great economic importance were introduced in the course of the war. The ackee tree came to Jamaica from West Africa in 1778. The famous gastronomic marriage which gives Jamaica its most characteristic dish dates from that time. As had often happened in the past, the ships which brought slaves to the West Indies brought also the plants with which they were to be fed. The first ackee slips were bought by Dr. Clarke, the first island botanist of Jamaica, from the captain of a slaver. More important still was the mango, an Asiatic tree which now grows all round the world within the tropics. The mango has had a long association with the slave trade. To this day in some parts of Central Africa lines of mango trees planted by Arab slavers mark the routes down which slave caravans were driven to the coast. The first plants to reach the West Indies were part of a collection despatched to the French islands from Mauritius at the command of the French government, in 1782. The ship carrying the collection was taken in prize by an English frigate, H.M.S. *Flora*, Captain Marshall. The admiral commanding on the station — the great Rodney

himself — recognising the potential value of the capture, sent
the plants to Jamaica, where they were propagated in Mr. East's
garden at Gordon Town. Like the ackee, the mango flourished
spontaneously and has spread throughout the West Indies.
Many improved varieties have since been introduced, and
possibly no single plant is now more important in feeding the
very poor during the summer months.

Not only West Africa, but the Far East and the Pacific were
laid under contribution. Cook's voyage had revealed a wealth
of plant life hitherto unknown to Europeans. The breadfruit
tree, found and described by Cook at Tahiti, especially caught
the public imagination, and in 1787 H.M.S. *Bounty* was ordered
to Tahiti to collect breadfruit and other plants. She was commanded by William Bligh, who had been Cook's lieutenant.
The mutiny of part of the ship's company prevented Bligh from
accomplishing his task; but in 1793 he was despatched upon a
similar errand in the even more appropriately named *Providence*
brig, and this time returned with a cargo of manna which included
several hundred young breadfruit trees. The trees were planted
in the government botanical gardens at Bath in St. Thomas, and
from there distributed all over the island. Incidentally the
foundation of a number of botanical gardens in various parts
of the West Indies at this time was evidence of the importance
attached to the problem of introducing new forms of cheap
starch for feeding field labourers, as well as of a general interest
in botany for its own sake. Bligh received handsome recognition
of his services from the Jamaica Assembly; but the slaves
perversely refused to eat the breadfruit, preferring the more
familiar yams and plantains. Breadfruit was fed to pigs for fifty
years. It was not until after Emancipation, in the middle of the
nineteenth century, that it came to be widely adopted for human
food.

From the food of slaves one passes naturally to their discipline
and management. The plantation routine was maintained partly
by habit, partly by coercion. That slaves were flogged for mis-
demeanours should not be cause for surprise. At that time all
people living under set discipline, from soldiers and sailors down
to schoolboys, were liable to be flogged if they rebelled or mis-
behaved. In the last half-century or so of West Indian slavery
the treatment of slaves undoubtedly grew milder; partly,

L

perhaps, because of the steady increase of the proportion of creole slaves, born in the islands — people who knew 'the ropes' — and the language — and were less likely to fall foul of authority than slaves fresh from Africa; partly because accumulated experience of slave management taught less savage and more effective ways of making them work. The barbarities described by Sloane were unknown, or at least very rare, a hundred years later. Roughley, a man with twenty years' experience of sugar-planting and with no axe to grind, wrote in his *Jamaica Planter's Guide*, 'There is no class of people in their sphere, in the universe, whose faults and natural tendencies to crime are more abridged, their comforts attended to, nay, their very existence, where tender infancy or decrepit old age requires care and succour, more humanely and rigidly looked after.' The slave was indeed assured, like an ox or a mule, of food and shelter, and in Roughley's day was legally protected from gross neglect or physical cruelty; his lot might even be envied — as West Indians repeatedly pointed out — by some of the European victims of industrial laissez-faire, who had no such assurances. Roughley, however, wrote in the last decades of slavery, when anti-slavery agitation had compelled colonial assemblies to make laws for the protection of slaves against cruel and irresponsible masters. In the eighteenth century the picture was darker. In 1748, for example, the Jamaica Assembly had rejected a bill which would have prohibited the mutilation or dismembering of slaves by their owners without the consent of a magistrate. It was not that planters were necessarily barbarous — the owner of a useful animal does not, as a rule, wantonly damage it; it was that slaves were property, and owners would tolerate no interference with their property rights. The mere existence of a possibility of appeal, they believed, would weaken discipline. Slavery as a rule was not so much deliberately cruel as arbitrary. The slave's expectation of decent treatment depended upon his owner, who was likely to act in conformity with current opinion and custom if he were resident; but many owners were not resident; and, resident or not, an owner's wishes were interpreted, again arbitrarily, by the overseer, by the book-keeper, and by the driver with his cart-whip in the field, who was himself a promoted slave with all the promoted slave's temptations to exercise a petty tyranny.

Mutiny or the fear of mutiny was a constant feature of plantation life in most West Indian islands. Most risings were
quickly put down, but a few were successful, and nearly all were
bloody and indiscriminate. The Danish island of Saint John,
for instance, was the scene of a rising in 1733 in which *all* the
resident Europeans were murdered, with the exception of a handful who fled to St. Thomas. In due course troops were sent from
Martinique, who methodically hunted down and shot the rebels,
so that the island was deserted except for a handful of fishermen,
until recent times, when it has become an expensive and exclusive
resort for wealthy North Americans. Both Jamaica and Saint-
Domingue had bad reputations as the scene of frequent mutinies.
This may have been due partly to the presence in the mountain
forests of villages of 'maroons' — the descendants of many
generations of runaways — whose jungle freedom might inspire
slaves with the desire to imitate, and who sometimes harboured
fugitives; though in Jamaica the two maroon 'wars' of 1734 and
1795 had terminated in treaties whereby the maroons were to be
available as mercenaries to track down runaway slaves; and very
savage auxiliaries they were. Considering the slovenly and
haphazard discipline of many plantations, and the small number
of white inhabitants, it is surprising that revolts were not more
frequent still; conversely, considering the dark undercurrents of
resentment, the lurking danger of revolt lying beneath the
smiling scene that casual visitors so often described, it is astonishing that the resident whites were not more vigilant. Habit and
long familiarity no doubt supplied the chief explanation, on both
sides; plantation slavery also, impersonal and wholesale though
it was, did not entirely preclude the growth of affectionate
loyalties, particularly where household slaves and stable hands
were concerned — a love of horses can be a surprisingly powerful
bond between master and servant. But the chief civilising factor
among the slaves — a factor which in normal times made for
peace and resignation — was the teaching of missionaries.

The eighteenth century was not a conspicuously religious age.
Neither French nor English colonial governments — unlike the
Spanish in earlier times — made serious provision for the
religious instruction of slaves. The *Code Noir* did indeed pro-
claim its chief end to be 'maintenir la discipline de l'Eglise
catholique'; but the chief methods of giving effect to this aim

consisted in negative measures such as the expulsion of Jews, the prohibition of Protestant worship in public, the confinement of public office to Catholics, and so forth. In the British islands the eighteenth-century torpor of the Established Church was more pronounced than in England itself. The West Indies — absurdly — were part of the diocese of London. The clergy were often indolent or absent; few of them paid much attention to catechising slaves. Nor did private piety provide much stimulus to effort. The bequest of the Codrington estates in Barbados — complete with their labour force of slaves — to the Society for the Propagation of the Gospel, was very exceptional. Codrington had no imitators on a comparable scale, and his benefaction was rendered almost ineffective in the eighteenth century by mismanagement of its funds. The Christian instruction of slaves in the British islands was left largely to sectarian missionaries, who achieved their biggest eighteenth-century successes in Jamaica.

As early as 1754 four Moravian missionaries had arrived in the island, the first of a devoted and successful band. The American negroes who introduced the Baptist creed about the end of the War of Independence were not people whom the most humane planters could regard with much confidence, and the first English Baptists did not arrive until 1814. Before that the Methodist mission made its beginning in 1789 and the Scottish Missionary Society in 1800. The missions provoked intermittent opposition, which became more obstructive and violent as planters began to associate missionaries, rightly or wrongly, with the spread of anti-slavery ideas; but opposition could not prevent the alteration in the tone of society which the missions in Jamaica and Antigua slowly brought about. The missionaries might not be able — and some of them certainly were not willing — to teach slaves to rest content in their slavery; but they could, and did, teach slaves ways of life which discouraged murderous mutiny.

Making all allowance for these various palliatives, legal, economic, religious and humane, it is clear that the slave society of the sugar islands was, at best, vaguely restless, inarticulately unhappy; at worst savagely and explosively resentful. Slave labour was unwilling, wasteful, inefficient. It was expensive, both because of the high capital cost of buying slaves, and of the high recurrent cost of feeding, clothing, supervising, and coercing them. It was employed because there seemed to be no alternative way of making sugar. What, then, of the people who ran the system, and — in a financial sense at least — profited by it? How did dependence on slaves affect the slave-owners? For one thing, it drove them away. Next to slavery itself, the most striking characteristic of West Indian society was absentee ownership. This was especially true in the largest and most prosperous of the sugar colonies — Saint-Domingue and Jamaica; but it was true to a greater or less extent wherever sugar was grown. There were considerable numbers of European smallholders in some islands; but the economic and social state of the *petits blancs* in Martinique and Guadeloupe, of the 'red-legs' in Barbados, was not such to tempt other Europeans to imitate them. Except among merchants, shopkeepers, and a handful of professional men, the ambition of most white West Indians not born to property was to manage an estate, then to own one, and ultimately to retire to Europe on the proceeds. The general disinclination to reside continuously in the West Indies was attributed to many causes: the unhealthy climate (a much exaggerated cause); the lack of cultured society and entertainment (though this was as much a consequence as a cause of absenteeism); the lack of educational facilities for children. To these should probably be added the insecurity and — to any moderately sensitive person — the unpleasantness of living at close quarters with a slave society based on coercion; the large number of West Indian properties which fell into the hands of residents in England through the foreclosure of mortgages; and the discovery that growing sugar was less lucrative than dealing in it. A considerable number of successful planters — the Pinneys of Nevis, the Lascelles of Barbados, to quote only two examples — returned to Europe not immediately as country gentlemen but as factors, selling sugar on commission, and advancing credit to their planter correspondents. Some of them did very well at it, thus increasing four- and five-fold the fortunes which originated in the cane-fields of the West Indies, and made possible — for the skilful or the lucky — landed opulence, public office, and political influence in England.

The absentee proprietor has long been the scapegoat of the West Indian economic scene; and before examining the economic inefficiencies of absentee ownership it is only fair to recall that without it the West Indies would have been unable to present their difficulties and needs to their home governments with force and success, as they did, in fact, for many years. The absentee was not only a powerful advocate at home; he was also a link with European culture. To him the West Indies largely owe their lovely heritage of eighteenth-century buildings — now, alas, fast crumbling into ruins — and a considerable body of historical, scientific, and literary work. Absenteeism, it should be remembered, is a relative term. Estates — especially slave-worked sugar estates — do not run themselves. Absentee proprietors often found it necessary to visit their West Indian properties, to see conditions for themselves, to check the dishonesty or incompetence of their representatives and employees, to take their place in local society and be entertained with the lavishness and deference due to their possessions. More sensitive than resident planters, many of them (like 'Monk' Lewis in Jamaica) used their visits to effect improvements in the conditions and treatment of their slaves; and their visits were usually periods of festivity on their estates. Usually the visits were short, however — a year or two at most. Having set matters to rights, the owners returned to Europe, and plantation life slipped back into its old slovenly routine. Many of the elegant 'great houses' stood empty most of the time, or were occupied by overseers, often with their slave concubines and a troop of mulatto children. The resident planters and the handful of resident professional or business men stood attorneys for the absentees. A single attorney might be responsible for a dozen estates, exercising a cursory supervision over the overseers. Every overseer wanted to become an attorney. Overseers were paid annual salaries — not very generous as a rule, considering their responsibilities, and the hard and lonely life they had to lead, in the fields all day, and half the night in the boiling house in crop time. It is not surprising that many of them made ends meet by means of illicit perquisites, using their employers' slaves for their own undertakings, feeding their own animals upon their employers' produce, and so on. Attorneys moved in a different social class and had opportunities for peculation on a larger scale, especially if they happened to be merchants as well as planters. Sometimes a planter would act as attorney for an

The 'great house' of an eighteenth-century sugar estate in Jamaica: Good Hope, Trelawny, now a hotel

[Courtesy of Jamaica Tourist Board]

absent friend without remuneration, but most attorneys received a commission for their trouble, calculated upon the gross shipments of sugar; a system of payment which constantly tempted them to sacrifice the long-term interests of the estate to considerations of immediate profit. Thus, not only was estate labour expensive and unreliable; estate management also, being inadequately supervised, was often inefficient and dishonest. Owners, attorneys, and overseers often drew more income between them than the estates could bear. The more prudent invested their profits, but in Europe, not in the West Indies The more feckless squandered in good times, borrowed in bad, and carried on their business under an increasing load of debt.

The resident planter-attorneys, little groups of local Pooh-Bahs, were the real rulers of island society; they filled the public bodies — not only the nominated councils, but also the elected but no less oligarchic assemblies, which had existed from the beginning in the British islands, and were introduced into the French by decree in 1787. Through these bodies they were able, as a rule, to impose their views upon the royal representatives, and especially to prevent any serious modifications of slavery. They supplied the officers for the local militias in the British islands, and for the *maréchaussées* created in the French islands after the Seven Years War. In the British islands, planters also filled, in effect, most of the public offices; for though the more important officials — colonial secretaries, attorney-generals, provost-marshals, and the like — were appointed by letters-patent in England, the actual work was commonly done by deputies resident in the islands, who were remunerated by fees and who paid a rent for their deputations to the principals. The principals tended to be friends of ministers, persons politically prominent or useful in England. Their appointment was a kind of pension. Office, like land, was thus a form of property, often owned by absentees; a circumstance which helps to explain the venality and incompetence of eighteenth-century colonial administration, and the sense of frustration which afflicted all energetic and conscientious governors.

West Indian society was elaborately stratified. Naturally a clear legal and social line divided free men, participants in society, from slaves, the instruments of wealth. Another line, less sharp but still important, divided white from black or brown among those who were free (white men had almost disappeared from the ranks of those who were not free). Among the free and white there were still further sub-divisions based upon wealth and social standing. In the French islands a recognisably sharp division separated the *grands blancs*, who were considerable proprietors, from the *petits blancs*, who were smallholders, small shopkeepers, artisans, or beachcombers. In the British islands the attorney did not, as a rule, sit with the overseer nor the overseer with his poor devils of book-keepers. In both sets of colonies full participation in local political life was naturally confined to those who were both free and white and who owned property. There were distinctions among slaves too — brown from black, creole from African, skilled from unskilled, household from praedial, to say nothing of the differences between tribes among those recently arrived from Africa. It is impossible to say how much these distinctions meant to plantation slaves, especially since some of them arose from the economic needs of the estate rather than from social differences; but many risings were organised and led by creoles, often trusted household slaves with some smattering of education. Toussaint, as we shall see, was such a person. A favoured place in the slave hierarchy did not necessarily make a man more contented with slavery.

A slave could buy his freedom under certain conditions — the rules varied from place to place — or he could be manumitted by the act of his owner. Some planters freed their slaves and turned them adrift when they became too old to work, in order to be rid of the expense of feeding them. Some inserted clauses in their wills granting freedom to favourite slaves; though this was held by some to be a dangerous practice, because it tempted slaves to hasten their freedom by poisoning their masters. Owners often liberated their slave concubines or their mulatto children; and *petits blancs*, especially in the French islands, quite often married slave women, who thus became free. By one way or another, a large class of free coloured people grew up in the course of the eighteenth century. Some of them acquired property and became prosperous. They developed a characteristic dislike and contempt for slaves and for black people generally; but at the same time they attracted the envy and hatred of the poor whites without acquiring *entrée* into the society of white planters. Thus, whereas in the early part of the century society had been stratified almost entirely according to wealth and status, in the latter part colour in itself became a more and more important element in stratification. The dislike and suspicion with which white people regarded the *gens de couleur* was partly due to social prejudice or economic envy, but still more it arose from fear; the coloured minority might one day make common cause with the black majority, perhaps even lead a slave insurrection against the whites. This powerful mixture of motives found expression in legislation, designed both to preserve social differences between white and coloured and to keep the *affranchis* disarmed and politically impotent. Legislation based frankly on colour was something of a novelty in the West Indies, especially in the French islands. The *Code Noir* had granted to *affranchis* all the rights of free men, irrespective of colour; but in 1766 the Minister of Marine declared: 'Tous les nègres ont été transportés aux colonies comme esclaves; l'esclavage a imprimé une tache ineffaçable sur leur postérité; et par conséquent ceux qui en descendent ne peuvent jamais entrer dans la classe des blancs. S'il était un temps où ils pouvaient être réputés blancs, ils pourraient prétendre comme eux à toutes les places ou dignités, ce qui serait absolument contraire aux constitutions des colonies.' Accordingly, *gens de couleur* in Saint-Domingue were debarred from office in courts or militia, and from certain lucrative professions; they were forbidden to use fire-arms without special licence, or to wear side-arms — the badge of gentility — at all; the cut and material of their clothes were prescribed, to distinguish them from white persons; and from 1779 they were subjected to extremely irksome curfew regulations. These successive abrogations of rights conferred by the *Code Noir* were enacted on the insistence of the white colonists in the *Conseils souverains*; it was one field of legislation in which *grands blancs* and *petits blancs* found themselves in agreement. The assemblies in most of the British islands legislated in the same spirit, though usually with less attention to sumptuary detail. Naturally such attacks provoked the most bitter resentment among a class of people who were beginning to approximate, in wealth and numbers, to the position of the resident white planters in many islands. The injured pride of free persons of colour was potentially as explosive as the resentment of slaves against their enslavement.

This brief and general description of the state of the West Indian colonies in the later eighteenth century admits, naturally, of many exceptions, and applies fully only to those places where sugar was the major crop. A small but interesting exception was the territory of the logwood camps — Belize or British Honduras. The Baymen owned slaves, but in small numbers, and masters and slaves worked side by side, cutting the logwood in the dry weather and floating it in bundles down the creeks in the rains — hard, exacting work, but productive of a comradeship quite different from the master-slave relation of the sugar islands. Other exceptions to the general rule were the ceded islands of the Windward group, which had become the refuge of smallholders squeezed out from the sugar colonies. They produced a considerable variety of crops, including spices such as nutmeg (still a major crop in Grenada), and grew most of their own food. It is true that in the last decades of the eighteenth century sugar — and with it, plantation slavery — was gaining ground in the ceded islands, and continued to do so throughout the French wars; but it never dominated their economy, and in the nineteenth century it almost disappeared. More significant, and on a far larger scale, were the differences between the Spanish islands and the rest of the West Indies. Cuba, Santo Domingo and Puerto Rico never commanded the close attention of their home government in the eighteenth century, as Saint-Domingue and Jamaica constantly did. Economically and politically (though not strategically) they were unimportant fragments of a great land empire. They were relatively poor, Puerto Rico especially. They had a predominantly white population, including many small proprietors, who had occupied themselves since the sixteenth century in tobacco growing and cattle ranching. Fine tobacco was the principal export of Cuba. Santo Domingo grew and exported sugar, as it had done for three centuries, but not in very large quantities. The social pattern of these colonies, therefore, was quite different from that of Jamaica and Saint-Domingue. Since 1762, however, the pattern had begun to change, especially in Cuba. Sugar and coffee were gaining ground, slaves were being imported (many through Jamaica), *latifundia* of the characteristic West Indian type were being established, the virgin lands of Camagüey and Oriente were beginning to be colonised. In the nineteenth century Cuba was to outstrip all other West Indian islands in the production of slave-grown sugar.

All the West Indies, but especially the French and English sugar islands, depended heavily upon the outside world, both for their livelihood and for their defence. They imported much of their food and almost all their manufactured goods. They lived by selling a small number of tropical products in European markets, and depended on the protection of those markets by preferential duties and other means to maintain the price of their exports. Trade with their home countries was their lifeline; if it should be cut off they starved, and its maintenance demanded constant heavy expenditure of naval force. Rich and vulnerable as they were, they could not even defend their own coasts. Their free population was too small to provide an adequate militia. Planter-militiamen made reluctant volunteers, understandably unwilling to serve away from their homes, and to leave their wives and children at the mercy of their slaves. The islands could not, in fact, simultaneously defend themselves against foreign attack and against the possibilities of servile mutiny; and so they needed professional troops for their defence. This was true of all the islands — even of the Spanish islands with their much larger European populations; and while the French and British planters supplied slaves to construct forts, and paid — albeit tardily, stingily, reluctantly — for the maintenance of their garrisons, the Spanish islands relied on subventions from Mexico to pay for the vast fortifications which their defence required.

The question was, how long would home governments go on granting special privileges to colonies whose economic system was being denounced as inefficient, whose social structure was an anachronism, but whose leading landowners were by-words for ostentatious wealth? The Europe which romanticised the noble savage, and which exchanged glib phrases about the Social Contract and the Rights of Man, had little sympathy with the West Indians, and little understanding of their very real difficulties. The England of Wesley and the revivalists had even less. Sugar, it is true, was still a very valuable product, but less valuable, relatively, than it had been; and other parts of the world were beginning to produce it for export. How long could the West Indians hope to maintain absentee ownership and estate slavery by means of preferential duties and costly naval and military defence? By a curious irony of history, the French Revolution and the resulting wars brought a reprieve to the West Indies, except to Saint-Domingue; but the reprieve could only be brief. Bryan Edwards rightly expressed the apprehensions of his class and time when he proclaimed in the House of Commons in 1798 that 'The time in which we live will constitute an awful period in the history of the world; for a spirit of subversion is gone forth, which sets at nought the wisdom of our ancestors and the lessons of experience.'

CHAPTER XI

REVOLUTION AND WAR

THE PLANTERS OF JAMAICA and Saint-Domingue were well aware of the dangers of a 'spirit of subversion'; though it is curious that on the very eve of the French Revolution many people in Saint-Domingue thought that the Jamaicans were in greater danger than they were themselves. There was not much to choose, however. De Rouvray, the officer commanding the troops in Saint-Domingue, and also a big proprietor, wrote to a friend in 1783, 'Une colonie à esclaves est une ville menacée d'assaut; on y marche sur des barils de poudre.' It was a trite metaphor, one much used at the time. History is full of examples of the extraordinary carelessness with which people who live in powder magazines handle naked lights. If ever a body of responsible people played recklessly with fire, it was the planters of Saint-Domingue — or at least a vociferous group among them — between 1788 and 1791. These were the people who insisted on sending delegates to the 1789 meeting of the Estates General, and who in 1791 openly defied the French government, upon whose support they depended, in the long run, for both livelihood and safety.

There was nothing inherently surprising in the spectacle of a land-owning, slave-owning aristocracy raising the cry of 'liberty', in the sense of liberty to run their colony in their own way. Something of the sort had already happened in some of the English North American colonies, and was to happen soon in Spanish America. The Saint-Domingue planters, however, were very vulnerable to attack. The 'liberty' which they sought from the Estates General was obviously liberty to proceed even more drastically than before against slaves and free persons of colour; but the institution of slavery was under fire in France, particularly from the *Amis des Noirs*, a body recently formed in imitation of Clarkson's abolition society in England, but more radical and more vociferous. The 'Rights of Man' were fashionable table talk; there was every possibility that the Estates General, if asked for 'liberty', might interpret the term in a sense very different from that desired by the *grands blancs* of Saint-Domingue. The situation in the colony was full of danger. At any moment the planters might need regular troops to deal with servile outbreaks. Their best policy was to lie low (as Isle-de-France and Bourbon successfully did), to say nothing which might bring colonial affairs into the public eye in France, to rally all respectable owners of property behind the existing government of their own colony. The more prudent among them understood this; but to the more hot-headed the meeting of the Estates General seemed too good an opportunity to be missed. The matter was openly and endlessly discussed. 'Even at table,' wrote Baron de Wimpffen in high alarm in 1790, 'surrounded by mulattoes and negroes, they indulge themselves in the most imprudent discussions on liberty etc. To discuss the "Rights of Man" before such people — what is it but to teach them that power dwells with strength, and strength with numbers?'

The extremists won their point, as extremists are apt to do in times of trouble. Irregular, and probably illegal, meetings of landowners in Saint-Domingue and in France prepared lists of nominations, and the Colonial Assembly allowed itself to be goaded into electing representatives, some of whom were resident in the colony, some in France. The assemblies of Martinique and Guadeloupe did the same; and eventually six of these colonial deputies, after much argument, were admitted to the Estates General in their tennis-court days — the first occasion in European history on which colonial representatives had sat in a metropolitan legislative assembly. They at once became involved in a long oratorical duel with the *Amis des Noirs*. Their demands for colonial autonomy were met by counter-demands that the National Assembly (as it now styled itself) should legislate on the rights of free persons of colour. The dangers of such a course were ably set out by Moreau de Saint-Méry, who represented Martinique in the assembly, and who published his *Considérations* — the ablest of the many expositions of the colonial point of view — in March 1791. 'If the National Assembly,' he wrote, 'has the misfortune to legislate on the mulatto status, all is over. The colonists will believe themselves betrayed; the mulattoes, instigated by their friends, will go to the last extremity. And then the slaves, who possess the same friends and the same means of action, will seek to attain the same results. The colonies will soon be only a vast shambles: and France ——— ? Yes! The mulattoes themselves are but pawns in a larger game. For if once our slaves suspect that there is a power other than their masters which holds the final disposition of their fate; if they once see that the mulattoes have successfully invoked this power and by its aid have become our equals — then France must renounce all hope of preserving her colonies.'

Moreau's forebodings worked themselves out in Saint-Domingue with the grim inevitability of classical tragedy. The National Assembly at first promised not to legislate on colonial matters unless invited to do so by the colonists, but it wavered under rhetorical bombardment and finally came down, albeit timidly, on the side of the *Amis des Noirs*. Its decree of 15 May 1791 provided that persons of colour born of free parents, if qualified in other respects, should be entitled to vote for the provincial and colonial assemblies, which had been established by royal decree only four years earlier. The white inhabitants of Saint-Domingue perceived in this decree the thin end of the egalitarian wedge, and their reaction was frankly mutinous. The colonists refused to obey the decree; the governor refused to enforce it; and there was much wild talk of secession from France. The mulattoes in some parishes were already in arms, demanding what they regarded as their rights; indeed the execution upon the wheel of one of their leaders, a young Parisian-educated zealot named Ogé, had greatly influenced French opinion against the colonists. The dispute over the May decree apparently absorbed the attention of both whites and mulattoes so completely that most of them ignored the premonitory rumblings of slave unrest. They were taken by surprise when, in August 1791, in answer to signals conveyed by drum-beats or through nocturnal ritual gatherings, the slave population of the northern plain rose in revolt, systematically setting fire to cane fields and houses and murdering the white inhabitants. Within a few weeks the whole plain was a smoking ruin, given over to bands of prowling savages.

The northern rising was the first concerted slave revolt on a large scale in the history of the West Indies. It was a terrifying revelation of the explosive force of stifled savage hatred. Once it had begun, it clearly could not be suppressed by the few thousand white inhabitants and the handful of regular troops available, without help. The mulattoes feared the slaves as much as the whites did; but suspicion and prejudice amounting to hatred prevented any effective alliance. The almost incredible savagery with which the fighting was conducted on both sides was described by Bryan Edwards, who was in Cap Français at the time. Edwards estimated that in the first two months 2,000 whites were killed, 180 sugar plantations and 900 coffee and indigo settlements were destroyed; and 10,000 slaves died, either fighting, or by famine, or at the executioner's hands. The total white population of the province cannot have been more than 10,000 as against at least twenty times that number of slaves. Cap Français and a string of fortified camps in the western mountains were soon the only places under white control in the north province. In the west there was as yet no slave revolt, but whites and mulattoes were at war with one another, and the mulattoes under their leader Rigaud were gaining the upper hand, except in Port-au-Prince, which was terrorised by a poor-white mob under criminal leaders. In the south the white planters had armed their slaves — who had remained obedient — against the mulattoes. Everywhere, *grands blancs* and *petits blancs*, royalists and revolutionaries, mulattoes and blacks, *affranchis* and slaves, fought and plundered in shifting alliances and bloody confusion. The only hope of restoring order lay in the despatch of troops from France. The Jacobin party in the National Assembly, however, resolutely opposed any move in support of slave-owning colonists and a royal governor; they found chaos in Saint-Domingue (with the consequent rise in the price of sugar and coffee) a useful stick to beat the government with: they made resounding speeches about the sufferings of the slaves and the oppressions practised by the colonists, and effectually blocked all attempts to send troops to the colony. It was only in September 1792, after the Jacobins had gained control of the Assembly, that an army reached Saint-Domingue, and then it was a revolutionary army, under the orders of Jacobin 'commissioners' sent out to enforce the rule of liberty, equality and fraternity. In this they were fanatically sincere; but the practical results of their efforts were immense bloodshed and complete disorganisation. Their leader, Sonthonax, faced with royalist resistance, had no choice but to associate himself with the revolted slaves, who in June 1793, at his instigation, entered and sacked the town of Cap Français. In August he proclaimed a conditional emancipation. This decree, when subsequently confirmed by the republican government in France, had momentous consequences; but its immediate effect was small. It alienated the mulattoes, many of whom were, or had been, slave-owners; it did not affect the slaves who — in the north at least — had already thrown off all civil authority. Of the surviving whites in the north, those who could get away fled either to the United States or to other West Indian islands — to Cuba, to Jamaica, and particularly to Puerto Rico, where the west-coast town of Mayagüez retains its French peculiarities to this day.

These events in Saint-Domingue naturally caused grave alarm to the Spanish government in Santo Domingo and the British government in Jamaica. The miseries and resentments of slavery were international. Among the slave leaders in Saint-Domingue, Boukman came from Jamaica, Christophe from St. Kitts. Colonial governments might well fear the contagious spread of rebellion. When in 1793 both Spain and England became involved in war with revolutionary France, both governments sent expeditions to invade Saint-Domingue. The immediate purpose of these invasions was to rescue the white colonists and help them to suppress the slave rising; incidentally to embarrass the French government; and ultimately — for the English at least — to annex all or part of the colony. A small British army, backed by a naval squadron, entered the country through the port of Jérémie in the south; a district which had long been in close contact, commercial and cultural, with Jamaica. Everywhere the British were welcomed as deliverers by the French colonists. In March 1794 they took Port-au-Prince; but the question whether, under British rule, the slave-worked sugar estates and coffee walks of Saint-Domingue could recover their old productivity was never answered. The outbreak of the second maroon war in Jamaica in 1795 — inspired by the example of the French islands and, it was believed, by actual French agents — thoroughly alarmed the government of Jamaica

M

and prevented adequate reinforcements being sent from that island; and though considerable forces eventually arrived from England, they were all fresh 'unseasoned' troops. After four years of wasting war, the invasion petered out, defeated by yellow fever, by force of numbers, and by the military skill of François-Dominique Toussaint.

Toussaint 'L'Ouverture', the first of a remarkable series of Haitian negro leaders, had been a slave on a north-plain estate. He took little or no part in the 1791 rising, but in the subsequent confusion became the leader of one of the many marauding bands which roamed the plain. On the outbreak of war between Spain and the republic he entered the Spanish service as a royalist mercenary, and built up a force of some four thousand irregular but very effective negro troops. In 1794, however, alarmed by the progress of the English and the restoration of slavery which an English victory might entail, and moved also, no doubt, by personal ambition, he deserted with his troops from the Spanish army, murdered the Spanish officers who opposed his defection, and offered his services to the battered and discredited army of republican France. His defection in itself was enough to disorganise the Spanish forces in Saint-Domingue. In 1795 the Spanish and French governments in Europe made peace at the Treaty of Bâle. The Spaniards rid themselves of responsibility by ceding Santo Domingo to France; but no action was taken by the French to occupy the colony, and after Napoleon's accession to power the Spaniards were left in possession. Toussaint's energies, meanwhile, were directed against the English invaders and their allies, the French planters in Saint-Domingue. He quickly became the dominant figure on the republican side. By 1798 he had so worn down the invaders that the English commanding officer, Maitland, was glad to withdraw his depleted forces in return for an amnesty to his partisans and — significant clause — a commercial treaty. In signing such an agreement Toussaint acted like an independent ruler; and so, in fact, he was. His ascendancy among the negro population was unrivalled. He commanded an army devoted to his person and enjoyed the respect, indeed the friendship, of powerful people abroad. It was his friendship with John Adams that enabled him to secure from the United States the ships and supplies he needed to fight the English.

The English expelled, Toussaint turned upon the mulatto faction of the west and south, defeated its leader Rigaud, himself a soldier of considerable ability, and sacked the town of Les Cayes which had been its headquarters. There followed a systematic round-up, mutilation, and murder of some ten thousand mulattoes, men, women, and children. As if to complete the tragedy of that black year, torrential rain fell all through the autumn of 1800. The irrigation dams of the Artibonite and Cul-de-Sac, weakened by ten years of neglect, were broken. The whole prosperity of west and south depended on these irrigation works; but they were never repaired, and the area they served became the eroded wilderness it is today.

Politically, by 1800 Toussaint was supreme within the colony. He was able to secure either the compliance or the removal of all officials sent out to the colony from France. He had, already in 1799, been formally appointed governor-general by the Directorate — a face-saving gesture, for his real power was military and personal. In Saint-Domingue, as in France, the fashion for liberty, equality and fraternity was, by that time, outmoded. After 1800 Toussaint put a stop to indiscriminate massacres, respected his contracts (such as the commercial treaty with England) and ordered his mobs of ex-slaves back to work. With the docility of men weary of war, idleness and famine, they obeyed him; he even induced some of the white *émigrés* to return to their estates, and between 1800 and 1802 the shattered economy of the colony began slowly to survive. In 1801 he drew up a constitution, some clauses of which have a remarkably modern ring. Saint-Domingue was declared to be 'une seule colonie qui fait partie de l'Empire française, mais qui est soumise à des lois particulières'. This document was submitted to the French government for confirmation, but promulgated in anticipation of approval. In it Toussaint proclaimed that his own tenure of office was to be for life; a step which Napoleon himself had not yet ventured to take.

There was no room within the French empire for two dictators; and Napoleon's irritation at the prestige and pretensions of 'gilded Africans' was partly responsible for Toussaint's fall. Napoleon had other motives, however, more practical than mere irritation. His political plans called for alliance with Spain; but Toussaint in 1801, in defiance of Napoleon's orders, had carried out a rapid and successful invasion of Spanish Santo Domingo, and showed no disposition to relinquish his conquest. Napoleon, moreover, shared with Pitt, and most other statesmen of the day, an exaggerated — because out-of-date — estimate of the value and importance of West Indian possessions. Saint-Domingue had been in the past a source of great wealth to some French-men, and indirectly to France; it could be so again. Geographic-ally and strategically Saint-Domingue was the centre from which measures for rebuilding the French colonial system in the Americas could best be taken. France had once more recovered Louisiana from Spain. Napoleon — as later became evident — intended to restore the old system, slavery and all, in Saint-Domingue and Guadeloupe. None of these plans could be executed while Toussaint ruled Saint-Domingue, and his re-moval could be achieved only through a military reconquest of the island.

The formidable army which General le Clerc, Napoleon's brother-in-law, brought to this task in 1802 was considerably larger than the force which the English had employed eight years before, and le Clerc, in a series of capable but very costly jungle campaigns, achieved his first task, that of reducing Tous-saint to obedience and taking over his office as governor-general. Most of Toussaint's supporters — Dessalines, Christophe, Mau-repas, and the rest, came over into French service, each with his band of followers, and Toussaint himself was arrested, or rather kidnapped, and shipped to France, where he died in prison. But le Clerc soon found that campaigning in the mountains and forests of Saint-Domingue was very different from fighting in Europe. His army could not live off the country, for the country had little or no food. Everything had to be bought at famine prices, in uncertain quantities, from Yankee traders. Then, the same enemy which had wasted Maitland's army — yellow fever — took its daily toll of le Clerc's men; and his hard-won prestige with the leaders of the negro bands was presently destroyed by the news which came from Guadeloupe. Napoleon's General Richepanse had regained control of that island, and had re-introduced slavery and the slave trade. Thousands of excited, resentful negroes in Saint-Domingue sprang to arms once more, believing (correctly) that le Clerc's instructions contemplated similar action there. At this critical moment le Clerc himself

A negroes' dance in the island of Dominica, by Brunias, published by Thomas Palser, Westminster Bridge, London, c. 1810

died of fever. Napoleon in 1803 broke the Peace of Amiens, resumed the war in Europe, and washed his hands of the Saint-Domingue affair — indeed, of the whole scheme of American empire, for Louisiana was sold in the same year. Le Clerc's successor never got the reinforcements he had been promised; at the end of 1803, with his starved, ragged, fever-stricken remnant of an army, he surrendered to the British in Jamaica. Meanwhile Dessalines, ablest, most savage and most ruthless of Toussaint's former vassals, embarked on a campaign of literal extermination against the surviving whites, in a country ravaged from end to end by war.

Dessalines, unlike Toussaint, was African born. At the outbreak of the revolt he was a slave on the plantation of a free negro, whose name he assumed and whose property he seized as soon as the insurrection gave him the opportunity of murdering his master. He quickly rose to power in the *entourage* of Toussaint, and was Toussaint's enthusiastic agent in the massacre of mulattoes in the south in 1800. He was the obvious successor to Toussaint; and in 1804 he proclaimed himself an independent ruler — Emperor of Haiti, choosing the Taino word for 'mountainous' to replace the name of Saint-Domingue. He ruled until 1806. After his death, and for the rest of the war period and beyond, the country was divided between his rival successors, the negro Christophe and the mulatto Pétion. Christophe's régime in the north was an astonishing *tour-de-force*, of which his great citadel stands as a grim witness to this day. Without administrative machinery to his hand, he held his kingdom together by sheer force of will, ruling through a kind of military feudalism based on forced labour, without the name of slavery. While he lived (till 1820) he kept the great estates going and delayed the running-down of the economic machine. Pétion, more easy-going, permitted in the south the popular but economically disastrous subdivision of the land into small peasant plots, which became in time the pattern all over Haiti. As a result, sugar production dwindled almost to nothing. Coffee — largely a peasant crop in the mountains — diminished too, though less seriously and with more hope of revival. After 1810 it was the principal crop. The export figures for Haiti as a whole are eloquent witnesses of all these changes.

	Sugar	*Coffee*
1791	163,405,220 lb.	68,151,180 lb.
1802	53,400,000 ,,	34,370,000 ,,
1804	47,600,000 ,,	31,000,000 ,,
1818	1,896,449 ,,	20,280,589 ,,
1825	2,020 ,,	36,034,300 ,,

These two men, then — Christophe, the illiterate black warrior, and Pétion, the cultivated, unpractical mulatto — between them presaged the whole indigent, disorderly history of independent Haiti.

In the early years of the revolution events in the smaller French islands appeared to be taking the same course as in Saint-Domingue; but Martinique and Guadeloupe were older, more unified, socially stronger. They had a much higher proportion of resident planters and did not suffer in the same degree as Saint-Domingue from the ferocious hatreds of race and class. On the other hand, they were important commercial centres as well as plantation colonies. There was a sharp divergence of interests between the merchants of Saint-Pierre and Basse-Terre and the white planters who were often their debtors. The free mulattoes (who here as elsewhere were agitating for a recognition of equality) were a third element in the conflict, tending, however, to follow the white planters, because some of them were planters themselves, and all of them feared slave insurrection. Left to themselves, the planter assemblies, with mulatto support, could probably have controlled the situation; but in 1792 Jacobin commissioners arrived from France, rallied commercial and poor-white support for the republic and compelled the governors to submit. Their activities drove the royalist planters into the arms of the English.

Both French and British governments assumed that without their sugar islands they could not pay for the war, and neither dared leave the other a free hand in the Caribbean. The West Indies were inevitably once again the scene of heavy fighting. Both sides made serious miscalculations. The French, during the revolutionary years, underestimated the destructive forces let loose by premature declarations of emancipation and equality. The English overestimated the effective support they would get from predominantly royalist French planters. The French had the advantage of a revolutionary battle-cry which rallied the forces of social and economic discontent; the English had the superior force at sea. The French could make revolutions, but not always control them; the English could capture islands, but not always hold them. Both sides sent fleets to the West Indies in 1793. The British captured Tobago in that year, and Martinique, Guadeloupe and St. Lucia in 1794. In Martinique their alliance with the royalists was effective. Slavery and internal peace were both maintained, and with access to the British market the sugar industry of the island entered upon a period of notable prosperity. Guadeloupe and St. Lucia, it is true, were quickly recaptured through the efforts of the Jacobin commissioner Victor Hugues, who arrived with a fleet shortly afterwards. Hugues proclaimed immediate emancipation and engineered a concerted rising of slaves, not only against the English but against the local planters. He set on foot also those intrigues with the maroons of Jamaica and the Caribs of St. Vincent, which contributed in each island to a desperate outbreak in 1795. Abercromby's expedition recovered St. Lucia in that year, however, and the inclusion of the United Netherlands and Spain within the French system gave the British an excuse to seize Demerara and Essequibo in 1796, Trinidad in 1797. The year 1801 found Great Britain supreme in the Caribbean, with the French practically confined to Guadeloupe and the Spaniards to Cuba and Puerto Rico; the whole island of Hispaniola being then in the hands of Toussaint L'Ouverture.

All conquests except Trinidad were returned by the Peace of Amiens in 1801, and Napoleon used the respite for an attempt to re-establish metropolitan control of the French West Indies. In Guadeloupe General Richepanse overthrew the mulatto group who had seized power after Hugues' departure, and restored the old régime, slavery and all, with dire consequences, as we have seen, in Saint-Domingue. After the failure of le Clerc, however, Napoleon gave up the West Indian situation as hopeless, and on the renewal of hostilities in 1803 the British reoccupied all that they had held before the peace. After Trafalgar they had nothing to fear in that area from French or Spanish arms. The final settlement of 1815 added St. Lucia, Tobago, Trinidad, and (by purchase) Demerara, Essequibo and Berbice to the British Empire. Martinique and Guadeloupe were restored to France, partly because of the over-riding British desire for security on the Channel coasts, which made 'Antwerp and Flushing out of the hands of France' worth — as Harrowby put it — 'twenty Martiniques'. The restoration was a drastic one, for Louis XVIII re-introduced the administrative, constitutional and social structure not of 1788 but of 1763.

For the British islands the long war — despite the alarms of the revolutionary years — brought an economic reprieve. Before the slave rising of 1791 Saint-Domingue had been exporting nearly as much sugar as the whole of the British West Indies. Its removal from effective competition was exactly what the British planters had hoped for for half a century. The price of muscavado in London rose from 54s. 3d. a hundredweight in 1792 to 69s. 2d. in 1796. The price of coffee doubled in about the same period; and Jamaican exports of both commodities greatly increased, despite war-time rises in costs of production, freights and insurance, and despite the steady increase in duties on colonial produce. There were, as usual, violent fluctuations. Muscavado dropped to 25s. 6d. at the end of 1802, but rose again with the resumption of hostilities and continued to rise until 1807. In that year there was another sharp drop, due partly to the conquest of foreign sugar colonies and partly to the carrying of foreign sugars directly to Europe in American ships, but the rise was resumed the following year; the embargo, the Non-Intercourse Act, and eventually the Anglo-American war forced prices higher and higher, and in 1814 muscavado reached a peak of 100s.

Not only sugar and coffee but cotton also reached record levels of production and price during the war. For most of the eighteenth century Great Britain had bought most of its raw cotton from the East. The rapidly increasing demand for cotton, noticeable in Lancashire and Lanarkshire by the end of the 'seventies could not be met from Eastern sources. The chief beneficiaries of it were the West Indian colonies, which by 1790 were supplying over 70 per cent of British needs. After that date the competition of the green seed cotton of the southern states of the Union, cleaned by Whitney's patent gin, steadily overcame the more expensive hand-cleaned sea island cotton of the West Indies; for West Indian cotton never enjoyed the degree of protection accorded to sugar. But at least until about

1810 cotton remained an important and profitable West Indian product, especially in captured Guiana, where the saline mud of the Courantyne coast was particularly suited to its cultivation.

Finally, the disturbed state of the Spanish colonies, and the English foothold in Spain after 1808, allowed an increase in trade with Latin America, sometimes legal, but more often not. The Anglo-American war and the blockade of American ports temporarily removed a dangerous competitor. British exports to Cuba, for instance, more than trebled during the two years of the war. Jamaica and Trinidad both profited greatly from this increase of Latin American trade between 1808 and 1815.

All in all, then, the war dealt kindly with the British West Indies; but their war-time prosperity could only be temporary. The hey-day of West Indian cotton was over before the end of the war. The prices of sugar and coffee would inevitably drop with the coming of peace; but duties would remain, since the war must be paid for; and the East India interest in England might at any time succeed in reducing or abolishing the preferential margin which had hitherto favoured West Indian against East Indian sugar. Even if this danger could be avoided, it was fairly certain that British West Indian sugar would once again be confined to the British market. Beet sugar was already being produced on a small scale in France; and larger, newer plantation colonies were producing cane sugar more cheaply than Barbados or Jamaica. Saint-Domingue, it is true, was out of the running, apparently for ever, but Cuba had taken its place as the most dangerous West Indian competitor. Demerara and Trinidad, newly acquired and undeveloped, might compete with Cuba in producing cheap sugar, if they could get slaves; but the slave trade had been made illegal for British subjects by Act of Parliament in 1807, while the Cubans could still get all the slaves they wanted from Spanish and Yankee slavers. Moreover, the British West Indian planters had every reason to fear that, once the war ended, the attack on the institution of slavery itself in British territory would be resumed. In this respect also the war had allowed them a respite, for the excesses of revolution in France had brought all radical ideas into disrepute, and events in Haiti had shown what could happen when slaves were loosed suddenly from control. But these warnings would be forgotten with the peace; humanitarian, religious and economic objections to slavery would be voiced again with redoubled force and conviction. Very few West Indians believed that sugar could be produced without slaves. After their war-time Indian summer, therefore, the men who ran and lived by the plantation system of the British West Indies looked forward to a bleak economic future and a long rearguard action against the forces of change.

CHAPTER XII

ABOLITION AND EMANCIPATION

FROM THE EARLIEST TIMES of West Indian settlement sugar had been grown by slave labour. The sugar trade — incomparably the most important business activity of the West Indies — and the slave trade, 'its great pillar and support', were, so it seemed, inseparably linked. Until the late eighteenth century most people in England — or France, or Holland, or Portugal — accepted without question the necessity of slavery and of the slave trade. Overseas trade in general was held to be the chief source of national wealth and power. The slave trade, because it made large profits, supplied essential labour, and employed many ships, was necessary, just as child labour or the press-gang were necessary. Only a few cranks doubted the propriety of the trade. George Fox, as early as 1671, had urged the Quakers in Barbados to treat their slaves kindly and to free those who had served long and well. A few years later the first formal and public protest against slavery was made by the Quakers of Germantown in Pennsylvania, and slavery was forbidden in that state; but the attitude of these Quakers was exceptional. It was not shared even by all Quakers, and certainly did not reflect any general moral misgivings about slavery and the slave trade. If positive justification of the trade were needed, it could be found in the fact that the victims were slaves before the traders bought them; their removal to the West Indies, it might be argued, took them from barbarous owners and brought them into contact with civilised society and Christian belief.

In the later eighteenth century economists began to question the validity of the assumptions on which the regulations of the old colonial system had been based. Already when Adam Smith wrote, the economy of Britain was being transformed by the growth of large-scale industry. People were moving from the land into the towns, and from the craftsman's work-shop into the factory. Beside the old society of land-owners, farmers and labourers there was growing up a new urban society, divided no less sharply between industrial employers and factory hands. Mechanical inventions like the spinning-jenny, the water-frame and the power loom promised to English industrialists the power to clothe the whole world in factory-made textiles; and nothing less than the whole world must be their market. It might be true that 'five hundred thousand negroes are constantly clad by the clothiers of Yorkshire and Wiltshire. . . . London, Birmingham, Bristol and Carron supply alike the mill-work, the nails, the hoes, the tools, the utensils of domestic life and the implements of husbandry'; nevertheless, the market offered by a few thousand planters parsimoniously buying osnaburg to clothe their slaves was trifling compared with the expanding societies of North and South America and the vast populations of the East. Moreover, an industrialised society demanded, above all things, cheap food, and West Indian sugar was not cheap. The British West Indies could not possibly compete in open trade, in a world market, with the larger sugar-producing regions that were coming into production — with Cuba, with Mauritius, and with the East Indies. The West Indian monopoly was becoming an expensive anachronism.

While the economists and the industrialists were attacking West Indian monopoly, the reformers, humanitarians and intellectuals were attacking West Indian slavery. Rousseau and his successors had sentimentalised the savage and popularised the gospel of liberty, equality and fraternity. Their ideas had influenced American leaders in the War of Independence and had helped to prepare the way for revolution in France. The example, the theories and the slogans of the French Revolution had influenced more strongly still the leaders in the Haitian revolt. The same ideas had affected England also; but in England radicalism was less political, less intellectual, and at the same time less violent. The ideas of liberty and equality there received force and religious sanction from the evangelical movement in which Wesley and Whitfield were the leaders. Their appeal was to conscience; slavery was wrong because all men were the sons of God. Out of this movement came the missionary societies; the Baptist Missionary Society in 1792, the London Missionary Society in 1795 and the British and Foreign Bible Society in

1803. Out of this movement also came the humanitarians like Howard, Elizabeth Fry and Shaftesbury with their campaigns against the abuses in prisons and against child-labour. There were others, men of strong religious convictions like the 'Saints' or the 'Clapham sect', who used their political power to attack slavery and who founded the first English colony in Africa by organising and financing a company in 1787 to establish Sierra Leone as a home for freed slaves. Closely associated with this group were many of the leaders in the campaign against slavery: Thomas Clarkson, Granville Sharp, James Ramsay, William Wilberforce.

The initiative for the abolition of the slave trade came from within English society, and not from within West Indian society. The story of the long campaign for abolition shows how swiftly and how profoundly the new political and religious ideas were affecting Englishmen, and how powerful and far-reaching were the economic changes that were in progress. It also affords one of the earliest and best illustrations of the modern methods of influencing political decisions by organising and mobilising public opinion.

The first man to begin public agitation against the slave trade was Granville Sharp, who began life as a draper's assistant in London and later held a government post at the Ordinance Office. At this time there were some ten thousand negro slaves in England, the property of West Indians who lived in England. Granville Sharp came into contact with one of these slaves, Joseph Strong, whose master was a lawyer from Barbados, David Lisle. The owner had turned Strong adrift because he was ill and useless. The slave would have died but for the help which Granville Sharp and his brother, a doctor, had given him. With care and treatment he recovered, and found employment. Then, one day, some two years later, Lisle came upon Strong, claimed him as his property and sold him for £30 to a Jamaican planter, who had him put in prison until he could be shipped to the West Indies. Sharp took up the case and managed to have Strong set free. He was a persistent man, and did not stop with this success; there might be other cases like that of Strong, and so he decided to press for a court decision on whether slavery was permitted in England. After several unsuccessful attempts to obtain a decision he took up the case of James

Somerset, who, like Strong, had been turned adrift by his master. Somerset recovered with Sharp's help, and on recovery he was claimed by his master. Sharp resisted the claim and the case finally went before the Chief Justice, Lord Mansfield, who, on 22 June 1772, declared that in the absence of positive law on the subject the right of property in slaves could not be upheld before the courts in England. This celebrated judgement had the effect of immediately liberating, in law, all who had been held as slaves in England. It was the first major victory in the attack on the slave trade, and the opponents of the trade now began to organise themselves. The Quakers formed an anti-slavery society, and they were joined, among others, by Sharp, Clarkson and by James Ramsay, a clergyman who had worked in the West Indies for nineteen years and who wrote and spoke with great effect of the abuses and cruelties of slavery. Clarkson soon became one of the leaders of the abolitionist cause, and he used every method of publicity to influence and rouse public opinion and to press for political action. In its political sphere the movement found a leader of conviction, in some respects a genius, William Wilberforce. Up to the time of his conversion in 1784 Wilberforce had shown no interest in the abolition movement. Witty, eloquent, and wealthy, he had lived an active political and social life but had not identified himself with any particular interest or cause. He was generally popular and was the close friend of Pitt. Now, having come under the influence of John Newton, once captain of a slave ship and now a clergyman, and having read Clarkson's book, he decided to devote his life to the campaign against slavery and the English slave-trade. The first step was taken in 1788 when Dolben, who had been horrified at conditions he had seen on board a slave ship in the Thames, introduced a Bill to limit the number of slaves ships might carry in proportion to their tonnage. Public interest was mounting and was maintained by a spate of pamphlets and by devices like Wedgewood's cameo which showed a negro kneeling in entreaty for freedom, the chains hanging from his wrists and fettered legs. Anti-slavery groups were organised, and sent hundreds of petitions to the House of Commons, the first occasion on which this form of political pressure had been tried on such a scale. With this support in the country, and with considerable sympathy in the House, Wilberforce, with the assistance of Fox and Pitt, won the agreement of the House to the proposal that the slave trade ought to be abolished, and that it should come to an end after four years.

Many different forces in England contributed to the campaign against the slave trade and helped to bring slavery itself into disrepute; but from the point of view of the West Indian planter, all abolitionists and emancipationists had two things in common, ignorance of West Indian conditions, and indifference to West Indian interests. The British islands had come to depend almost entirely on the sugar trade for their livelihood. The way in which the sugar was marketed, and the planter financed, tied the West Indian economy very closely to that of England. The crop grown on a West Indian estate was consigned to a factor in England who acted as the planter's agent, sold the goods on his behalf, deducted his commission, and credited the planter with the balance. In addition he bought such goods as the planter needed, shipped them to him, advanced money to him, and financed him as a bank would nowadays. Since sugar-planting was a hazardous business, subject to sudden losses by hurricane and drought and other natural or man-made disasters, and since planters often made matters worse by extravagance, estates were usually heavily encumbered, and often fell into the reluctant hands of factor or banker by way of foreclosure. In 1772, for example, there were 775 working sugar estates in Jamaica; twenty years later just over one half were still in the hands of their owners as going concerns. About two-fifths had been sold for debt or thrown up. While the sugar trade flourished, said Postlethwayt, 'both planters and merchants grew immensely rich and the trade and navigation of Great Britain was carried on to a much greater height than ever it was before'. When it languished, he might have added, merchants grew less rich, and many planters were ruined.

Any threat to this trade, therefore, united planter and merchant, and the combination had great political influence. The sugar business, after all, represented some £50,000,000 of capital invested in estates alone, to say nothing of the working capital of the factors. More than half of these investments were held by people resident in England. The wealth and social standing of the absentee proprietors enabled them to influence the colonial legislatures and gave them also a direct entry into the House of

Commons as members and as lobbyists. The West India interest was powerful and well organised, experienced and skilful both in the control of production and in the use of political influence. Some of its members, it is true, adopted a comparatively liberal view and supported proposals, such as those of Ellis, for improving the social condition of the slaves and giving them full legal protection, in an effort to lift the birth-rate above the death-rate and so reduce the importation of new slaves. The majority, however, seeing themselves threatened with rising costs, falling prices, and eventual ruin, resisted bitterly the proposals for abolishing the slave trade. The legislature of the Leeward Islands, in resolving 'that no power shall endeavour to deprive us of obtaining slaves from Africa', expressed the dismay and indignation of the planting community in general.

It was not West Indian defiance, however, so much as international circumstances, which turned Wilberforce's estimate of four years into fifteen. The French Revolution and the Napoleonic Wars demanded the full attention of government and people. The slave trade was reprieved or forgotten, and abolition, thanks to the indiscretions of Clarkson, momentarily shared the disrepute of the radical political ideas current in France. It was in those years that Wilberforce became indispensable to the cause he had embraced, grimly moving his resolution against the trade year after year. In 1803 his Bill passed the House of Commons but was defeated in the Lords. Finally in 1807 a fortuitous circumstance, a turn of the political wheel, made victory possible. The Act for the abolition of the slave trade came into force on January 1, 1808.

The Abolition Act put Britain out of the slave trade at a time when more than one-half of the trade was in British hands. It did not put an end to the trade itself, for others moved in to take what the British gave up. The United States government declared the trade illegal in 1808, a measure which commanded widespread public support, for cotton was not yet king, and at that time there were many in the south who would have echoed Patrick Henry's declaration about slavery: 'I tremble for my country when I reflect that God is just.' Many Americans, however, continued to engage in the trade, evading the law by selling their ships nominally to Spain. English traders also, tempted by the profits, sometimes became slave smugglers, but they were subject to laws which became increasingly severe; in 1811 an Act of Parliament made slave trading a felony and in 1827 it was declared to be piracy and so punishable by death. Other nations also legislated against the trade. Denmark had done so even before Britain, in 1804; Sweden followed in 1813 and Holland in 1814. France declared the trade illegal in 1818 and Spain did the same in 1820, but both of these powers were half-hearted about the matter and slave dealing was for long an open business in ports like Nantes, which had some eighty slave ships and where the profits from the trade were said to have amounted to 90,000,000 francs in the year 1815. The total number of slaves taken from West Africa after the Abolition Act of 1808 may in fact have been greater than the total of those taken before that date; it is certain that both Cuba and Brazil imported greater numbers after 1808 than they did during the earlier period. Cuba was importing slaves up to 1865, Brazil even later.

In Cuba and in the United States the demand for slaves increased after 1808 because of the greatly expanded production of sugar, cotton and tobacco. Slave labour enabled Louisiana to become a sugar State which, by 1830, was able to supply one-half the sugar required in the United States. Slave labour, the cultivation of improved types of cotton, and Eli Whitney's invention of the saw-gin which cleaned short-fibred cotton well and cheaply, enabled the South to become the world's greatest supplier of cotton. The West Indies never had a chance to keep the British market. From 1796 to 1800 they had supplied Britain with 70 per cent of its cotton; in 1803 they supplied 57,000 lb. against 45,000 lb. from the United States; but between 1816–20 the United States was supplying 47 per cent of the cotton imported into Britain, while the West Indies supplied 7 per cent. Slave labour also enabled tobacco planters to spread the cultivation of the crop from Virginia into Kentucky and Tennessee, and slave labour transformed the fertile plains of Cuba into great sugar estates. In Cuba and in the southern States production was on a scale beyond that of which the British West Indies were capable, and the prosperity which flowed from the mass-production of one or two crops united the southern States in support of slavery in the same way that the West Indies and the British government had been united in favour of slavery throughout most of the eighteenth century. An illicit slave trade

N

sprang up even in the British Caribbean and continued up to the time of the Emancipation Act. The Slave Trade Consolidated Act permitted an owner leaving one of the islands to take with him one or more domestic slaves to attend him on the voyage. This gave a chance for dishonest persons to sell slaves illegally from one island to another. A Barbados official complained in 1827 that many slaves had been taken from the island in that year alone, and that the trade was increasing.

Meanwhile in England public opinion, after a period of relative indifference, was beginning to show interest in the conditions of slavery itself. In the years immediately following the French war the British government sponsored a policy of amelioration and urged the West Indian governments to enact legislation in conformity with this end — to give slaves religious instruction, put a stop to Sunday markets and Sunday labour, permit and legalise the marriage of slaves, prohibit flogging, and limit the owner's power to punish. There were at this time about three-quarters of a million slaves in the British Caribbean territories, about one-half of these being in Jamaica and one-tenth in the newly acquired mainland territory of Guiana. Self-interest alone dictated greater care in conserving these numbers, when they could no longer be replaced by fresh imports; but planter-legislators, already in desperate financial straits, and exasperated by the unremitting attacks of people in England who knew little, and cared less, about their troubles, would not see their interest in this light. They were, moreover, difficult to coerce. Newly acquired places like Trinidad, British Guiana and St. Lucia, it is true, had no independent legislatures. They were governed by Order in Council and the members of their legislatures were nominated, not elected. The Crown, therefore, was able to introduce reforms in these 'Crown colonies' without much difficulty. In the older colonies, on the other hand, the assemblies resisted the amelioration policy as long as they were able; and even when they had been induced, with many grumbles, to pass Amelioration Acts, the problems of enforcement were formidable. Planters were still very much the masters within the bounds of their own estates, as far as the slaves were concerned. The officials who were to carry out reforms were often in sympathy with the planters and sometimes were themselves slave owners. These two factors contributed to the relative failure of the policy of amelioration and the increasing demand in England for outright abolition of slavery itself.

An impoverished and increasingly discredited West India interest thus found itself engaged in a long defensive action against the forces of change. It had to face charges of inefficient estate management as well as of cruelty and general immorality where slaves were concerned. Abolitionists and economic theorists alike proclaimed that slavery was wasteful and inefficient, as well as inhumane. The supporters of slavery could only reply that, inefficient though the system might be, there was no other known way of growing sugar. Nothing reveals more clearly than this the intellectual as well as financial bankruptcy of West Indian society at the time. Nobody now dared attempt a philosophical defence of slavery as an absolute good, as a means of civilising the savage or evangelising the heathen. The best that the West Indians could claim for their most important social institution was that it was a necessary evil.

While in England government after 1823 was subjected to increasing pressure from the abolitionists, led by Wilberforce and Buxton, within the West Indies the pressure on the local legislatures came from the missionaries, the free mulattoes and the slaves. The missionaries brought the evangelical movement from Britain to the West Indies, though some of the early contacts with Quakers and Baptists were with the United States. In Jamaica, for example, the Baptist Church was founded by two negroes, George Lisle and Moses Baker, who were brought to the island in 1783 by loyalist families who left America after the Declaration of Independence. Lisle set up a chapel in Kingston, and persecution and imprisonment failed to prevent him from preaching. He converted Moses Baker, who came from the Bahamas, and in turn Baker began to instruct the slaves and to set up churches; but as their movement grew both Baker and Lisle appealed to the Baptist Missionary Society for help, and in 1814 the first Baptist missionary was sent out from England. The Methodist and Baptist missionaries were bitterly opposed by many of the planters on the ground that the 'Chapels and meeting houses were centres of subversive activity and that religious instruction was a pretence for stirring up the slaves to rebellion'.

The fear of mutiny can never be far from the thoughts of a

small minority of slave owners; and in the circumstances it is not surprising that any gathering of slaves was suspect. Governor Bentinck, writing from British Guiana in 1812 to Liverpool, expressed this general feeling in these words: 'In a country like this where on an extent of coast of near 150 miles there is a population of only 1,746 white inhabitants and 847 people of colour that could in case of necessity be called on to repel an insurrection of 31,484 male slaves, if such a calamitous event should ever arise, too many precautions cannot be taken to prevent as far as possible the assemblage of negroes in considerable numbers under any pretence whatsoever.' Woodford, governor of Trinidad, said that his principal objection to the Methodist preacher is 'that he teaches and allows the slaves to preach'; later, having 'heard and seen nothing of the Methodizzies since the last took himself off, I hope I am quit of them, but let me entreat you to do what you can about a Bishop for us'.

In England, during the turbulent and troubled period of reform, the evangelical movement had generated the forces of change while at the same time teaching and encouraging good order and respect for authority, and so it had been one of the most powerful influences for stability. Similarly, in the West Indies, there is evidence that the missionaries laboured to give religious instruction without inciting the slaves. They were, in fact, a restraining influence, and the slave risings of this period were remarkably free from excesses of cruelty and bloodshed. But as the emancipation movement in England grew more powerful and as the slaves began to grow more restive, the feeling against the missionaries became stronger and more hostile; not only planters, but the clergy of the established church and some officials made common cause against them.

In Barbados a riotous crowd pulled down a Methodist chapel, the missionary, Shrewsbury, escaping to St. Vincent. In Jamaica, in 1832, the Colonial Church Union was formed 'to resist by all constitutional means, the encroachments of their enemies', and they soon showed what they meant by 'constitutional means' by burning non-conformist chapels and attacking missionaries on the theory that 'to get rid of the rooks you must destroy their nests'. The issue was no longer whether or not religious instruction should be given, but whether the system which prevented religious instruction being given should be destroyed. Seeing this, the Baptist missionaries sent William Knibb to England to discuss the problem with the Baptist Missionary Society. Knibb was a man of remarkable foresight and courage; he had been one of the first to be attacked by the Church Union, who destroyed 'that pestilential hole, Knibb's preaching shop'. When he arrived in England and heard of the passing of the Bill for the reform of the House of Commons he cried, 'Thank God, now I'll have slavery down.' When his society tried to prevent him from campaigning for abolition he told them that he would go forward even if he had to take his wife and children by the hand and walk barefoot through the kingdom. So effective was Knibb's agitation that his biographer Hinton said the planters 'had flung the firebrand from their hearths but it had fallen on the powder magazine'.

The free mulattoes were comparatively few in number, and were for the most part more concerned to secure for themselves the privileges enjoyed by white people, than to advance the cause of the slaves. They included men of substance and culture, and so were bound by common interests with the planters. In Grenada in 1823 they obtained most of their demand for full citizenship, but in Jamaica the assembly obstinately withstood their claims. Rebuffed by the assemblies in Barbados and in Jamaica, they appealed to the British government. Finally, in Jamaica in 1832 most of them sided with the missionaries and negroes and advocated emancipation.

The slaves themselves grew more and more restive and impatient and the eighteen-twenties saw outbreaks in Guiana, Barbados and Jamaica. Just as negroes in Haiti, under the leadership of Boukman, had caught the whisper of the watchwords of the revolution, so in the British territories the words and acts of the British Parliament were whispered throughout the region. Simon Taylor of Jamaica complained in 1807 of the imprudence of his neighbours in talking about Pitt and Wilberforce. Sailors may have passed on word of the debates and discussions in Britain. Missionaries told of what was happening. So, at Le Resouvenir in British Guiana in 1823 negroes demanded immediate emancipation and killed two overseers who resisted them. Martial law was enforced, a hundred rioters were killed, and Smith, an 'independent' missionary at Bethel Chapel, was arrested, tried, sentenced to death and thrown into prison, where he soon died.

In Jamaica, too, there was a rising, and the Earl of Manchester reported that 'all those executed were fully impressed with the belief that they were entitled to their freedom and that the cause they had embraced was just'.

In 1831, in Jamaica, this very belief that their freedom had been granted but was being withheld from them drove the slaves in the western part of the island to rise. The rising was savagely repressed, scores of Methodist and Baptist chapels were burnt, and the assembly resisted more stubbornly than ever any attempt to revise the law in the interests of slaves. In England, too, there were rioting and disorders, in the autumn of 1831, when the House of Lords threw out the Reform Bill. The various aspects of reform were linked together in the minds of English liberals. Opposition to the abolition of slavery was becoming as dangerous politically as opposition to parliamentary reform. The abolitionists had public opinion behind them, for a variety of religious, humane, and economic reasons, and they had convinced, tenacious and skilful leaders. Wilberforce, it is true, had relinquished his leadership to Buxton, and some of the older leaders were dead; but George Stephen and Zachary Macaulay were among the most vigorous minds in the public life of the time, and the policy of the Colonial Office itself was already strongly influenced by James Stephen, most upright and most conscientious of public servants, and devoted to the cause of emancipation. Agitation, mutiny, political pressure, and administrative skill, all played their part in preparing the Emancipation Act which finally became law in 1833.

The analogous movement for the emancipation of slaves in the remaining fragments of the French American empire followed a similar course about fifteen years later. Slavery had been abolished in law by the Revolution, but — except in Saint-Domingue — the abolition had not been effective; the institution of slavery was re-established by Napoleon, and retained under the restored Bourbons. The example of English legislation, and the warnings offered by a series of widespread conspiracies among the slaves (of which the most serious were those of Carbet in 1822, and again in 1824, and that of the Grande Anse in 1833, all in Martinique) forced upon the government a policy of amelioration similar to that pursued by the English government fifteen years earlier. Naturally the establishment of the July

Monarchy in 1830 made the adoption of such a policy much easier politically. In 1832 the tax on manumission was abolished, and the procedure for manumission simplified. In 1833 the registration of slaves was made compulsory, and mutilation and branding of captured runaways prohibited. In 1836 it was enacted that all slaves brought into France became free immediately. All this legislation was enacted by the central assembly in France, and not, as in the British islands, passed by local legislatures under metropolitan pressure. Like the corresponding British legislation, however, it was inadequate to the situation, and could not be consistently enforced because of the opposition of colonial magnates and officials. In France, as in England earlier, the conviction grew among those who disliked slavery that only complete emancipation would suffice. The *Société pour l'abolition de l'esclavage* was formed in 1834, and the first serious draft of an emancipation law was proposed in the assembly in 1838. The West Indian slave owners, being represented in the assembly, were able to oppose this and subsequent proposals more directly than their English counterparts had done, and they did so with more conviction, defending slavery not only as economically necessary but as socially desirable, given the savagery and idleness of the slaves. 'Ce n'est pas l'esclavage qui a rendu les races nègres paresseuses,' one of them roundly declared, 'c'est leur paresse qui les a fait tomber dans l'esclavage.' The arguments used on both sides were rational and secular. French abolitionists, unlike the 'Saints' in England, had no particular religious bent. Schoelcher, their most eminent and zealous leader, shared to the full Wilberforce's humanity, and was better informed — he had travelled in the southern States — but he lacked Wilberforce's evangelical fervour. The debate, with all its acrimonies and cries of ruin, raged intermittently until 1848. In that year Schoelcher proposed the final and successful enactment, abolishing slavery forthwith throughout the French colonies and authorising the payment of compensation to the former owners. By the middle of the nineteenth century, then, West Indian slavery survived only in the Spanish islands. In the French and British colonies there were no more slaves; but the task of equipping men for freedom still lay ahead.

CHAPTER XIII

'THE BEST AND WORST OF TIMES'

THE CASSIA TREE, WHICH grows throughout the West Indies, is a symbol of alternating despair and hope. Most West Indian trees are evergreen; but the cassia loses its leaves, and the bark peels from its grey-white trunk, as from a dead stick. Then suddenly, overnight, the tree becomes a cascade of golden flowers, as short-lived as it is lovely.

The period in West Indian history which followed emancipation was like the death and rebirth of the cassia tree. It was the best and worst of times. One disaster followed another; bankruptcy and financial chaos in the eighteen-forties, droughts and epidemics in the eighteen-fifties, rioting and bloodshed in the eighteeen-sixties. Yet in these disastrous years the initiative and courage of newly emancipated people were creating an independent peasantry. Radical constitutional changes were made in some territories, while the abolition of imperial preferences completed the destruction of the old plantation system. A rigid slave society marked by division and dominated by fear disintegrated and conditions were created for the growth, however slowly, of a new and dynamic society. The transition from slavery to 'full free' by way of apprenticeship, the rise of the free villages, the collapse of the plantation system, the encouragement of immigration and the extension of Crown colony government make this period one of the most fruitful and significant in West Indian history.

On the eve of emancipation the population of the British Caribbean was made up of three main groups. One of these consisted of a comparatively small number of white persons, all of them free: officials, plantation owners, merchants, professional men, attorneys, overseers, book-keepers, master craftsmen. They controlled the economic and political life of the country, and in the long-established colonies were practically self-governing in local affairs. There was a second group which consisted of free people of colour, whose rights as citizens were limited. They owned property, were permitted to carry arms and to give evidence in a court of law, but had not the right to vote or to offer themselves for election. Below them in standing were the slaves, who had no direct part whatever in the political life of the islands

This description is generally accurate for those islands which had been British for some time and where the plantation system was well-established. Trinidad was a notable exception. In 1783 the island was largely undeveloped, and its population was very small: 126 white persons, 295 free persons of colour and 310 slaves. These were all subject to Spanish law, and this provided that free persons, white or coloured, should have full rights of citizenship after five years' residence. The population grew rapidly. Some white planters were attracted from other islands by the abundance of available land, and a number of free persons of colour took refuge there from Saint-Domingue. By 1809 the group of coloured persons who were free formed one-fifth of the total population of about 30,000, while the group or whites was less than one-twelfth. In 1829 there were 4,326 white persons, 16,412 free coloured, and 22,436 slaves. The coloured group never suffered to the same extent from special political disabilities, as did the group in Jamaica, for the British retained the system of administration which they found in Trinidad. In 1828, as a result of agitation in the West Indies and in England, all civil and military distinctions between free British subjects of any colour were abolished by Order in Council in all the Crown colonies. Jamaica legislated in the same sense in 1830, Barbados in 1831. The slaves got the benefit of this later, for upon full emancipation they became, in most British colonies, equal before the law with any other British subjects.

In the British Caribbean, as a whole, the third social group was by far the largest. It included about three-quarters of a million slaves. Some of these were occupied with domestic duties; others were the technicians of the plantations, the carpenters, masons, boiler-men for example; and about three-fourths of the full number were praedial or field workers, or belonged to 'jobbing gangs' which might be hired out. The slaves had certain rights which were theirs by custom, and other rights which were theirs by law; they were entitled to allowances of food and clothing; in Jamaica they had the use of land on which to grow food, and were supposed to have every Sunday and every other Saturday for their own work; and usually they were allowed to keep small stock.

The three groups were separate and distinct from each other, each having its own religious and political institutions, its own customs and traditions, its own set of values and codes of behaviour, and its own status. Emancipation was the beginning of a gradual shift of political and economic power from the small dominant group of owners and a slow but steady change in the concept of social status.

This shift in social relations began with emancipation, and was emphasised in the labour problems of the period. One of the most difficult questions for those concerned with the Emancipation Act was how to grant full freedom and at the same time ensure that the plantations would have the labour they needed for their very existence. Also, should the change from slavery to freedom be sudden or should it be gradual? These two questions were well put by Governor Smith of Barbados in his letter to the Colonial Office in July 1833: 'after an attentive consideration of the difficulties which present themselves in giving effect to any scheme of negro emancipation so as to ensure their labour and yet to clear them of a cruel bondage, my greatest apprehension of failure and disorder has been from the unfitness of the slaves themselves to bear the great transition from slavery to civil rights.'

James Stephen at the Colonial Office was given the task of drafting, almost overnight, a plan for emancipation which would meet these two difficulties. The resulting Bill of 1833, which became an Act of the Imperial Parliament and binding upon all British colonies, provided that children under six years of age should be free but that all other slaves might be required to serve a period of apprenticeship. For field workers this period was to be six years, and for others it was to be four years. During their years of apprenticeship the newly emancipated people had to work for their former owners for three-fourths of the week (40½ hours) without pay. They were to be paid for the remaining fourth, and from their earnings they were to be able to buy their freedom at any time before their apprenticeship ended. Special magistrates were to be sent out from England for 'The effectual superintendence of the said apprenticed labourers, and the execution of this Act', and they were given jurisdiction over every 'Question, matter, being or thing incident to or arising out of the relations subsisting between such apprenticed labourers and the persons respectively entitled to their services'.

When the Secretary of State sent the Emancipation Act to the legislative colonies he pointed out that no scheme of probation other than the apprenticeship system would be allowed, but that they were free to shorten the period of apprenticeship or to do away with it altogether. Antigua took the bold and imaginative step of declaring full and immediate freedom, and although there were some disputes over rates of pay no serious labour trouble developed. In 1837 Sturge reported that the experiment had succeeded 'beyond the expectations of its most sanguine advocates.'

Apprenticeship was adopted in all the Crown colonies and in the other legislative colonies. The British government looked on this as a period of transition during which labourers would be prepared for full freedom by a series of social reforms and by the enjoyment of fuller rights. Many planters, however, regarded the system as 'a part of the compensation, a short and partial reprieve granted that they might squeeze the last juice out of compulsory labour before the great ruin of freedom set in.'

As Mathieson points out: 'the Act which abolished slavery did not emancipate the slaves. . . . As a social institution slavery disappeared . . . and it came back as a system of industry, the negroes . . . having to work as slaves for so many hours a week.' Yet there was from the start this fundamental difference, that those who had been owners of labour had become the buyers, and those who had been slaves were now the sellers of labour. It took time for the owners to recognise their loss of power, and there were difficulties and misunderstanding when at one and the same time freedom was proclaimed and forced labour demanded. In St. Christopher martial law had to be proclaimed and a number of ex-slaves punished before the apprentices would work. There was some unrest and dissatisfaction among the apprentices in Trinidad, Tobago, British Guiana and in Jamaica, but on the whole the system worked. The disputes were generally about wages and the continuance of rights, particularly with respect to the growing of food and the use of land. This problem was not acute in Barbados, where food was imported. The hope had been expressed in Nevis in 1782 that 'in a year or two this island will be able to raise much provision towards supporting its own slaves but hitherto it has been our invariable custom to depend almost entirely on America'. This was true of all the Leeward Islands, so that here and in Barbados scarcity of land compelled labour to work on the estates to get wages to buy food. Labour disputes were acute in Jamaica where it was customary to give the slaves 'grounds' on which to grow their food. This had been one way in which the estates kept their costs down and, at the same time, 'anchored' the slave to the estate. The custom had been a stabilising factor under slavery. Under apprenticeship, with labour and production costs rising, some planters saw a chance of keeping wages down by charging rent for the 'grounds' and they caused resentment and ill-will when they evicted those who would not or could not pay these rents.

The contrast is indicated by Gurney, who visited the West Indies in 1838. In St. Kitts a stipendiary magistrate reported that the negroes 'will do an infinity of work for wages', and in Antigua the late Speaker of the Assembly had declared that 'the free labour system is the cheapest', whereas in Jamaica 'the question of tenancy has been mixed up with that of labour' and evictions had caused bitter resentment.

One of the best accounts of the difficulties of this period of transition is given by Sir Charles Metcalfe, when governor of Jamaica, in a despatch to the Secretary of State in 1839. He wrote: 'When the freedom of slaves was established, the great question that agitated the island was, on what terms free labour could be obtained for the cultivation of the estates, from which the wealth of Jamaica has hitherto been derived. It naturally became the interest of the owners of properties to obtain labour on the cheapest, and that of the labouring population to sell it on the dearest terms; and a struggle with these opposite views commenced between the two parties.

'The practice which prevailed in slavery, of granting grounds to the labourers, from which they derived the means of subsistence in esculents for themselves and their families, and by the sale of surplus produce, gave a great advantage to the labourers when they acquired freedom, as it rendered them in a great degree independent of labour, and enabled them to hold out for terms. The proprietors could not hold out with the same safety, for the want of labour on their properties, at some, if not all, periods of the year, must have been ruinous. The wages of labour, therefore, have been hitherto settled more at the will of the labourer than at that of his employer, and this must continue to be the case until a great increase of the labouring population shall make labour cheaper, or until labourers shall be more dependent on labour, or until such a number of properties shall be thrown out of cultivation by the impossibility of meeting the expense as may produce the same effect as an increase in the labouring population. . . .

'As a counterpoise to the power of the labourers over wages, the proprietors have that of charging rent for the houses and grounds tenanted by the labourers, and this right is often exercised with a view to counterbalance, as much as possible, the payment of wages, and not with reference purely to the value of the house and grounds. Thus in many instances the rent of a house is charged, not as a rate fixed for the house, but at a rate fixed for each occupant of the house. These counter-claims for rent and wages keep up much irritation and litigation, but will, it is to be hoped, in time, be settled on the basis of mutual interest. . . .

'The conduct of the labouring population is represented by the stipendiary magistrates, whose reports are the most frequent channels of official information possessed by the government, as being orderly and irreproachable; and I see no reason to doubt the truth of their representations. . . . The stipendiary magistrates are a class, with individual exceptions, offensive to the proprietary interest. This is not surprising. The magistracy of the country consisted, formerly, exclusively of proprietors, or their representatives, performing their duties gratuitously. . . . During the apprenticeship and since the recent granting of freedom it was scarcely possible to entrust the dispensation of justice entirely to those who were themselves so much interested in the questions likely to arise for discussion. Nevertheless, the establishment of stipendiary magistrates was extremely grating to the landed interests; and added to the abolition of slavery, became a second revolution in the island. The annoyance was aggravated in a great degree, partly by the inexperience and unfitness of some of the stipendiary magistrates, and partly from their receiving a bias from the purpose for which they were appointed, and by their regarding themselves rather as protectors of the labourers than as dispensers of equal justice to all parties. . . .'

The system of apprenticeship for field workers was terminated in 1838, two years earlier than had been intended. In islands where there was a higher proportion of resident owners and where labour relations were, therefore, generally better, and where there was very little land available for further cultivation, the system seems to have worked fairly well. It is indeed possible that islands like Barbados and St. Kitts did not need the system and might very well have followed the example of Antigua, since the plantations dominated the economy of the islands and the labourers had few other sources of livelihood. In other islands like Montserrat and Dominica there were only a handful of white planters with limited resources and the demand for labour was, therefore, small. In these, apprenticeship mattered little. It was in British Guiana and in Jamaica, where there was land and where the estates were powerful, that friction and dissatisfaction arose. This was inevitable, for the system was an attempt at a compromise between two irreconcilables: slavery and freedom. It set out to provide forced labour, to limit the mobility of labour, and to continue the system of allowances — rent-free gardens and supplies of fish and meat — all of which had been characteristic of slavery, while at the same time requiring payment for labour and causing competition between employers for such labour as there was. Wage agreements between masters and apprentices were made difficult because some indulgences were a legal right, and some were not; as a result, the apprentice often demanded as a right what the master withheld as a wage. Nor could disputes be fought out by outright refusals to do any labour, because the apprentice was compelled to give his $40\frac{1}{2}$ hours per week; or by the threat of dismissal, for the apprentice was fixed to the estate. In short, the coercive power of the master, the essential force of slavery, had been removed; and the full freedom to bargain, the essential force of free labour, had not been substituted. The efforts of the stipendiary magistrates, the unskilled interpreters of a vague law, though often brave, could hardly have solved the difficulties inherent in the system.

In those places where the estates were powerful and where land was also available there developed a remarkable movement in the establishment of an independent peasantry. The movement began before emancipation, and sprang from a desire for land and liberty. During slavery negroes had broken away from the Surinam and Guiana plantations to establish settlements in the interior, and they had escaped from the sugar estates on the Jamaican lowlands to maroon villages in remote mountain valleys. These settlements were active and corporate units. Their success owed much to the efforts which had been made by governments in the late eighteenth century to introduce new food crops, particularly starchy ground provisions such as cocos and improved varieties of yam, and tree crops such as ackee and breadfruit, which produced over long periods with little effort, conserved water, and provided shade for the peasant cultivator. Yams, plantains, ackees and later breadfruit were the chief Jamaican peasant foods. Accounts from Guiana tell of the cultivation of rice, yams, tannias and tobacco by the bush negroes and of the 'encampments' of run-away negroes on the east coast of Demerara. The establishment of free villages was not begun as a result of emancipation, but with freedom it became possible for many people to do legally what a few hitherto had done illegally. So, along the banks of the Berbice and Demerara rivers in British Guiana there sprang up settlements of newly emancipated people who pooled their resources, bought land, 'parcelled it out, and so called a regular Negro Colony into existence'. The same process took place in Trinidad, where, in Montserrat Ward for instance, peons from the mainland and newly freed negroes squatted and established villages. In Guiana, the movement was on an impressive scale. In Berbice, in 1838, out of a population of 20,000 there were 15,000 who were newly emancipated and none of these owned land. Four years later over 1,000 of these families owned 7,000 acres purchased at a cost of more than $100,000.

A vast land-settlement scheme was in fact put through in Guiana by people who acted very largely under their own leadership and by pooling their resources. The result was that up to the end of 1848, over 400 estates had been bought, and more than

10,000 houses had been built and occupied by 44,443 persons. By 1852 it was estimated that there were more than 70,000 persons of the labouring class in British Guiana and that these owned property in houses and lands for which they had paid £1,000,000.

There was a similar wave of settlement in Jamaica, where also land space exceeded the supply of labour. In Guiana the expansion was on to land that was fertile and rich. The choice was more restricted in Jamaica, and it seems likely that a large number of persons would have preferred to live in their old villages and to cultivate their grounds. Many estate owners, however, thought that they could compel labour to accept their terms if they could deprive them of the use of these 'grounds' and so they drove them from the estates by high rentals and by ejections. Missionaries like Knibb, Phillippo, Clark, Dendy and Burchell gave a lead in the establishment of free villages, and the general result of this process which transformed the emancipated slave into a peasant proprietor is described by Sir Charles Metcalfe in 1840 in a letter to Lord John Russell: 'The accompanying statement shows that a large increase has taken place from 1838 to 1840 in the number of proprietors of small freeholds in the several rural parishes of this island, the increase consisting almost entirely of emancipated negroes. It appears that the number of such freeholders assessed in 1838 was 2,014; and in 1840, 7,848. There was no assessment in the intermediate year, owing to the suspension of ordinary taxation.'

Five years later William Knibb described the progress of settlement in these words: 'By the census taken during last year, I find that there were full 19,000 persons, formerly slaves, who had purchased land on which they were erecting their own cottages. In St. James' parish there were 10 new villages, with 1,020 houses; in Trelawny, the parish in which I live, there were 23 free villages, and 1,590 houses; in St. Mary's, 15 free villages, with 632 houses; in St. Thomas, in the Vale, 10 free villages with 1,780 houses.' By the middle of the century the communities of peasant farmers had grown up throughout the islands. They were practically self-supporting, getting the cash they needed by the sale of the ground provisions which they cultivated.

While these settlements of smallholders were being established the plantation system was crumbling. The boom in sugar at the beginning of the century had been caused by the collapse of sugar production in Saint-Domingue and by the exceptional circumstances of war. After the war prices fell disastrously. The disturbed state of Europe lessened the demand and the interruption of trade with the United States made it difficult and costly to obtain timber and food. The American trade was re-opened in 1822, but by then competition from Cuba and the East Indies had increased and there was a rising demand for the removal of the preferential duty of 10s. per cwt. which West Indian sugar enjoyed over East Indian sugar. In the boom years much marginal land had been planted in cane, and in addition the general cost of production was high. In the middle of the Napoleonic war it cost the planter from 35s. to 36s. to produce 1 cwt. of sugar. The result was that when prices fell to what had been the normal 30s. to 35s. and even below, only the most efficient estates could stay in business, and production steadily declined.

Production costs had been increased by the abolition of the slave trade in 1807, and the Emancipation Act of 1833 had the effect of increasing the shortage of labour and so sending up its cost. In Barbados and St. Kitts, where labour was in excess of land-space, production was fairly well maintained, but in the other territories there was a fall in production during the period of apprenticeship and a further fall after full emancipation. Apprenticeship seems to have put a brake on the downward trend which had begun early in the century. The introduction of the Bourbon cane helped planters to lift the production of sugar per acre, but this on the credit side was not enough to counterbalance the heavy debit items of labour shortage and low prices.

Full emancipation caused a radical change in the way in which the plantations were financed. Under slavery the planter had been able to operate with comparatively little working capital. He did not have to pay wages, and he could cut his expenditure on food supplies for the estate by letting the slaves grow as much food as possible. He sold his sugar through an agent in London, who purchased supplies for him and advanced money to carry him over bad years. This method of finance suited the West India merchants in London because they could collect the interest on money they had lent by insisting that their debtors' sugar should pass through their hands. It suited the planters because it gave them the credit which they needed.

'Full free' meant payment for labour. The estate had to find cash to pay wages, as well as to equip the estate with labour-saving devices like ploughs and harrows, and with steam engines for the mills. The labour bill for an estate in the eighteen-forties might be as much as two-thirds of the total cost of production and it was a bill that had to be paid on time, so that the planter needed two or three times more working capital than formerly. The West Indies had always been short of currency, and coins of almost every variety had been in circulation before the abolition of slavery — Spanish dollars, doubloons, pistoles, escudos, and, latterly, United States dollars. Now planters had to find cash, much of it in small denominations. Most West Indian planters were already heavily in debt to their London agents, and could not expect much further accommodation from that source. They had been paid £20,000,000 in compensation for the loss of their slaves, it is true; but little of this went into the planters' pockets. Most of the money went to the merchants to pay off mortgages and sub-mortgages. There was little left for capital development or for working the estate and some planters could not even raise the cash to pay their labourers. The banks which were founded in the eighteen-thirties to meet the desperate need for capital — the Colonial Bank for the West Indies in London in 1836, the Planters' Bank in Jamaica in 1837 — were very shaky affairs. Under slavery a man's wealth had been reckoned by the number of slaves he owned. Now it was reckoned in terms of money, and money was even shorter than labour.

Prices continued to fall. Sewell says that 'between 1805 and 1825 the price . . . fell 25 per cent . . . between 1825 and 1835 it fell another 25 per cent . . . between 1835 and 1850 it fell away 25 per cent again.' The ruin was completed by the introduction of free trade and the removal of the preferential duty on West Indian sugar between 1846 and 1854. In 1847 also there occurred a commercial crisis in the United Kingdom which sent thirteen West India houses into bankruptcy within twelve months. The West India bank with its headquarters in Barbados failed, and so did the Planters' Bank in Jamaica. The West Indian planters were desperate. The figures for Jamaica, which produced one-half of the sugar sold in the British market at the time, show how catastrophic was the collapse of the industry in that island. From 71,000 tons in 1832 production fell to 25,000 tons in 1852. In 1840 the price had been £49 per ton in bond in England. It fell to £23 in 1846. Between 1846 and 1852, 474 sugar and coffee plantations and 132 grass pens valued in 1841 at £2,441,000, were wholly or partly abandoned. The value of property fell sharply. In 1777 Rose Hall Estate, consisting of 1,095 acres with 260 slaves, had been sold for £18,000. In 1857 one-third of the same estate was sold for £300.

George Price, writing in 1866, described the collapse of the sugar estates in Jamaica in these words: 'In the district around, about 300 square miles, I found in 1842 nineteen sugar estates in full operation, having on them the usual white managers and people — other whites, attracted by the considerable amount of money in circulation, being also settled in the district. In 1864 all these estates had long ceased cultivation, except that with which I was connected; trees were growing out of the walls and roofs of nearly all the buildings; and all around was bush. With the exception of three or four, all the whites had vanished.' There had in fact been two movements — the flight of labour from the estates and the flight of capital and of white owners. In 1844 there had been 15,775 white persons in the island and in 1861 the number had fallen to 13,815.

Britain at this time was putting its surplus capital into expanding industries, new developing overseas territories, and the railways and steamships that were revolutionising transport. The West Indies, grown shabby and threadbare, could not hope to attract new capital. Any industry would have been hard put to it to face a combination of increased labour costs and falling prices; add to these the lack of capital to cover day-to-day expenses and essential reorganisation and the reasons for the collapse of the sugar industry in the British West Indies became plain. Jamaica appeared to be following, by less violent stages, the same path as Saint-Domingue.

At this crucial period of transition from slavery to freedom, owners usually were not present to initiate reforms or to supply leadership. The Marquess of Sligo complained that the Jamaica House of Assembly was made up almost entirely of attorneys and overseers. The drain on local resources is shown by the fact that the exports from Jamaica were normally nearly double the imports in value, the difference representing the profits drawn by absent owners. When prices fell and profits diminished owners began to sell out, but many estates went into chancery because, by law, the estates remained subject to any encumbrances or liens which had been put on them. The buyer purchased both the estate and any charges to which it was subject. St. Lucia was the first island to change this by setting up a mortgage office in 1829 and by passing a law in 1833 which authorised the seizure of real estate property and the sale of this property without encumbrances. The benefits were immediate. Between 1833 and 1843 sixty-nine out of the eighty-one estates in the island were sold free of mortgages. Then in 1854 the first West Indies Encumbered Estates Act was passed, and the principle of encumbered estates being sold without encumbrances was adopted by St. Vincent in 1857 and by Jamaica in 1861. The estates were sold out or were broken up and sold to smallholders.

The position of the sugar industry was better in some British territories than in others. For all of them the critical years were from 1845 to 1854, the year of the complete equalisation of the sugar duties. In 1854 the price fell to 21s. 5d. per cwt. in bond, but after that it began to rise again and in 1857 it reached 35s. 7d. per cwt. Production rose, and by 1860 the islands and British Guiana had weathered the storm. Barbados was able to do this mainly because labour was available; Trinidad and British Guiana managed to achieve comparative prosperity because of Indian labour. Many owners and attorneys had seen that the labour shortages which began with the passing of the Abolition Act of 1807 would become more acute with the passing of the Emancipation Act of 1833. In Barbados, Antigua and St. Kitts the problem was not so much one of the scarcity of labour as of its irregularity, but in Trinidad the development of the island had been retarded by the acute shortage of labour. The shortage was also acute in British Guiana and in Jamaica. Many of the emancipated people disliked estate labour and preferred to grow food on their own 'ground', working only for such cash as was needed and nothing more. Moreover, the position was affected by the withdrawal of women and children from the estate labour force, the reduction in hours of labour, the increased mobility of the worker and his preference for other kinds of work. The planters believed that the answer to the problem was immigration — finding new sources of labour and bringing them into West Indies on contract.

Immigration was in keeping with the spirit of the age. The eighteenth century had seen the movement under compulsion of vast numbers of people from West Africa to the Americas. The nineteenth century saw an even greater free movement of people from Europe and Asia. In the sixty years after Waterloo some 7,000,000 people went from the United Kingdom alone to the colonies. In the ten years immediately after 1815 the population of Canada rose from 80,000 to 150,000. At the same time, in the East, the Chinese were making their way down through Indo-China to Java and the islands of the Pacific. The emigration of Indian labour on a large scale began in 1830 when a French merchant took 130 Indian artisans to Bourbon. By 1847 there were 7,000 Indians in Mauritius and the movement of Indians into Africa had also begun.

In the West Indies it was natural that the planters should press for immigration on a large scale. Jamaica desired European immigration so as to settle the highlands of the interior with white smallholders who would be a counterbalance to the negroes, but — not unnaturally — the efforts failed. In 1834 and 1835 batches of labourers were taken from Madeira into British Guiana, while from Trinidad and from Guiana the planters sent agents into the British islands to recruit labour. This immigration has continued up to the present time in spite of legal barriers; in 1952 it was found that there were some 11,000 illegal West Indian immigrants in Trinidad alone. Efforts were also made, with some success, to bring free Africans to the West Indies. African immigration, however, was insignificant in comparison with East Indian. It lasted for thirty years and involved 36,000 people, one-third of whom returned to Africa. On the other hand, East Indian immigration involved more than ten times as many persons and covered a period of about eighty years.

The British government was not unnaturally suspicious of any scheme that might conceivably lead to a revival of slavery, and it did not grant any substantial concession until John Gladstone became interested in the recruitment of Indian labour and obtained permission to bring Indian labourers into Guiana on five-year contract. Ill-treatment and sickness caused many deaths, and Lord John Russell informed the Governor of British Guiana in 1840 that he would be unwilling 'to adopt any measure to favour the transfer of labourers from British India to Guiana, after the failure of the former experiment'. Nevertheless, the planters persisted in their attempts to attract labour from overseas and by 1842 very nearly 5,000 Madeirans had been brought in. The history of Trinidad and of Guiana is dominated by the labour question at this period and by the attempts to solve it by immigration. Under pressure from the West Indies and the Colonial Office, the embargo on immigration from India was lifted and a second attempt was made during the years 1845-46 to bring Indians to the West Indies. This attempt also failed.

Up to 1850, then, the results of these attempts to encourage immigration were disappointing. During the years 1841-47 British Guiana alone spent £360,655 on immigration, and in return obtained 12,237 labourers from India, 12,898 from the West Indian islands, 8,645 from Africa, and some 16,000 from Madeira — a total of about 50,000 persons. The Africans showed a strong and understandable tendency to walk off into the bush and set up as peasant squatters. The Madeirans suffered from an appallingly high mortality rate, due largely to their own indifference to — or ignorance of — the most elementary rules of health in the tropics. Only the Indians worked steadily on the sugar estates and so contributed directly to the labour supply, and their numbers were inadequate to the need. Things went from bad to worse with sugar and finally the House of Commons lent £250,000 to help the industry, four-fifths of the amount to be spent on immigration. The mortality rate had been high among indented Indian labourers also — though less than among the Madeirans — because large numbers of uneducated people had been removed from the things they were used to, thrown on their own in a strange land, given inadequate medical attention and insufficient food. The local commission which was appointed to spend the loan money emphasised that immigration from India was the only way to save the sugar industry and arrangements were made to bring Indians into the country under improved conditions, with compulsory provision of housing and medical attention. Much of the 'barrack' housing in British Guiana dates from this time. Between 1884 and 1914 some 239,000 Indians were brought into British Guiana under indenture and only about one in every four of these were repatriated. Already in 1883 Indians formed more than one-quarter of the population of British Guiana — 65,000 out of 250,000. In Trinidad, similarly, by 1883 East Indians formed about one-third of a total population of 153,000.

In Trinidad and British Guiana the steady increase of the East Indian population was reflected directly in the figures of sugar production. In British Guiana production dropped steadily from 60,000 tons in 1830 to 23,000 tons in 1846. It was hard hit by the crisis of 1847 and by the equalisation of duties, but from 1848 it began to rise, and thereafter it rose equally steadily: 38,000 tons in 1851, 63,000 in 1861, 92,000 in 1871. The trends in Trinidad were similar, on a smaller scale, and both colonies showed a striking contrast with Jamaica, where production declined throughout the century from a high figure of nearly 100,000 tons in 1805 to a low figure of under 13,000 tons in 1888. In Jamaica, lack of labour was probably a less serious difficulty than lack of capital; there was considerable opposition to Indian immigration, or rather to the spending of money on immigration, and in 1883 there were only 13,000 Indians in a total population of 580,000.

The East Indians contributed other things to West Indian life besides estate labour. They were largely responsible for the great increase in consumption, and the considerable increase in production, of rice throughout the area. Rice had been grown in Jamaica since the seventeenth century — Sloane mentions it — but in very small quantities. With the coming of the East Indians it became an important crop, and in time a daily food for all classes of society. Connected with rice-growing, but of great importance for sugar also, was the age-old traditional Indian skill in irrigation. The revival of the Jamaican sugar industry in the twentieth century has been made possible by irrigation, and on almost every irrigated property, until very lately, the 'waterman' was an East Indian.

The East Indians, on the other hand, posed a social problem. There were, in the early days, few people of education among them. They came, for the most part, as labourers, an amorphous, leader-less mass, which proved extremely difficult to absorb into the general life of the community. In the estate barracks, and later as small settlers, market-gardeners or merchants, they naturally stuck together. They retained their religion — Hindu, or less frequently Muslim — their social habits, to some extent their languages. They did not quickly adopt European religion and habits, modified to suit their needs, as the African had done. Such provision as governments could make for public education in the nineteenth century — which was little enough — tended to pass the East Indians by. Of all the races thrown into the West Indian melting-pot they found — and find — the greatest difficulty in regarding themselves as West Indians. Their ability and their willingness to overcome that difficulty is one of the most important conditions for the social and political health of the British West Indies today.

CHAPTER XIV

PATTERNS OF COLONIAL GOVERNMENT

THE BRITISH WEST INDIES in the middle nineteenth century formed a rich and varied museum of antiquated constitutional and administrative devices. The stagnation of the economic life of the islands and the neglect with which they were treated at that time by the British government led to an ossification of their political life in eighteenth-century, indeed sometimes in seventeenth-century, forms. The forms were as varied as they were old-fashioned. Different parts of the British West Indies had at different times been settled and governed by Spaniards, Frenchmen, Dutchmen, and Englishmen, and traces of the different systems of administration survived repeated changes of masters, because nobody bothered to alter them.

The preservation of old variety was most evident, as might be expected, in the field of local government — the municipal and parochial structure, which everywhere in the West Indies had preceded the establishment of central administration. The people who went out from England in the early years to settle and plant in St. Kitts and Nevis, in Antigua, Barbados and Jamaica, transferred to these lands the pattern of local government to which they were accustomed. Within a few years of its settlement Barbados was divided into six parishes, each with its vestry. The freeholders met each year to elect the 'trustees' for the following twelve months; these had the power to levy rates for the poor, for the support of the clergy, and for the upkeep of the roads. In Jamaica and in the Cayman Islands also the parish vestry began to function at an early date. A characteristic extract from the vestry book of the parish of St. Elizabeth in Jamaica deals with the raising of revenue in 1695: 'At a meeting of the Justice and Vestry of the first Tuesday in February . . . ordered that Negroes young and old be valued at ten pounds a Head and Cattle of all sorts at Thirty Shillings a head and sheep and goats at five pounds a score and that the tax be leveyed at 12s. 6d. for every hundred pounds and if that be not sufficient to defray the parish charge then the Vestry meet and levy the said tax to be at 15s. for every hundred inhabitants.' The vestry minutes show how local government, the method by which a community learns to manage and direct its own business, had taken firm root in these early colonies. The vestry licensed teachers, maintained roads, paid the parson, punished vagrants and looked after the poor, and the freeholders of the parish were taxed for these and other purposes.

This development of local government in the older West Indian territories is in contrast with the highly centralised administrative system which the Spaniards established in Trinidad. The Spanish governors in Trinidad had autocratic powers that were limited in two ways: the necessity of having most of the sentences pronounced by the governor confirmed by the royal *audiencia* in Caracas, and secondly by the *residencia* — the special inquiry held at the end of a governor's term of office, either by his successor or by an official sent out from Spain, who reviewed the governor's actions with a view to redressing grievances. The *cabildo* or municipal council of Port-of-Spain also exercised some influence on the government, and so there was a measure of local government through the municipality but none through the parish. The British retained the Spanish system for some years after they took Trinidad in 1797, without the administrative checks that have been mentioned, and so they helped to establish tradition of a strong central government without any effective system of local government.

British Guiana and British Honduras introduced yet other variations. At the beginning of the seventeenth century the main stream of English settlement had been towards Virginia, the Caribbee islands and the coast of Guiana, but the danger of Spanish and Portuguese attacks, and the decision of the Pilgrim Fathers to cross the North Atlantic to New England, had turned the main flow to North America and away from South America. The Dutch, on the other hand, had turned from New Amsterdam on the Hudson to enlarge their holdings in South America. In 1667, by the Treaty of Breda, they took over Surinam, which had been settled from Barbados under the leadership of Francis Lord Willoughby. Much earlier in the century they had pushed up the Guiana rivers, the Cayenne and the Essequibo, founding Fort Kijk-over-al at the place where the Mazaruni and Cnyuni meet the Essequibo.

> *There runs a dream of perished lost foundations*
> *Through these Guiana rivers to the sea,*

and there runs through the law of British Guiana today the influence of its former rulers. The Dutch system of administration was planned for controlling trade depots, and not for creating settlements of free planters. Trade was the main object. When settlements grew up the profits of the Dutch West India Company were the first concern, and the company ruled until 1792, when Guiana was put under the control of a council set up by the States General. At no time was local opinion allowed to have much influence on the government of the colony. The company had a Court of Policy, made up of its officials, for each of the provinces of Essequibo, Demerara and Berbice. The first opportunity for the settlers to participate was when, in 1738, a planter was appointed to the Essequibo Court of Policy. Later, one unofficial member was also appointed to each of the Courts of Policy for Berbice and Demerara. Then, in 1743, Gravesande set up the College of Kiezers or Electors. The members of this were elected for life by resident planters who owned more than twenty-five slaves, and they only had to give a double nomination to the Director General of the Colony when the unofficial member died or left the colony. Rarely in a democracy can so little have been given to so many by so few. Agitation led to a reform in 1787, the Plan of Redress, by which Essequibo and Demerara were given one Court of Policy, and the planters were given more representation through the College of Kiezers. Later, in 1795, the governor accepted the proposal made by the planters for a 'Combined Court' made up of six 'Financial Representatives' elected for two years by resident planters and the members of the Court of Policy. The planters argued that the Court of Policy, as it stood, with its official majority, gave them no voice in the levying of colonial taxes. The Combined Court, on which their representatives had a majority, was to vote on the raising of taxes and examination of accounts but was to have no other powers. The British, when they took over the government, were confronted with the task of making this intricate system work. It could hardly be expected to work well. Since the Combined Court had a majority of settlers, and the Dutch Crown had capitulated, the colonists claimed that legislative rights had passed to them and that no change could be made in the constitution without their consent. It was not until 1831, for instance, that local consent could be secured for so obvious a measure as the union of Demerara, Essequibo and Berbice in the single administration of British Guiana.

The fundamental weakness in the Dutch system of administration was the separation of powers; the official majority in the Court of Policy was responsible for governing while the unofficial majority in the Combined Court controlled the purse. This same weakness was the main defect also in the British islands with Houses of Assembly. Charles II declared that Englishmen who settled in Jamaica and their children 'shall from their respective births be reputed to be free denizens of England; and shall have the same privileges, to all intents and purposes, as our free born subjects of England'. Within a few years of this declaration the Crown took over from the proprietors the government of the Caribbee Islands also, but retained the constitution, with governor, council and assembly. When the administration of the Leeward Islands was separated from that of Barbados in 1672 one governor was appointed with a council and assembly in each island. The pattern of government in all these British West Indian islands was very much like that of England in miniature. There were, wrote Long, 'three estates of which the governor (as representing the King) is head. Having no order of nobility here, the place of a house of peers is supplied by a council of twelve gentlemen appointed by the King, which in the system of our legislature forms the upper house. The lower house is composed (as in Britain) of the representatives of the people, elected by the freeholders'. There was this essential difference, however, between the constitution of Britain and of the West Indian colonies — that the English system represented a stage in national development, a process in which full power finally passed into the hands of the House of Commons. The West Indian system remained fixed and rigid for very nearly two centuries. In England those with or without the franchise were free citizens, and public opinion could be used to compel constitutional change. In the West Indies the free citizens were a small section of the community and it was vital to them to preserve the situation which existed. They were cut off from an appeal to more than a very limited section of the public in a society with a rigid social and economic structure.

Another basic weakness of the West Indian constitution was that the power to govern lay with the assembly and the responsibility to govern lay with the governor. The instructions which were given to the Earl of Carlisle when he was appointed governor of Jamaica show how much was expected of him. He was captain-general and vice-admiral of the fleet; with the Legislative Council he was the supreme tribunal in civil matters; he had the final voice in the passing of legislation; he had to preserve good relations with the assembly and keep the machine of government working. If a Chinese philosopher were told of the many tasks that a governor had to perform, says Edward Long, he would point out that they were for a superman who had been specially trained to undertake them.

The Legislative Council was a pale reflection of the House of Lords. It advised the governor when sitting as an executive body, formed the upper house of the legislature, and with the governor was the highest court of appeal in civil matters. The really effective body was the House of Assembly. The independence of colonial assemblies sometimes provoked the governors to bitter outbursts like that of Sir Richard Dutton to the Barbados assembly in 1681: 'I have never heard that the King hath granted you a new Magna Charta, though you dispute all his commands as though he had.' They claimed privileges similar to those of the House of Commons; they controlled finance, and used the power of the purse to encroach on the prerogatives of the council and of the governor. In Jamaica the Assembly had been designed to play a minor role and its powers were limited in the governor's instructions, but by 1752 Governor Knowles reported that 'the Assembly of Jamaica had succeeded in making itself the predominant element in Government'. Lord Hamilton declared in 1760 that 'it is extreme vanity in them to assume all the privileges of the House of Commons' but, vanity or not, the claim was made good by the strangle-hold which they obtained on finance. He who pays the piper calls the tune, and the Assembly would not vote money if it objected to the governor's policy. It went further, and prevented him from using his power of dissolution to govern without it, by voting money for not more than six or twelve months at a time. Another method it used for getting its way was that of 'tacking' a measure it wanted on to a money bill; if the governor wanted the money he had to take the measure that was 'tacked' to the bill. In 1791, for example, the Jamaica House of Assembly 'married' a clause giving help to the Haitian planters during a rebellion to a money bill. The council objected and the Assembly branded the objection as 'officious, indecent, and irregular'.

The assemblies in their old shape could never have become the instruments of genuine self-government. They had power, but it was power to obstruct. The governors were entirely responsible for carrying on the government, and, as Wrong points out, the result was that 'In all the islands, large and small, the machinery of government groaned and grated and deadlock ensued deadlock. . . .' The local legislatures resented interference from the British Parliament, where the absentee proprietors and West India merchants had a powerful influence; though they were thrown into close alliance with the West India interest in England on the struggle over the abolition of the slave trade.

The number of these independent, factious and quarrelsome West Indian assemblies was multiplied after 1763 when, by treaty with France, the islands of Grenada, Dominica and St. Vincent were ceded to Britain. The government in them was modelled after that of the Leeward Islands. The original plan was for one governor-general and one legislature, but this was too much for the planters and merchants of each island. Chiefly because of their pressure the ceded islands, within twelve years, had three separate governments. The Board of Trade, mindful of the difficulties which had arisen in Barbados, the Leewards and Jamaica, tried at first to limit the powers of the assemblies in the ceded islands and for nearly five years after the first assembly met all the laws that were passed in the islands were disallowed by the Privy Council. The attempt at imposing restraints failed. In 1772 the governor was given authority to sign any bills that were based on the precedents of legislation in the Leeward Islands.

Though the assemblies in the ceded islands successfully enlarged their powers they never had the prestige and importance of the assemblies in the older islands because they represented smaller communities, each with a few hundred English residents. Small or large, however, the British Parliament did not generally interfere with the decisions of the colonial assemblies. The loss of the American colonies was a sharp reminder of the difficulties caused by interference. But during the first quarter of the nineteenth century a change took place. The Quebec Act of 1774 had provided that French Canadians should keep their own system of law and religion, but had placed all legislative power in the hands of the Crown, and the Crown delegated only very limited powers to the Legislative Assembly which it set up. This was a useful precedent for dealing with the West Indian territories that became British at the turn of the century — St. Lucia and Trinidad, Berbice and Demerara. In each of these conquered territories the laws and institutions to which the people were accustomed were retained, but in Trinidad and St. Lucia, and in British Guiana as far as possible, the Crown kept legislative power firmly in its own hands. Trinidad was allowed to retain most of the system of government which Spain had established there, though in fact there were about 1,700 French and British settlers in the island in 1803 as compared with some 500 Spanish. The governor had autocratic powers such as the Spanish governor had possessed, but without checks imposed by the Spanish use of the royal *audiencia*. Then, in 1810, after some years of dissatisfaction and agitation Liverpool announced the decision to keep the power in the hands of the Crown, since the British Parliament would find it easier to protect the 'people of colour' and to enforce legislation in connection with the abolition of the slave trade. The despatch is explicit, stating that 'It is essential, for this purpose, that in a new Colony, the Crown should not divest itself of its Power of Legislation, and that neither the Crown nor Parliament should be subject to the embarrassments which, on such an occasion, might perhaps arise from the conflicting Views of the Imperial Parliament, and of a Subordinate Legislature'.

This was one of the reasons why the British government's policy of ameliorating the condition of the slaves was carried out more effectively in Trinidad than in Jamaica or Barbados, where the general stand taken by the assemblies was well expressed by a member, who remarked: 'It is impossible for any reflecting man to pursue, without dismay, a Despatch from the Secretary of States for colonies threatening, in most direct terms, to legislate for us in England, unless we adopt, in toto, and without hesitation, a certain plan of government for our slaves. . . .'

In the first half of the nineteenth century, then, there were two fundamentally different systems of government in the British West Indies, that of the legislative islands and that of the Crown colonies. During the latter half of the century the old representative system fell to pieces and disappeared, except in Barbados, and Crown colony government became general. Subsequently, in the twentieth century the change began from Crown colony to representative and responsible government.

During this first half of the nineteenth century, also, there began a reform in administration. In the eighteenth century there had been no professional civil service, and absenteeism was characteristic of government in the West Indies just as it was of industry. Society accepted political patronage or clientage as normal, and one way in which the government rewarded its supporters was by giving them sinecures and colonial patent offices. Long, in 1774, stated that 'the most executive offices in this island (the governor's excepted) are granted by the Crown to persons residing in England, and by these patentees are farmed or rented to deputies and sub-deputies acting in Jamaica, who remit annually several thousand pounds to their principals.' Even in the early Crown colonies the practice prevailed, for Rodway mentions a colonial secretary of British Guiana who, in 1824, had never been to the colony but was drawing £13,000 a year in fees. Out of this amount he paid two deputies.

Within the British West Indies the variations and contrasts in the pattern of government multiplied after emancipation. The old representative system was replaced by Crown colony government in many of the islands but was retained in Barbados; the system of Crown colony government which was introduced in British Guiana and Jamaica differed from that in Trinidad; yet other variations developed in British Honduras; a federal system managed to survive in the Leeward Islands but never developed in the Windward Islands; finally, a century after emancipation, responsible government became the deliberate aim of the political parties of the West Indies and of the government of the United Kingdom, and the federation of the British West Indies became a live political issue.

The old representative system decayed and perished in Jamaica and in the other parts of the West Indies for three main reasons. The first was absenteeism, which deprived the West Indies of the services of people of position and ability who might have identified themselves with the community. The West Indian assemblies recognised this, and tried unsuccessfully to check absenteeism by such proposals as putting higher taxes on the property of absentees. Emancipation was another and powerful reason. In the West Indian slave society of the eighteenth century, when slaves were property, they were technically represented by their owners. Emancipation wrought a vast social and political change; it set three-quarters of a million people free, without making any attempt to train them for the duties of citizenship. Its effect was to render the oligarchic rule of planter-attorneys more of an anachronism than ever. Henry Taylor at the Colonial Office advocated a policy of 'trusteeship' that involved abolishing the House of Assembly and introducing Crown colony government. He summed up the whole paradox of the situation in this way: 'To effect by force from without the greatest of all social changes and yet to leave the political framework of this totally different society the same as it was, would seem, even in a more theoretical view, to be in the nature of a political solecism.' The suggestion was then to sweep away the old representative system and in 1839 a Bill was in fact introduced into the British Parliament to suspend the House of Assembly for five years. Peel spoke against this Bill in parliament and Burge, Q.C., agent for Jamaica, appeared at the Bar of the House of Commons and of the House of Lords in defence of the ancient constitutional rights of Jamaica. Mutilated in the House of Lords, the Bill eventually merely empowered the governor, with the consent of the council, to enact measures for the government of Jamaica two months after the House of Assembly had thrown them out. The third factor was the Act (1846) of the British Parliament which provided for the progressive equalization of duties on British and foreign sugar. The wealth of Jamaica had been based on a monopoly propped up by differential duties; this final blow to the Jamaican economy went far to destroy the Assembly's power, for the Assembly had built up its power by control of the purse, and the purse was now empty.

P

The Jamaica Assembly at that time contained two recognisable parties; one was the Planters' Party, reinforced by the professional and mercantile elements, and it took the lead in a policy of retrenchment; the officials who received fixed salaries were the favourite targets for attacks by those gentlemen. The second was the 'coloured party' which also supported a policy of retrenchment, because it hoped by so doing to render offices less attractive to Europeans. The coloured politicians did not want the old assembly abolished, because they hoped that soon they would command a majority in the Assembly and they hoped to keep the greater part of the revenue dependent on annual grants. In 1853 when Sir Henry Barkly became governor he brought with him proposals from the Duke of Newcastle, then Secretary of State, that all public monies should be levied and disbursed, and all public accounts audited, by paid officials responsible to the Crown. These proposals implied that the Assembly was to abdicate its financial powers, since at that time 'It imposed the taxes, supervised their collection, voted their appropriation, expended the money voted and audited the accounts'. It was further suggested that annual estimates of revenue and expenditure should be framed on the responsibility of the governor and the initiation of money votes should be made under his authority and direction. The Duke of Newcastle made it clear that if the Assembly refused to consider those measures then they were not to assume that they would continue to enjoy the power and privilege of paralysing government. In 1853 a Bill was drafted providing for an executive committee, the component parts of which were three members of the House of Assembly, and one from the Legislative Council. They were to be the authoritative emissaries of the governor in disclosing the policy of the Crown and they had the duty of proposing money votes in the name of the Crown. The Act made it clear that the responsibility for the government of the colony was still the governor's, and the chairman of the West India Committee described this new form of government as an attempt to have responsible and representative government without party. Though it had certain advantages, the new constitutional experiment failed because it did not define with any precision the locus of responsibility. Of the executive committee Wrong says: '. . . when there was any fundamental disagreement between the

Governor and Assembly the new Committee had either to act as the undignified messengers of the Governor to a hostile Assembly, or as the impotent spokesman of the Assembly to the Governor whom they could not control, and in each case they were equally powerless.' The first faltering steps taken in Jamaica in the direction of responsible government led to a blind alley. But despite the inadequacy of the machinery of government, it might have functioned, as it did in Barbados, where an executive committee was established in 1886.

Jamaica, however, lacked the first and essential attribute of responsible government — a real public opinion. The electoral figures for the year 1864 illustrate this. The population was roughly 450,000; the number of voters on the register was 1,903, and the people who actually voted were 1,457. There was no foundation on which the structure of responsible government might be raised. In Jamaica, as in most of the other West Indian islands at this period, there was an almost complete lack of candidates able and willing to devote themselves to the task of government. Total apathy towards political matters and a supreme indifference pervaded the West Indian atmosphere. With the disappearance of this inertia, there was revealed a society completely lacking in balance and stability. Violent passions, bitter animosities and a complete absence of toleration overwhelmed the island in the outbreak of 1865. Only then was the political bankruptcy of the island revealed and the problem of government squarely faced.

The end came suddenly, as a result of the rising which took place in the parish of St. Thomas in October 1865. On the 12th of December, the assembly signed its own death warrant. The Speaker of the House of Commons remarked, cynically, 'The only good law the Assembly passed was that by which it abolished itself.' By the Jamaica Act which was passed on the 12th of December 1865, and an Imperial Act of the following year, the Queen was empowered to prescribe a new constitution in such a form and with such powers as Her Majesty saw fit. This Act of 1866 is an important statute, for it is the authority for all subsequent constitutional amendments in Jamaica. By an order in council under the act, Crown colony government was established in Jamaica and power and responsibility now passed into the hands of the governor.

The old representative system was soon discarded in the other legislative colonies, with the exception of Barbados. This island had never suffered to the same extent from absenteeism as had the other islands, nor had the economic consequences of emancipation been as severe as in Jamaica because the island was fully developed. There was no vacant land to tempt squatters into the bush. The Barbadians formed a compact community, whose members recognised their dependence upon one another in spite of racial and social divisions, and had worked out an accepted method of living together. The economic stability of the island was shown by the way in which it weathered the economic storms of the eighteen-forties and maintained its production of sugar. A constitutional crisis developed in 1876 but this was over the political issue of federation with the Windward Islands. In the riots which occurred eight people were killed, and at one time it looked as if the old constitution would be abolished and Crown colony government introduced. There was a bitter quarrel between governor and assembly, but after the governor had been transferred and the federation issue dropped tempers cooled. The device was adopted of setting up an executive committee rather after the fashion of the Jamaica pattern of 1853 and the old constitution was retained.

With the exception of Barbados the British colonies in the Caribbean were now Crown colonies — that is, in each the Crown retained control of the executive. Trinidad and St. Lucia were models of complete Crown colony government, with an executive council consisting of the chief officials and a few unofficial advisers, and a Legislative Council made up of the principal public officers and a number of unofficial representatives nominated by the governor, official members being in the majority. Jamaica, too, had pure Crown colony government from 1866 to 1885, and a modified form thereafter. In British Guiana elements of the old oligarchic system remained down to 1891, with an oligarchy based on a very limited franchise, using its control of the purse to protect the interests of its own section of the population. As in the older legislative colonies control was separated from executive responsibility. Executive power was exercised in Crown colony fashion.

Crown colony government performed useful tasks in the West Indies, particularly in the field of public works and services. It was paternal and impartial. It put an end to the bickering and frequent deadlocks which had been characteristic of the old representative system in its later years, and gave full scope to the constructive activities of vigorous governors such as Sir John Peter Grant and Sir Henry Blake in Jamaica. It prepared the way for social and economic development, for it introduced a policy of trusteeship for the whole community; its basic principle being 'the direct protection by the Crown of the unrepresented classes, which takes the place of representation'. This was not mere window-dressing. All in all, the system functioned reasonably well, considering the daunting economic situation with which it had to deal, and the social resentments which it inherited. It was, by its nature, however, a temporary and expensive makeshift, without roots in public support. Even before the end of the nineteenth century it underwent modifications of detail in several colonies. In Jamaica a 'moderate step in advance' was taken in 1884, in the formation of a Legislative Council consisting in the governor and an equal number of official and unofficial members. The latter were to be elected on a restricted franchise, and could only be outvoted by the official members if the governor certified that the passage of a particular Act or vote was a matter of paramount importance. A somewhat similar change took place in 1891 in British Guiana, where the unofficial members of the Court of Policy (the legislature in other than financial affairs) were thereafter to be chosen by direct election. In general, however, Crown colony government was not drastically modified, or even widely criticised, until after the First World War. The re-establishment of representative government, or the establishment of responsible governments, on the old narrow franchise, would have been politically difficult, if not impossible. It was not until after the First World War, however, that local nationalisms became clamant on a wider basis, and that people in the West Indies and in England began to consider the possibility of inexperienced, largely illiterate negro electorates taking direct part in the political life of the islands.

The institution of Crown colony government in many British possessions was a somewhat exceptional episode, in an empire which had always possessed — and was later to recapture — a strong tradition of decentralisation. In the French empire, on the other hand, the dominant tradition was that of centralised government. The French West Indian islands, down to the very eve of the Revolution, possessed no legislatures of their own, for the *Conseils Souverains* were advisory bodies. Colonial assemblies were instituted in 1787; and in the early years of the Revolution the colonies also secured representation in the National Assembly — a device characteristic of French constitutional ideas and quite foreign to English. Under the restored Bourbons, colonial government had reverted to the system, not of 1789, but of 1763; the remaining remnants of the French-American empire — Martinique, Guadeloupe, Cayenne — lost both the power of legislating for themselves and the opportunity of influencing metropolitan legislation. Under the July monarchy a liberalising policy was resumed. Free persons of colour were granted full civil rights in 1831 (in Jamaica the corresponding date was 1830). In 1834 Colonial Councils were created in Martinique and Guadeloupe, whose members were to be elected on a restricted franchise. At the first election in Martinique, 750 persons were qualified to vote, and 650 voted; 25 free persons of colour were qualified to vote, and 6 voted; no coloured person was elected. The legislative powers of the councils were very limited, and they could at all times be overridden by the National Assembly. The revolution of 1848 in France, however, was followed by the grant to the colonies, once again, of direct representation in the National Assembly upon a greatly enlarged franchise. Each island elected three representatives, and the first group of deputies elected included Schoelcher and Pory-Papy, along with others who had been prominent in the movement for emancipation. The group comprised one white Frenchman (Schoelcher) and one white *Martiniquais*, Perrinon. The other representatives were all coloured West Indians, and one of them (Bissette), elected as a replacement in 1849, was an extreme left-wing member of the emancipation party, a rival of Schoelcher, who had served two terms of banishment for seditious propaganda. Since then, the West Indian senators and deputies in Paris have usually been coloured, though certainly no less French for that. The parliamentary representation of the West Indies was suspended in 1854, but restored in 1871, after a period of rioting in Martinique which reflected the troubles of the Commune in Paris. Schoelcher, now an old man, was one of the deputies elected in 1871.

The events of 1848–49, which marked the end of slavery, fore-shadowed also the end of white political supremacy — though not economic power — in Martinique and Guadeloupe. They marked also the rejection of any attempt to develop decentralised autonomy, and the acceptance of the opposite policy of inte-grating the colonies more closely with the home country. The French West Indies were on the way to becoming departments of metropolitan France, as they are, in law, today.

CHAPTER XV

THE SPANISH ISLANDS IN THE NINETEENTH CENTURY

OF THE THREE SPANISH colonies in the West Indies, only one, Santo Domingo, was seriously and directly affected by the events of the French Revolution. The city of Santo Domingo, once the capital of the Indies, had become in the course of the eighteenth century a somnolent backwater. Its administrative importance had disappeared, for the authority of captain-general and *audiencia* was now confined to the island. Commerce had passed it by. Its countryside displayed none of the feverish activity and savage hatreds so characteristic of French Saint-Domingue. Its mountains were uninhabited; its fertile savannahs were divided among great estates, patriarchal, isolated, self-sufficing, lazily producing cattle and a little sugar on portions of their land, with the help of relatively small gangs of slaves. The colony had twice the area of Saint-Domingue, and less than half the population. It was an easy prey for the semi-militarised mobs which came swarming over the frontiers from Haiti in 1801. For four years, from 1801 to 1805, the territory was given over to plunder and sporadic massacres at the hands of the followers of Toussaint and Dessalines. From 1805 to 1808 a remnant of le Clerc's French army, under General Ferrand, supported by occasional French ships from Martinique, gained control and expelled the Haitians; but in 1808 the news of the Bonapartist *coup* in Spain brought about a local revolt, aided by British warships, against the French, in the name of Ferdinand VII. The leader of the revolt, Sánchez Ramírez, was confirmed by the Council of Regency in Spain as intendant and captain-general, but was replaced by a peninsular Spaniard as soon as Ferdinand, with the help of Wellington's army, had climbed back on to his throne; colonial administration, marked by irksome restriction in small matters and procrastinating incompetence in great, held sway until 1821, when a fresh revolution in Spain unseated Ferdinand once more. The mulatto president of Haiti, Boyer, who inherited Toussaint's policy and much of his ability, selected this moment for a fresh invasion, and in 1822, after a few more weeks of independence and a futile proposal of union with Bolívar's Great Colombia, Santo Domingo fell once more under Haitian rule; a régime of extortion by illiterate officials and soldiers, hostile to everything Spanish and everything white, which lasted until 1844.

The two periods of Haitian domination, and a third, unsuccessful, invasion by the megalomaniac savage Soulouque in 1849, created a mutual hatred between the two neighbouring peoples, which is still alive and in quite recent times has broken out in ugly incidents. They caused also the emigration of many of the Spanish inhabitants, so that Santo Domingo, which had possessed a fairly numerous white aristocracy, became largely mulatto, and so remained, though under later republican governments some of the white exiles returned to their abandoned lands. Santo Domingo came also to resemble Haiti in its poverty, its disorganisation, and the violence of its public life. After a successful national rising had expelled the Haitians, the new Dominican republic entered on a long period of faction fights in which the principal chieftains were the uncouth mulatto *caudillo* Santana — a tough and merciless fighter, both for independence and for his own hand — and Báez, his more cultivated but hardly more scrupulous rival. In 1861 Santana persuaded the Spanish government to reoccupy Santo Domingo, and became himself the new captain-general; but the occupation was a failure, unpopular with the Dominicans and burdensome to Spain, which had constantly to spend money on suppressing revolts, and on reinforcing a garrison depleted by yellow fever. These expenses, and rumbles of disapproval from the north at the end of the Civil War, caused the Spaniards to withdraw in 1865. The only result of the reoccupation was an increase in the white population.

Three years later Báez, despairing as Santana had done of respectable independence, persuaded President Grant's government to annex the Dominican republic to the United States; but the treaty drafted for the purpose was rejected by the United States Senate. Báez went into exile and the country slipped further into anarchy, in which the contending factions were distinguishable chiefly by the labels 'red', 'blue', and 'green'. Anarchy led naturally to dictatorship, in the person of Ulises Heureaux, who was the perfect type of tropical tyrant, astute, fearless, vindictive, corrupt. Heureaux governed with considerable success — in the sense of enforcing order and suppressing revolts — for eighteen years; but his private army, his spy system, and his many mistresses were more than the country could afford, and he himself was irreplaceable. His assassination in 1899 left the republic without organised government and burdened with a public debt on which it inevitably defaulted. Various European governments applied diplomatic pressure, in varying degrees, on behalf of creditors who were their nationals; and the upshot was gradually increasing American control, fiscal at first, then political, culminating in 1916 in American military government.

Cuba — larger, richer, more populous, and better known — offers an interesting contrast with Santo Domingo in many ways. Its political history in the nineteenth century — at least in the first two-thirds of the century — was less confused and certainly less turbulent, for the Cubans had no rapacious foreign neighbours within their island. The economic history of Cuba in the nineteenth century, on the other hand, was more intricate, certainly more vigorous. A distinguished social historian has recently described Cuban history as a counterpoint, in which sugar and tobacco are the contrasting, interwoven themes. The fine tobacco of Cuba is one of the most difficult crops in the world to cultivate. Martí wrote lovingly of the devotion of the tobacco-grower, caring for each individual plant 'with his protecting hands, against the excessive heat of the sun, the treacherous cricket, the rough pruner, the rotting damp'. The same patient manual skill is needed in the curing of the leaves and the manufacture of cigars. There is no place in the fine tobacco trade for slave labour, for mass production, for the heat and hurry of the great *central*. Tobacco — in Cuba at least — has always been traditionally a small man's crop. On the eve of the French Revolution there were more than 10,000 *vegueros*, each cultivating his small property with the help of his family, and perhaps one or two hired hands. They were concentrated in a few favoured districts: the famous Vuelta Abajo in Pinar del Río; Vuelta Arriba; and the neighbourhood of Santiago. Their number, and the total area of their holdings, was increasing, for tobacco fetched a good price in the twenty years from the end of the Seven Years War to the outbreak of the French Revolution.

The purchase and manufacture of tobacco, however, was a government monopoly. The royal *Factoría* fixed the amount purchased, and the price, in a completely arbitrary fashion, having regard only to increasing revenue. The *vegueros* were in a very weak bargaining position in dealing with the grasping and corrupt officials of the *Factoría*; and the vexations caused by the monopoly were among the causes of the sharp decline in production which coincided with the French war. There were other and greater causes, however, the most important being the war itself. The war cut off Cuban tobacco from its European market. At the same time, a great and expanding market, almost unaffected (at first) by the war, was opening up in North America; but North Americans did not want Cuban tobacco, which would compete with their own Virginian product. They wanted sugar and coffee; and Saint-Domingue, formerly their principal source of supply, was put out of effective competition by revolution. The war, therefore, produced a boom in sugar and a disastrous slump in tobacco. Cuban tobacco production by 1803 had fallen to one-sixth of what it had been in 1788. Sugar production more than doubled in the course of the war. It was still, in 1815, at 42,000 tons, not much more than half that of Jamaica; but Jamaican production stood still from 1815 to 1820, and then declined, while that of Cuba continued its astonishing increase. It was to reach 500,000 tons in the 'sixties and twice to exceed a million tons before the end of the century.

This remarkable growth of sugar production was made possible largely by the great extent of virgin land. Sugar planters purchased old cattle grants, which had existed since the sixteenth and seventeenth centuries and had never been fully used. It owed much, also, to official policy. The Spanish government, advised by the distinguished planter-economist Arango y Parreño, appreciated the possibility of Cuba becoming a source of wealth comparable with Mexico and had the wit to adjust its economic policy to that end. It declared an open trade in slaves in 1791, and greatly reduced the duties upon them; it allowed traders, of whatever nationality, who imported slaves to Cuba, to export rum and certain other trade commodities free of duty.

It permitted the import of North American provisions to feed slaves. A little later, it abolished import duties on tools and equipment used in producing sugar and coffee, even if they were of foreign origin. Technical development in the Cuban sugar industry, fostered by this policy, was very rapid. French refugees from Haiti are said to have popularised overshot water mills, and to have introduced enclosed furnaces in place of open hearths. The first steam-driven mills were installed in 1819, and the vacuum pan was generally adopted at an early date. Cuba was the first sugar-producing area to recognise the economic effect of large capacity, and from the establishment of Alava, the first of the great *centrals*, was far in advance of any other country in this respect. Refineries also were established during the war, and the refined product might be exported to any part of the empire. No government, in a mercantilist age, could be expected to go much further.

Economic development, especially the development of a large-scale industry employing slave labour, must exact its social price. On a vastly increased scale, in mechanised nineteenth-century conditions, the old story of West Indian economic history was repeating itself once more — sugar driving out tobacco, big properties driving out small cultivators, slaves driving out free peasants, black labour driving out white labour. Like the other islands, Cuba was to run the risks of an exporting monoculture. Already at the beginning of the century there was formed the close connection with the North American market which was to make the island at once the greatest single sugar producer in the world, and an economic dependency of the United States. The consequences of dependence were to follow as the century progressed; dealer would dictate to producer, foreign capital would replace native capital, absentee control would replace local ownership.

The census of 1817 — the first held in Cuba — revealed a population of 630,000, of whom 291,000 were white, 224,000 slaves, 115,000 free persons of colour. Already the whites were a minority. The implications of this situation, to people with Haiti fresh in their minds, were clear, and the energetic intendant Ramírez, with the advice of Arango, set to work on measures designed to redress the balance. The tobacco monopoly was at last abolished; legislation was enacted protecting the titles of smallholders; free passages, free land, and other privileges were offered to European immigrants. A decree of 1818 finally removed all prohibitions of trade with foreigners — a matter of great importance to the tobacco growers (though import duties still discriminated heavily in favour of Spanish shippers). More surprising, in 1817 the Spanish government agreed to a treaty with Great Britain providing for the suppressing of the slave trade. Some of this legislation, notably that which sought to encourage white immigration, had considerable effect. The growing demand in Europe for Cuban cigars, together with the freeing of trade, sufficed to rehabilitate the tobacco industry. On the other hand, those decrees which struck at powerful vested interests, as might be expected, proved very difficult to enforce. In particular a clandestine but barely concealed slave trade continued to flourish. Most Cubans regarded the treaty of 1817 as an attempt on the part of Great Britain to prevent the rise of a competitor in the sugar trade, and the Spanish government was lukewarm, if not insincere. The number of slaves brought annually to Cuba mounted steadily in the 'twenties and 'thirties, to reach a peak of 12,000-odd in 1837; and the trade was not effectively suppressed until 1865.

The steady increase in the numbers of slaves, and the fear of servile mutiny, were important factors in preventing the growth of a serious independence movement in Cuba in the early nineteenth century. Cuba, also, being an island and the principal base for Spanish naval and military operations against the mainland colonies, offered little opportunity for revolt; and the leaders of Cuban society were too fully occupied in making money to devote much attention to political agitations. The loyalty of the 'ever-faithful island' was not entirely proof, however, against the influence of the separatist movement in the rest of Latin America, and the political disorganisation of Spain itself, at that time. Events on the mainland, and divided counsels in Spain, were inevitably reflected in unrest and occasional conspiracy in Cuba. Most of the conspiracies sought, not separate independence, but annexation by Colombia or by the United States. In 1823 the government discovered and suppressed several subversive organisations, including one known as the *Soles y Rayos de Bolívar*, of which the young poet Heredia was a member. The leaders, including Heredia, were exiled. The outcome of these commotions was a decree of 1825 conferring upon the captain-general 'todo el lleno de las facultades que por las reales ordenanzas se concedían a los gobernadores de plazas sitiadas'. This meant virtually absolute power; specifically, the power to deport, without trial, any person whose presence the governor thought undesirable. It was the colonial counterpart of the rigid absolutism of Ferdinand VII, who after the liberal revolutionary interlude of 1821–22 had been restored to full power with the help of a French army.

The decree of 1825 accentuated the already serious ill-feeling between the Cuban creoles and the peninsular Spaniards resident in Cuba. The *peninsulares*, whether officials or business men, resented the social exclusiveness of the wealthy creole families: the creoles disliked the rapacity and the petty tyrannies of peninsular officials and regarded themselves as entitled by their social standing to a greater part in the conduct of political affairs. Havana, like most Spanish-American cities, had its liberal periodicals, its reading-circles, its political discussion groups. The creoles naturally resented the absolutism of the 1825 decree; the *peninsulares* welcomed it, as a means both of putting the local people in their place and of enforcing discriminatory regulations and duties in favour of Spanish trade. The slave trade in particular was mostly in the hands of peninsular Spaniards, and officials, mostly *peninsulares* also, connived at it, or were lukewarm in enforcing decrees against it. Many creoles, on the other hand — including even some proprietors of sugar estates — had serious misgivings about the steady increase of the negro population and wanted the trade controlled or suppressed.

On its political side, the decree was not at once made a weapon of serious oppression. Under Vives, the easy-going captain-general of the time, and under his successor, Ricafort, government was inert and incompetent rather than repressive; and in 1833 public attention was taken off politics by a devastating epidemic of Asiatic cholera. The selection in 1834 of the inflexible, unpopular, but extremely able martinet Tacón as captain-general, brought an electric change. Tacón's appointment was the immediate consequence of the death of Ferdinand VII, the accession of the child Isabel II, and the reliance of the Regency upon a liberal, constitutional ministry to rally support against the Carlists. Spanish liberalism, then as on many subsequent occasions, stood for centralisation, for Benthamite efficiency; liberals in Spain had little sympathy with the wealthy, conservative, slave-owning creoles, who had so consistently shouted their loyalty to Ferdinand VII; and no Spanish government, liberal or otherwise, could contemplate even a suspicion of separatist intrigue in Cuba, the last remaining source of extensive colonial wealth and patronage. Most of the Spanish liberal politicians of 1834 believed, or professed to believe, that the concessions granted by the Cortes of 1812 had led directly to the loss of the Indies. So instead of repealing the decree of 1825, the liberal ministry reissued it, and appointed a captain-general who would make use of it — a soldier who valued discipline and firm administration as ends in themselves, who regarded the talk of liberal intellectuals with intense suspicion, and who notoriously disliked the Cubans.

Tacón's four years of office were years of relentless activity in which he took from the Cubans all the political and social influence which they — or at least their leaders — desired, and showered upon them administrative reforms, many of which they did not want and would never have thought of. He effected great improvements in police administration, in the maintenance of order and the prevention of crime, in the organisation of markets, in street cleaning, sanitation and water supply. He was an indefatigable road builder, and encouraged the construction of the first Cuban railway, from Havana to Güines. His public buildings ranged from a national theatre to the vast, new, sanitary fish market, which still bears his name. At the same time he was ruthless in the suppression of disaffection and arbitrary in matters of justice. Newly constituted military courts, with summary jurisdiction, took over much of the criminal work of the *audiencia* and the municipal magistrates. He used his absolute powers to exclude creoles from places of responsibility and profit and to promote peninsular Spaniards. He antagonised the young liberals by condemning to exile their leader, the eminent writer and pamphleteer José Antonio Saco, author of the *History of Slavery*. He insulted the venerable Arango, whose loyalty and respectability were beyond question. He offended creole conservatism by his outspoken contempt for local social precedence, and undermined the colonial social structure traditionally centred in the captain-general's palace; for an outraged aristocracy refused to accept palace invitations. The hostility between creole and Spaniard, long latent in the social and political life of Cuba, became bitter and open in Tacón's day, especially after 1837, when the sole remaining constitutional right of the Cubans, that of representation in the Spanish Cortes, introduced in 1834, was finally withdrawn. Conspiracy was the inevitable answer, and in the cafés of New York and Madrid exiles from Cuba were beginning to hatch plots for the termination of Spanish rule.

Tacón had no successor of his own stamp; after him, colonial administration relapsed into venal and incompetent inertia. The fault lay not so much with the captains-general, some of whom — Valdés and Concha, notably — were able and energetic, and most of whom were conscientious, as with unreliable subordinates. There was still no serious independence movement, however. The Cubans were too afraid of their slaves, who increased in number year by year throughout the 'thirties and early 'forties as the sugar industry expanded. There was good reason for alarm. The treaty of 1817 with Great Britain had made the slave trade illegal in Cuba. A fresh and more explicit treaty in 1835 reaffirmed the determination of both governments to end the trade. By 1840 the majority of slaves were, in strict law, automatically entitled to their freedom if they could prove to the satisfaction of the Anglo-Spanish mixed commission at Havana that they had been brought to Cuba after 1820. Events in the British West Indies between 1833 and 1838 had made a considerable stir in Cuba, and were well known to the slaves. The proprietors thus faced two different, but related, dangers: if the Spanish government gave way to British insistence, and fulfilled its treaty obligations, there would be a serious attempt to stop the trade, probably backed by British naval force and followed by a rush of manumissions; if it did not, there might be widespread servile revolts. The activities of British agents and the friendly relations between the governments of Espartero and that of Palmerston, seemed to point to the first possibility. In fact, however, the Spanish government stood firm, and the British, not wishing to intervene in a manner which would seriously offend the United States, retreated. Instead, in 1843, a series of revolts broke out among embittered and disappointed slaves, chiefly in the neighbourhood of Matanzas. The risings were suppressed with prompt and brutal severity, among those executed being a number of free coloured men suspected of complicity, including the mulatto poet Placido. The episode revealed to Cubans of property the dangerous instability of the internal situation of the island. It caused a strong revulsion of feeling against the further import of slaves; after 1845 the trade declined, though Spanish officials were still prepared to connive at it and a few thousand continued to enter the island annually down to 1865. The problem of slavery remained, however. Many white Cubans were ashamed of slavery, but almost all feared emancipation. With the example of Jamaica before them, they were convinced that sugar estates could not be worked without slavery. Much as they disliked Spanish officials, they preferred a Spanish colony to a black republic. The events of 1840–43, however, had shaken their confidence in the will and ability of Spain to protect them. They knew, or surmised, that British intervention for the purpose of abolishing slavery had been prevented largely by the attitude of the United States. They saw in the southern states a slave-owning society with problems similar to those of Cuba, but with vastly greater power. If independence was too bold an aspiration for the Cubans, and colonial rule was uncongenial, annexation to the United States seemed more and more to offer an attractive third alternative.

North American statesmen from Jefferson onwards had from time to time expressed interest in Cuba, but proposals for the acquisition of the island were not made in public by responsible people until the late eighteen-forties; a period remarkable for the territorial aggressiveness of United States' foreign policy in other directions also. The desire to annex Cuba was compounded of general and particular motives: a feeling that Cuba, like other territories adjacent to the United States, was 'destined' to become part of the Union; a desire, in the south, to acquire more slave territory; an understandable irritation with Spanish commercial discrimination and obstructiveness; and a characteristic itch to intervene wherever a colonial people was alleged to be struggling for liberty. To these positive motives was added a negative one: suspicion of Great Britain. The British government throughout this period was pressing Spain not only to co-operate in suppressing the slave trade but also to emancipate the Cuban slaves. British motives were partly moral and humanitarian, partly economic, because Cuban 'slave' sugar was underselling Jamaican 'free'. In urging emancipation on the Spaniards Palmerston in 1851 went so far as to say that it would 'create a most powerful element of resistance to any scheme for annexation to the United States'. It was partly to forestall the emergence of such negro 'resistance', and the extension of British influence, that Polk in 1848 approached Spain with an offer to buy Cuba, which was promptly refused.

The Cuban struggle for liberty at this time — in so far as it existed at all — consisted chiefly of agitation by committees of exiles in New York, and occasional ineffectual filibustering expeditions. Three such raids were organised between 1849 and 1852 by General Narciso López, with American arms and a largely American following. López failed to arouse enthusiasm in Cuba, and eventually he was captured by the Spaniards and shot, with some fifty of his followers. A diplomatic counterpart to filibustering was supplied by Soulé, the United States ambassador to Spain, who in 1854 induced his colleagues in England and France to join him in an open report to the Secretary of State, urging the acquisition of Cuba by purchase, or, failing that, by force. This document, the 'Ostend Manifesto', when its contents became public, provoked the celebrated European description of American diplomacy as 'a very singular profession, which combines with the utmost publicity the habitual pursuit of dishonourable objects by clandestine means'. The manifesto was repudiated by the United States government, as the López raids had been; but political agitation for the purchase of Cuba continued, until it was interrupted by the civil war.

Within Cuba itself the strongest support for annexation had come from slave-holding landowners. The civil war, by abolishing slavery in the United States, deprived them, and their counterparts in the southern States, of their principal reason for wanting annexation. Opposition to Spanish rule was not thereby silenced, however; it continued to grow throughout the 'sixties, and from being a movement for annexation led by landowners who sought chiefly to postpone emancipation, it became a movement for independence led by doctrinaire liberals — many of whom, in the coffee-growing areas at least, were also landowners — who were prepared to accept emancipation, and indeed to welcome and promote it. Its principal support was the *junta* of Cuban exiles in New York, which organised propaganda, gunrunning, and the collection of money; but the acknowledged political leader of the conspirators for independence in Cuba itself was Carlos Manuel de Céspedes, lawyer, landowner and liberal, who had already, in 1855, served a term of imprisonment for outspoken criticism of the government.

Céspedes' conduct of affairs was distinguished by courage and singleness of purpose rather than by the guile and the organising skill characteristic of successful conspirators. His declaration of Cuban independence, at Yara in 1868, preceded by the manumission of his own slaves and accompanied by the histrionics customary on such occasions, was premature. It was precipitated by heavy land taxation and by indignation at the manner in which government, in 1867, had evaded its promises of constitutional reform. No adequate preparations had been made, either to secure general support or to raise and equip an army. Consequently the Ten Years War which followed the declaration at Yara was not so much a popular uprising, as a series of irregular guerrilla campaigns in the wild country at the eastern end of the island. In the east, the fighting was bitter and its results devastating; but it never seriously affected Havana and the west. The leader of the insurgents in the field, Máximo Gómez, was not even a Cuban, but a Santo Domingan. Céspedes, elected 'president' by his followers in 1868, was thrust aside in 1873, and killed in a Spanish raid soon afterwards. He left a name for disinterested patriotism which is revered in Cuba to this day.

The Ten Years War would probably have ended much sooner, but for the internecine struggles distracting Spain itself at the same time. The Carlist War ended in 1876, and the Spanish government then took vigorous steps to stamp out the insurrection, despatching to Cuba its most distinguished soldier, Martínez Campos, who also displayed a capacity for negotiation and compromise uncommon in Spanish civil wars. The war came to an end with the Treaty of Zanjón in 1878. The insurgents surrendered. Martínez Campos promised a variety of constitutional and fiscal reforms, including representation in the Cortes — a useless and almost unworkable concession. Provision was made for the gradual emancipation of slaves; a decree to that effect, without compensation, was issued in 1880, and the process finally completed in 1886; meanwhile a vigorous policy of encouragement for white immigration, sponsored by the newly formed liberal party, was set on foot. In general, the treaty combined liberal provisions of an academic kind — some of which were afterwards repudiated or evaded — with a series of severe blows at the creole landowning interest which — in the eastern provinces at least — had supported the rising. It was a treaty of exhaustion. It was followed by seventeen years of uneasy peace.

The Ten Years War inevitably aroused great interest and indignation in the United States. Public sympathy with the insurgents was outspoken and widespread, and often took the form of filibustering and gun-running expeditions, against which the Spanish government protested vigorously but in vain. The war caused serious damage to North American property, and occasional interference with ships wearing the American flag. The most notorious case of this kind was that of the *Virginius*, which made a number of voyages under United States registry, carrying arms to the Cuban insurgents, until 1873, when it was intercepted by a Spanish cruiser and taken into Santiago. There, fifty-three of the ship's company — mostly American citizens — were shot, upon summary conviction by a drum-head court-martial. The remaining ninety-three were saved only by the intervention of the captain of a British warship which happened to be in the harbour. For a few weeks this ugly incident seemed serious enough for war; but the United States attorney-general decided that the *Virginius* was not entitled to wear the American flag. The Spanish government agreed to compensate the families of those who had been executed; and the matter dropped. The truth was that the United States government was not in a bellicose mood, its navy was in no condition to fight, and its attention was concentrated on internal troubles arising from the Civil War. It made no public pronouncements in favour of the insurgents. It never recognised them as belligerents, despite the efforts of Morales Lemus, the distinguished liberal who represented their interests at Washington. It would, indeed, have found great practical difficulty in conducting regular relations with the peripatetic administration of Céspedes and his successors.

The United States government could not escape the Cuban

problem, however. After the Ten Years War four possible lines of political development presented themselves to the Cubans: colonial government as before; local autonomy under a loose allegiance to the Spanish Crown; complete independence; or annexation to the United States. Each of these possibilities had its supporters, either in the openly organised political parties which first took shape at this time or in conspiratorial groups; the choice between them must inevitably be influenced, perhaps decided, by the attitude of the United States. At the same time, American economic interests and influence in Cuba increased steadily in the last two decades of the nineteenth century, and with it American resentment of disturbance and of fiscal discrimination. It was a period of great economic difficulty for the Cubans. The war itself had caused widespread devastation, especially in the east. The coffee industry was permanently ruined, and Cuba began to import coffee. The cost of suppressing the rising was made a charge upon the finances of the island, which was thus saddled with a heavy load of debt. The estates of landowners implicated in the rising were confiscated, and sold either to Spaniards or Cubans of known loyalty, or else to North American companies. The European market for Cuban sugar dwindled almost to nothing, even in Spain, as a result of the development of locally protected beet-sugar industries. The loss of these markets was balanced, it is true, by the rapid expansion of the North American market; but the distribution of sugar in the United States was increasingly controlled by big financial combines, culminating in the formation in 1888 of the Havemeyer group, which became the American Sugar Refining Company, or 'Sugar Trust', in 1890. For the next twenty years this vast concern supplied about 80 per cent of the refined sugar consumed in the United States. The effect of all these circumstances was a steady drop in the price of raw sugar to the Cuban producers, at a time when the industry was struggling to adjust itself to the abolition of slavery. The only remedy was the reduction of costs by greater efficiency, the separation of sugar-growing from manufacture, the concentration of manufacture in fewer and larger central factories, connected by private railways with the tributary plantations which supplied the cane. All this was achieved. The number of factories dropped from 1,191 in 1877 to 470 in 1895: sugar production rose steadily, and reached

1,000,000 tons for the first time in 1894. But new railways and bigger factories required more capital, and capital in the required amount could only come from abroad. In general, British concerns financed and built the railways, while capital for new sugar factories was found in the United States, chiefly among people concerned with the marketing of sugar. At the same time, United States tariff policy sought to protect home refineries by heavy duties on refined sugar, and admitted only raw sugar duty-free from Cuba. The expansion and modernisation of the industry was achieved therefore at the price of the extension of foreign control and the subordination of the producer to the dealer. An analogous development took place in the tobacco industry. The production of tobacco leaf increased steadily in the last two decades of the century; but in order to escape the McKinley tariff (which gave the president power to suspend imports into the United States from any country which 'unreasonably' taxed American exports to it), a considerable number of Cubans engaged in the manufacture of cigars were obliged to move their operations to the United States. It was among the émigrés of Key West that Martí found his most devoted adherents.

Throughout all these changes the Cuban Junta in New York continued its propaganda and its conspiracy for Cuban independence of Spain. Its leadership had by now devolved upon the journalist and philosopher José Martí, one of the most magnetic personalities of West Indian history and a visionary of uncommon power. Martí did not belong to the class of landed creoles who had made the earlier insurrections. He was the son of a Spanish sergeant who had become a captain of rural police in Cuba. Cuban independence, not merely autonomy, was for him a matter of youthful conviction, for which he had duly served a prison sentence during the Ten Years War. From 1880 to 1895 he was in exile, mostly in New York, acquiring a great reputation as a journalist throughout the Americas. He possessed, in unusual combination with his other qualities, considerable tactical skill in politics. His selection of the moment to strike was as skilful as that of Céspedes had been ill-judged. His propaganda was a potent force in rallying American support for a Cuba believed to be groaning under an antiquated tyranny. Cubans, ground between the millstones of Spanish taxation and

American tariff policy, came more and more to attribute both these troubles to their imperial connection, and to reflect that, were they independent, Spain could not tax them, and the United States would have no motive for discriminating against them. These reflections were given a sharper edge by the general depression of 1893, which especially afflicted primary producers such as Cuba; and by the Wilson tariff of 1894, which placed a new and crippling duty on raw, as well as refined, sugar. Poverty and hunger proved the best recruiting agents for the forces which the insurgents collected in the east of the island, where Martí raised the standard of revolt in 1895.

The horrors of this civil war surpassed all that went before. Martí, bent on seeing real action after years of campaigning with his pen, was killed in one of the first skirmishes, leaving the direction of the rising to old Máximo Gómez, and to the mulatto Maceo, who had won a considerable reputation as a *guerrillero* as a youth in the Ten Years War. The insurgents sought to drive the peasantry into their ranks, and to render Cuba valueless to Spain, by deliberate destruction of crops and holdings. Weyler, the captain-general, attempted to deny recruits to the enemy by the establishment of vast concentration camps, whose inmates he could not adequately house or feed. Atrocities occurred on both sides, and were greatly exaggerated, sometimes invented, by the North American press. Maceo was killed in 1896. Gómez, over seventy but vigorous and elusive still, fought on in the east, losing ground. He was saved by American public opinion, which vociferated against the camps and induced the Spanish government to recall Weyler and replace him with the less efficient and less ruthless Blanco. American property, as before, was suffering severe damage. In 1896 President Cleveland hinted at the possibility of intervention. McKinley, the following year, used stronger words, though disclaiming all thought of annexation. Two months later the United States battleship *Maine*, making what was termed a courtesy visit, was sunk by an external explosion in Havana harbour. Responsibility for the act was never fixed, but most Americans believed, or professed to believe, that it was deliberately planned by the Spaniards. McKinley, still negotiating vaguely to preserve peace, allowed himself in May 1898 to be pushed into war.

American victory was swift and complete; and the resulting

American military government was conscientious and ruthlessly efficient. For three years American governors gave the Cubans aseptic treatment, whether they liked it or not. Their administration was honest, in that they endeavoured to punish those of their officials who plundered the public: a thing the Spaniards had rarely thought of doing. The starving were fed, ruined houses restored, roads repaired, schools founded, placemen ejected, drains disinfected. Above all, yellow fever was traced to its insect source and conquered. The intuition of Finlay, a Scot settled in Cuba, was brought to scientific certainty by devoted American and Cuban physicians; and so the Panama Canal became a possibility.

With all this, the United States government stuck to its promise not to annex Cuba, though both the Spanish government and many wealthy Cubans urged it to do so, as a guarantee of peace and property. It annexed Puerto Rico, which was much poorer, though strategically even more important; but in Cuba it encouraged the establishment of a convention, which framed a republican constitution and made an agreement with the United States, including the famous 'Platt Amendment'. By this instrument Cuba granted coaling or naval stations (later reduced to one at Guantánamo) to the United States, undertook not to contract any debt without adequate provision from the ordinary revenue, and consented that the United States 'may intervene for the preservation of Cuban independence (and) for the protection of life, property and individual liberty'. In December 1902 the American governor, Wood, handed over the administration to the first elected president, Estrada Palma. Thoughtful Cubans, looking back to the years of prosperity before the Ten Years War, and reflecting upon the Platt Amendment, the fact of the Sugar Trust and the possibility of the Panama Canal, might have wondered whether they had not exchanged King Log for King Stork; but in the enthusiasm for 'Cuba Libre' these chilling doubts were not expressed.

CHAPTER XVI

THE BRITISH AND FRENCH WEST INDIES
1860–1918

THE PERIOD FROM 1860 to 1870 forms a watershed in British West Indian history. The labour shortage in Trinidad and British Guiana was being made good; a satisfactory scheme of immigration had been devised, and a rising tide of Indian labour was flowing into Trinidad and British Guiana. By 1870 there were 28,500 Indians in Trinidad, and by 1883 the number had risen to 48,000 — about one-third of the island's population. In the same year there were 65,000 Indians in British Guiana out of a population of a quarter of a million. This steady supply of labour enabled the sugar estates to expand production and put the two colonies on the road to prosperity. At the same time conditions developed which encouraged peasants to settle on the land, and this led to an increase in the number of smallholders and in their economic importance. It will be remembered that after emancipation free villages had been established and a landed peasantry had come into existence, but that by 1870 the strength of the first impulse towards community development through ownership and education had lost its strength and the leadership had disappeared. The royal commission of 1882 described the change in these words: 'The first few years which followed [emancipation] saw great activity and a good deal of expenditure by the imperial government and the local governments as well as by private humanitarian organisations and by the churches. By the 'fifties and 'sixties of the nineteenth century the first burst of enthusiasm waned, and education fell into the doldrums. . . .' Knibb and the other missionary leaders of the emancipation period had carried through plans for land settlement and had aimed at educating the labourer technically and as a citizen. The former slaves were held together partly by affection for their missionary leaders and partly by the religious organisations to which they belonged; but by the middle of the century many of the leaders were dead and there was no permanent organisation to keep alive the dynamic of the early years. The pace of settlement slowed down, for the savings of the years of slavery and apprenticeship had been spent, and the price of land had been pushed up. The managers of estates tried to stop the flow of labour from the plantations on to Crown lands or purchased lands. Burnley tells how, in Trinidad, squatters had been encouraged before emancipation to settle on Crown lands, but immediately after emancipation the planters tried to eject the squatters in order 'to condense and keep together the population in such a manner that it may always contain a due proportion of labourers'; and the government itself collaborated in this policy 'by diminishing the facilities of obtaining land . . . by fixing the price of fresh land so high as to place it above the reach of the poorest class of settlers'.

In the eighteen-sixties there was a change of policy. In British Guiana and in some of the islands the government divided portions of the Crown lands into small lots and sold them to peasants at low prices. This was done in British Guiana in 1868, and in the same year the governor of Trinidad, Sir H. H. Gordon, threw open some of the Crown lands to settlers. The Indian labourer enabled Trinidad to expand its sugar production from 20,000 tons in 1850 to 67,000 in 1879; and during the same period planters and smallholders trebled cacao production, pushing it from about 4,000,000 pounds to nearly 12,000,000. In Jamaica the banana trade began in 1870 when Captain L. D. Baker with a little 85-ton schooner stopped at Port Antonio on his way from Venezuela to New York and took a cargo of bananas. By 1890 the trade was fully established, and the banana became the main smallholder's crop. The combination of cheap land and of a profitable crop led to an increase in the number of smallholders in the island from one-sixth of the gainfully occupied population in 1881 to one-third in 1911. The emergence of the smallholder, his economic importance, and the adoption by governments of a policy of land settlement are among the most significant features of this period.

The best book about the West Indies of the eighteen-sixties is Sewell's *Ordeal of Free Labour in the West Indies*. He points to the difference between the other British territories and Jamaica.

Barbados and Antigua were comparatively prosperous, and Trinidad, with a population of from 70,000 to 80,000, was at the beginning of its prosperity. St. Vincent was recovering from the recent depression, arrowroot production had been increased, and the sugar planters, being now assured of labour and freed of debts, looked forward to a time of 'revived and redoubled prosperity'. Grenada, Tobago and St. Lucia were in some difficulty, but their position was not critical. Of all the islands, Jamaica seemed in worst case. 'I know of no country in the world,' wrote Sewell, 'where prosperity, wealth, and a commanding position have been so strangely subverted and destroyed, as they have been in Jamaica within the brief space of sixty years.' Kingston was shabby and impoverished: 'not a house in the city in decent repair . . . not a wharf in good order'; the people were in wretched plight: 'they perish miserably in country districts for want of medical aid; they are not instructed; they have no opportunities to improve themselves in agriculture or mechanics; every effort is made to check a spirit of independence'. What Sewell found was that 'while sugar cultivation in Jamaica has retrograded under a free system, in other colonies it has advanced', and that the country 'wanting nothing but capital and labour' was 'sparsely settled by small negro cultivators, who have been able to purchase their plots of land for £2 and £3 an acre'.

The reasons for the difference were clear. In Trinidad and British Guiana a steady supply of labour made it possible to expand sugar production, and Indian estate labourers provided a profitable market for the peasant who grew foodstuffs. In Jamaica the estates were short of labour. Immigration was negligible. Local labourers were often unwilling to work on estates, and even if they had been willing, the estates lacked the cash to pay them. Jamaican estates declined, therefore, both as sources of employment and as markets for produce, instead of expanding, as they did in Trinidad. Meanwhile, the population was growing; it was 370,000 in 1844 and rose to 406,000 in 1871, in spite of the heavy death rate during the cholera epidemic of 1851. Subsistence agriculture was the only immediate solution. Consequently, as the peasant population grew, more and more people wanted land, and although there were Crown and estate lands lying idle, this land was not readily available to peasants because of the difficulty of transfer and because, sometimes, owners thought that if the peasant was able to buy land he would become too independent. The pressure of the expanding peasant population on the geographical, economic and legal limits which confined it was one of the fundamental causes of the Morant Bay rising. Nor was the labourer who remained on an estate in much better case. He had no security, his employment, and consequently his house and provision ground, depended upon the will of his employer, and when differences arose he could not be expected to feel much confidence in the justice dispensed by a planter magistracy.

By the beginning of 1865 the danger signs were clear, and were pointed out to the Secretary of State for the Colonies by Underhill, the secretary of the Baptist Missionary Society, who drew attention to the increase in petty convictions and in applications for poor relief, the low wages and irregular employment, the failure of crops because of drought and the existence of the truck system. Underhill did more than point to the inflammable material. He showed how it could be reduced by political and legislative reform so as to give fair representation and proper protection; by organising the production of food for export; by improving roads, and so on. The governor at the time, E. J. Eyre, was a second-rate official, obsessed as many such people then were by recollections of the Indian Mutiny; and characteristically he proceeded to court unrest in Jamaica. In his comments on Underhill's letter he told the Secretary of State that the evils complained of did exist but that the main reasons for the prevailing distress were the 'idleness, improvidence and vice of the people'. He made Underhill's letter a public issue by his attempts to refute it, and he later added to the mischief by giving island-wide publicity to the so-called 'Queen's Advice', which was a harshly worded reply from the Secretary of State to a group of poor peasants in the parish of St. Ann who set out their distress and asked for land which they planned to cultivate co-operatively. They were told that it was from 'their own industry and prudence' in dealing with what they had 'and not from any such schemes as have been suggested to them' that improvement would follow.

One of Eyre's chief opponents was George William Gordon, whose father had been attorney of several sugar estates and whose mother had been a slave. Gordon educated himself, became a landowner in St. Thomas, and soon became politically active. He stood as 'the people's candidate' for election to the House of Assembly, and he was a member of the parish vestry. He also founded an Independent Baptist Church and was a vehement and vigorous speaker. He had already clashed with Eyre, who had engineered his removal from the magistracy, and he attacked Eyre strongly during the controversy over the Underhill letter.

During the summer of 1865 matters went from bad to worse, what with the drought, the high prices due in part to the American Civil War, and the obstinacy of Eyre. In St. Thomas there were special grievances over land and over the mal-administration of justice. On October 11 a crowd led by a local Baptist preacher named Bogle marched to Morant Bay, where rioting broke out, property was destroyed and twenty-one white and coloured persons and seven negro rioters were killed. The measures taken to suppress the riot and to pacify the disaffected parish were effective but brutal. Gordon, suspected — without proof — of complicity, was taken from Kingston to Morant Bay, court-martialled and hanged. Five hundred and eighty men and women were killed, six hundred were flogged, and a thousand houses destroyed.

The rising in Morant Bay was not a rebellion. It was neither nationalist nor racial in origin, though Bogle did raise the cry 'Colour for colour'. It was not a rising of negroes and mulattoes against the whites. It was not part of a general insurrection. It was caused by poverty and injustice, by lack of confidence in the central authority and by deep resentments and suspicions which were stirred and inflamed by rumours and by an appeal to religion. No labour movement sprang out of the rising as it did out of the 1937 and 1938 disturbances, because neither West Indian nor Jamaican society was cohesive enough to produce a national leadership or a national movement, and because the wage-earning group was too small to be organised as a labour movement in the way that English labour was being organised.

But the West Indian see-saw was in motion again. Though other crops like nutmeg, cocoa, and limes were important, sugar was still the main support of most of the West Indian colonies. Jamaica was exceptional. There the number of sugar estates in operation fell from 513 in 1848 to 211 in 1877 and to 77 in 1910.

The labour requirements of the estates fell from about 30,000 workers in 1860 to about 20,000 in 1910. In the same fifty years the population of the island rose from 441,000 to 832,000. The period was one of comparative prosperity, however, because of the growing trade in bananas. The smallholder made a substantial contribution to this development. Cumper estimates that 'In 1867 there were about 500,000 acres in cultivation . . . including land under holdings of less than 100 acres. Between 1867 and 1896 the cultivated area increased by 200,000 acres, and only 14,000 acres of this increase related to holdings of over 100 acres. Allowing for the higher proportion of grass and pasture on the larger properties, we are justified in supposing that by 1896 the holdings under 100 acres included more land under intensive cultivation than those of more than 100 acres. By 1910 the cultivated area had further increased to 895,000 acres.' These developments were greatly assisted by the road- and railway-building activities of governors such as Sir John Peter Grant and his successors under the Crown colony dispensation; for the abolition of the Assembly had removed one of the brakes upon the raising and spending of money on public works.

While Jamaica was moving towards some measure of prosperity, Trinidad and British Guiana were again experiencing severe hardships. First there had been strong competition in the sugar market from Cuba, though the Cuban war of 1868–78 reduced this. While the front was being held against Cuba, competition came from a new and unexpected quarter. Europe began to increase its production of beet-sugar and to subsidise it for export. The West Indies could not compete, though sugar was their main support. In British Guiana, Trinidad, Barbados, and the Leeward Islands sugar represented 75 per cent of the total value of exports in 1896, whereas in Jamaica it had fallen to 18 per cent. Britain bought in the cheapest market, and her import of colonial sugar fell from 63 per cent in 1861 to 14 per cent in 1886 and 2.5 per cent in 1900. The selling price of sugar also fell from 29s. per cwt. in 1881 to 4s. 9d. in 1896. Subsidised beet-sugar drove colonial sugar out of the market. British Guiana gained some benefit from the discovery of gold in 1897, but when a royal commission under Sir Henry Norman visited the British Caribbean in that year it found that 'a very serious

condition of things was rapidly approaching'. An account by
the owner of Palmiste estate in Trinidad shows the effect on the
West Indies of beet-sugar competition. The estate consisted of
2,200 acres and up to 1883 had four factories using the old
'copper mill' process to make muscavado sugar, the cost of
production being £14 2s. 7d. per ton. Falling prices compelled
the owner to modernise his factory in order to cut production
costs. He replaced the four factories by one central factory which
was able to produce 15 to 20 tons of vacuum-pan sugar daily,
and cut the production cost of sugar to £11 7s. 8d. per ton, but
he was still unable to compete with the subsidised beet-sugar.
The position was desperate, and the Norman Commission urged
the abolition of the bounty system. As immediate measures they
proposed that land settlement should be undertaken, minor
industries encouraged, means of transport and communication
improved, the fruit trade with the United States encouraged,
and production increased by harnessing science to agriculture,
providing agricultural education, and by making it easier for
planters to expand their cultivations through better systems of
rural credit.

The Secretary of State for the Colonies at this time was Joseph
Chamberlain, who looked on the colonial empire as a vast undeveloped estate and took energetic steps to develop it. There
was a good deal of haggling about bounty-sugar with the
European powers, with the result that in 1902 a sugar convention was signed by which the signatories gave up the payment of bounties on the production or export of sugar. This
gave some relief to the West Indian sugar industry; but Chamberlain went further. He saw that West Indian agriculture
needed scientific knowledge and brains even more than
fertilisers and manure, and so the Imperial Department of
Agriculture for the West Indies was founded in 1898, for teaching
and research. Some governments had moved in this direction some years before. Sir Anthony Musgrave had reorganised
the Jamaican Department of Agriculture in 1879 and British
Guiana, Barbados, and Jamaica had already appointed government botanists. A botanic research station had been set up
in Barbados and sugar-cane was successfully grown there
from seed in 1888. Soon improved varieties of cane were being
produced and cane planters were able to replace the old Bourbon

canes by new and better varieties. This work was of vital importance to an island like Barbados which had to increase its yield without being able to increase the land available, but it was also of special importance throughout the region since West Indian sugar had to compete on the world market. The white transparent and Bourbon canes gave way to better varieties, and when mosaic disease threatened to wipe out the industry a resistant South African variety, the Uba, was introduced. At the same time, factories were modernised, the *central* taking the place of a number of small and wastefully inefficient factories. The improvement in yield of sugar per acre was remarkable. In Jamaica, for example, the average yield in 1888 was 18 tons; in 1950 it was 32.4 tons.

The main flow of West Indian trade at this time was to Britain, the United States and Canada. West Indian sugar had a valuable market in the United States up to 1898, when the Spanish-Cuban war came to an end and the United States began its close trade relationships with Cuba. High preferences were given to sugar from Puerto Rico, Cuba and the Philippines, and a tariff wall kept out British West Indian sugar. The Canadian market remained, however. In 1897 Canada had given British West Indian sugar a special preference of 25 per cent and in 1912 a trade agreement with Canada gave further benefits to West Indian products.

Such were some of the chief developments in trade and commerce. This was also the period of migration, when British West Indians began to go to other countries to settle. This was a new development. The population spilled over from the islands on to the mainland, establishing themselves in Aruba and Curaçao and in Central America. In the eighteen-sixties Jamaican labour went to Panama to help to build the railway; they went in the eighteen-eighties to work with de Lesseps on the canal; and when the United States set about building the Panama Canal in the nineteen-hundreds West Indians furnished the labour. To this day thousands of people of West Indian descent on the Isthmus keep their Barbados, Antigua, Grenada and Jamaica societies. Along the coastlands of the Central American republics West Indians settled, working on the banana and coffee plantations in Costa Rica and Honduras, setting up shops and homes in Limón and Cristóbal, and they moved by the thousand to Cuba to work

on the sugar estates. They went further north to New York and
the other cities of the United States and Canada, establishing
themselves in the great industrial centres and playing a worthy
and important part in many spheres of American life. The story
of West Indian migration in search of wages and education at
this time is an epic of courage and adventure.

The picture that West Indian society presents during this
period is one in which different groupings begin to appear; a
class structure with the possibility of upward or downward
movement from one class to another. The social distances are
still considerable, but they are less than they were in the post-
emancipation period. The groups move a little closer to each
other, but they are still separate; there is a wider distribution of
money and of privilege but there is no pervading and dynamic
feeling of unity.

One way of measuring the growth of a community is by
examining its social services. In the West Indies of 1850 these
hardly existed. Before emancipation the estates had their own
health service and provisions for the care of the sick; but on the
whole people in the West Indies — and in Europe, too — knew
and cared little about the principles of sanitation and public
health, and still less about the causes of disease. Dysentery or
the 'bloody flux', typhoid and typhus, cholera and smallpox,
malaria and yellow fever, the dropsy and venereal disease killed
their thousands and ten thousands. In 1741 the British army
before Cartagena had lost two-thirds of its numbers from fever.
In Haiti at the time of the war of independence the English
troops were defeated by yellow fever. In 1851 cholera decimated
the population of Barbados, Jamaica and the Bahamas. Meanwhile in 1848 the Public Health Act was passed in England, and
health became the concern of the State. The Sanitary Commission of 1869 added years to the lives of people in England by
insisting on the improvement of water supplies, and by enforcing
precautions against bad food and epidemics. The West Indian
governments set up medical services, with district medical
officers and nurses; quarantine regulations were made, water
supplies improved, and water-works and water-mains installed. Preventive medicine has wiped out yellow fever, and
reduced the incidence of typhoid. The foundation work in
public health was laid during these years.

R

Education is a better measuring rod for our purpose because it is an expression of social purpose and of the values which people accept. During the eighteenth century education had been left to the home and to charity; schools were founded by benefactors, and this tradition was continued in the West Indies. Christopher Codrington left two Barbados plantations and some slaves for founding a college to teach medicine and theology, and in 1735 Harrison College was founded for twenty-four indigent white boys. In 1728 a jeweller of Kingston, John Wolmer, left money for founding a free school, and other Jamaican schools like Manning's, Rusea's, and Beckford and Smith's owe their origin to similar bequests. These were all grammar schools, founded by bequests, and attended by a handful of children, for neither the scholar nor the school was highly esteemed in the materialistic West Indian society of the period. Leslie says that in Jamaica in the seventeen-forties the churches were attended only for funerals, and that learning and scholarship were despised.

Planters generally sent their children to school in England. Long judges that in 1770 about three-quarters of the children of the proprietors growing up in Jamaica went abroad for education. The consequences were that 'all the real interests of such students centred in England, which became home to them as it had to their elders. Therein lies the lamentable lack of local pride and feeling already noted, and also to a great degree the reason for the vicious system of absenteeism.' Some West Indians went to the North American mainland also for their education. Between 1650 and 1790 there were at least eighteen West Indian and Bermudian students in North American colleges like Harvard, William and Mary, the College of Philadelphia and King's College in New York, which later became Columbia University; and in 1720 a Jamaican-born Jew called Judah Morris was lecturer in Hebrew at Harvard. Of all these West Indian students, the best known is Alexander Hamilton of Nevis, who went to King's, New York, and later became Washington's chief of staff and one of the architects of the American constitution.

The enslaved part of the population went through an education of a sort. Newly arrived slaves had to be 'seasoned' — that is, they had to be given time to adjust themselves physically to their new environment. They learnt their work under the direction of a driver or from a creole slave, and the trades were taught by craftsmen brought out from England. The purpose of training was to get as much value as possible in labour from the slave, and the same purpose directed the training of the children through the 'pickney gang'. The only people who thought that slaves should be taught to read and write were the missionaries. The planters regarded literacy as a sort of social dynamite, but in 1760 the Moravians were allowed to begin the instruction of slaves in the Christian religion because they taught acceptance of the rule of the master. As the evangelical movement gained in strength in England the habit of reading the Bible spread, and out of this there sprung a mass movement in literacy in England in the early nineteenth century. At the same time in the West Indies the missionaries pressed forward with their efforts to christianise the slaves. In 1797 the Barbados Consolidated Slave Act made it the duty of every Anglican rector to set aside a time every Sunday for instructing the slaves in the doctrines of Christianity, but it was illegal to teach reading and writing.

One of the first statements of the purpose and aims of education in the period just after emancipation was given by Lord Grey, the Secretary of State for the Colonies, in 1838. He pointed out to Lord Harris, governor of Trinidad, that the people who had been freed should 'look to labour on the estates as their main dependence'. He proposed that schools should be set up which would have a curriculum that was largely industrial and would encourage 'a love of employment'. Lord Harris, however, had a more liberal conception and demanded in 1848 that the aim of British policy should be not merely to free a race but to form a society. He put forward proposals for the training of teachers and for free schools paid for out of local rates, with free secondary education for those who passed the necessary tests. Lord Harris's scheme for local government and for secular education broke down on the indifference of local board members.

The Church, and the British government, made an excellent beginning after emancipation and it was reported that in 1838 there were more than 73,000 pupils in day and Sunday schools. Barbados had the most comprehensive provision, largely because of Bishop Coleridge, while St. Lucia and Dominica lagged behind the other colonies. Money came from Britain and from the churches. Two years after the British government gave its first grant for elementary education in England it gave £25,000 for the education of the West Indian people. The grant was increased to £30,000 in 1836 and further grants were made up to 1846. The churches bore the main burden of organising education and establishing schools, and some of the West Indian governments assisted with small grants. A long step forward was taken by setting up colleges for training teachers, the money coming from the Lady Mico Trust. The story is a romantic one. In 1670 Lady Mico left £1,000 'for the redemption of poor Christian slaves in Barbary'. When there were no longer Christian slaves in Barbary to be redeemed the money accumulated until in 1827 it amounted to £120,000. Sir Thomas Fowell Buxton formulated a scheme which the Court of Chancery accepted for using the money to promote 'education among the black and coloured population of British Guiana and the West Indies'. Schools were opened in Trinidad, Demerara, the Bahamas and St. Lucia and training colleges were founded in Jamaica and Antigua with money from the Mico Trust. Codrington College was completed in 1840 and this, with the Mico Colleges in Antigua and Jamaica, gave a permanent footing to education in the British West Indies. More schools and more teachers were needed. What had been done represented a beginning on a very modest scale, for Codrington started with few students, and the Mico College in Jamaica in its early years turned out only ten students a year. Herman Merivale of the Colonial Office saw that in building up colonial societies endowments for education should be put on a permanent basis, since these societies tended to take the short rather than the long view, and made laws to meet emergencies rather than for constructive action. What in fact happened was that when the United Kingdom grants ceased and the economic depression began very little money was provided by the governments for education. In 1861 Jamaica, which then had a population of nearly half a million, spent only £3,700 of public money on education. From the eighteen-seventies, however, the State began to play a more active part. Neglect had produced its results in ignorance, for in Jamaica in 1883 only 22,000 negroes out of 250,000 could write, and the 1891 census showed that about one-half of the people of the West Indies over five years of age were illiterate.

The difference, however, between what existed in 1860 and in 1900 was substantial. The number of pupils enrolled in 1868 in Trinidad was 2,836; in St. Lucia, 2,258; in Jamaica, 19,765. In 1809 the Trinidad figure had gone up to 24,866, while it stood at 6,833 in St. Lucia and 97,091 in Jamaica. Figures like these represented substantial progress; but there were serious deficiencies in the quantity and content of education. Technical and vocational education were poor relations — an interesting contrast with the development of education in many of the states in the south after the American Civil War; there technical and vocational education flourished because they were considered safe for the negro. In the West Indies the whole community depends for its very life on agriculture; but this means field work, which had been the lot of the slave under the old plantation system. The free man therefore wished his child to get as far away as possible from manual work. Those who became peasant farmers, it is true, found some fulfilment of aspirations, despite hard conditions, the inaccessibility of markets, and difficulties over tenure. In general, however, the way of the agricultural worker, subsisting on day labour and a backyard economy, seemed to offer neither dignity nor hope. Psychologically the land worker tended to reject his lot, and aspired to escape from it; consequently, he rejected also the idea that school should prepare children for the life which their parents had to lead. Instruction in such accomplishments as needlework, domestic science, handicrafts and horticulture, when introduced, was widely welcomed; but even in practical subjects the demand was — and to some extent still is — for training in techniques for ceremonial occasions rather than for daily life.

There is this further point, that the curriculum of the schools, and especially of the secondary schools, gave little place to the history of the West Indies and did not help the child to develop an interest or pride in its own environment or country. The common schools helped to bring about social cohesion. They increased social mobility by enabling men of any race or colour to take up professions like medicine or the law which gave prestige and security. They did not contribute as fully as they might have done to the development of a national outlook because they tended to neglect the environment and historical background of West Indian society. The primary-school teacher, however, furnished a leadership which was to make its influence felt in the nineteen-twenties and later, not only in teaching the three 'r's' but in all the social and economic activities of small rural communities. The primary-school teacher, at least in rural areas, holds the key to the orderly development of the British West Indies today.

Of the French West Indies, it would be an exaggeration to say, as one French historian put it, 'A partir de 1848 jusqu'à nos jours . . . la Martinique n'a plus d'histoire'. Politically speaking, however, from the restoration of representation in 1871 down to the period of the great world wars, the history of the islands was singularly uneventful. In form, government was representative on a wide franchise; in fact, the French governor was necessarily still the dominant power in government. Since French policy was made in Paris, and French economic help, especially the protected French market for sugar, was necessary for survival, the local elected general councils could not exercise truly responsible government; nor, as a rule, were the colonial representatives in the French assembly a significant force in the determination of colonial policy. The chief economic activities of the islands were still the making of sugar and the distillation of rum. The annual sugar export of Martinique fluctuated between 25,000 and 40,000 tons; it was 33,000-odd in 1860 and 32,000 in 1913, on the eve of war. The corresponding figures for Guadeloupe were 28,000 and 26,000. Neither the type of ownership nor the methods of the estates and their associated factories changed much during this period, though peasant smallholding made greater progress in Guadeloupe than in Martinique. Such things as primary education and social services hardly existed. Economically and socially the history of Martinique, and to a less extent of Guadeloupe, was one of somnolent stagnation punctuated by occasional riots or natural disasters. The most destructive of these cataclysms was the eruption of Mont Pélée in Martinique in 1903. It was far more disastrous in its effects than, for example, the earthquake which wrecked Kingston in 1907. The whole town of Saint-Pierre was engulfed in ash and lava, and almost all of its 30,000 inhabitants perished. Saint-Pierre was the chief centre of European wealth and culture in the island. It possessed the only secondary school of any reputation — the Lycée Saint-Pierre founded in 1882.

The destruction of the town greatly accelerated the decline of European population and influence, and the transfer of social leadership to a coloured élite. Nevertheless, both Martinique and Guadeloupe remained — and remain — staunchly French in culture and outlook. Both islands accepted military conscription with enthusiasm on the eve of the First World War. Both sent considerable numbers of men to fight in Europe; as, indeed, did the British islands also, without the spur of conscription.

Wars have always had the effect of stimulating West Indian economies by sending up the prices of primary products. This happened again to some extent during the First World War. In the course of the war the price of sugar, despite controls, rose to nearly five times its 1914 level. The French islands were unable to take full advantage of the rise because of lack of shipping, but in most of the British islands production rose sharply for the first time in eighty years. The value of cocoa, cotton, and copra was doubled, and the market for bananas held up well, allowing for shipping difficulties. The general economy of the region was strengthened also by the development of other crops and by the discovery of oil and other minerals. The East Indians on the Courantyne coast in British Guiana were extending their production of rice; the cultivation of sea-island cotton, which is the best long-staple cotton in the world, began again, after a lapse of nearly a century, in the Leeward Islands and St. Vincent; and Trinidad was busy expanding the export of oil and asphalt. The hopes of renewed and lasting economic prosperity encouraged by these developments proved premature, it is true, insofar as they related to agricultural produce; but at least there was hope to feed on. More important still, the war gave an impetus, as wars will, to West Indians' sense of their own community, and pride in their own place. The war record of the British West India Regiment was no mean one. A combination of nascent nationalism, constitutional and administrative reform, and renewed economic initiative was to work startling changes in the next thirty years.

CHAPTER XVII

THE UNITED STATES AND THE
INDEPENDENT ISLANDS

THE INTERNATIONAL LIFE OF the Caribbean area in the twentieth century has been governed chiefly by two interrelated facts: the overwhelming power of the United States, and the strategic importance of the Panama Canal. Under the pressure of these uncompromising facts the Caribbean has once again become, as it was in the old days of the rush to the South Sea, a closely guarded corridor, and the West Indian islands are once again the barbicans of a narrow gate.

The Isthmian Canal project was taken over by the United States in 1903 and the canal opened to traffic in 1914. It provided an immensely valuable new line of communication, in which the United States had a paramount and fundamental interest. The increasing sensitiveness of the American government with regard to the situation in the Caribbean, and the increasing determination which it displayed in preventing European intervention in that area, were closely related to the problems of the defence of the canal. There were three main types of threat to be feared. The most obvious was an armed assault upon the Canal Zone, or its approaches, by a hostile power in time of war. To guard against this possibility the United States began to acquire bases at key points, beginning in the zone itself and in Cuba. Another potential source of danger would be the cession of colonies in the Caribbean, by a neutral power or one friendly to the United States, to another power less friendly. The weapons against this danger were diplomatic or (as in the case of the Virgin Islands) financial. A third and more likely possibility was the occurrence, in any Caribbean country not under European or American tutelage, of disorder involving damage to foreign property, or a major default upon foreign debt, which might entail intervention by one or more European powers to protect the interests of their nationals. Such a situation arose in Venezuela, for example, in 1902. It was largely to discourage future interventions of this kind that T. R. Roosevelt in 1904 enunciated his celebrated 'Corollary' to the Monroe Doctrine; a pronouncement which logically implied the intention to exercise, where necessary, a degree of supervision over the internal affairs of independent states. The Roosevelt 'Corollary' not only expressed the understandable truculence of his own attitude, and that of his immediate successors, during the years when the canal was building; it also gave scope to the didactic purpose which has never been entirely absent from United States foreign policy. It confronted the State Department with a series of dilemmas. Successive United States governments have had to find ways of reconciling traditional respect for self-government and self-determination — both sacred words in the American vocabulary — with a desire to insist on good order and constitutional procedure, or else to establish United States control, in places dangerously close to vital strategic points. The issue has usually been complicated, moreover, by the presence of American business interests.

This problem of reconciling irreconcilables first presented itself in an acute form in Cuba, which is the nearest of all the islands to the United States and which experienced, in its early years of independence, the difficulty which revolted colonies often find in providing themselves with a stable administration. The United States government, true to its traditional principles, withdrew from Cuba in 1902, but safeguarded its freedom of action by the so-called Platt Amendment; an instrument which, by all the liberal rules, should have been as galling to Cuban pride as it was troubling to the American political conscience. In fact, the 'struggle' for freedom, self-government, and so forth, in many parts of the world has often proved to be a figment of the theorist's imagination. It exists, from time to time, in most places, but intermittently, not continuously. Peoples have had self-government thrust down their throats almost as often as they have struggled for it. In Cuba the first American invocation of the Platt Amendment was brought about deliberately by the Cubans, or by a group among them. In 1905 Estrada Palma, after his re-election as president, found himself faced with an armed revolt; attempts to reach a compromise agreement, by negotiation or through the efforts of American commissioners, having failed, the president and vice-president resigned, leaving the country without a government and with no alternative to anarchy but American intervention. This occupation lasted from the end of 1906 to the beginning of 1909, and ended with a general election under American supervision, followed by withdrawal.

After 1909 there were no more interventions in the strict sense of the word, and singularly little continuity in American policy towards Cuba. The Taft administration, whose Secretary of State was Philander Knox — 'a statesman', to quote Professor Dexter Perkins, 'distinguished for his limited knowledge of the psychology of the Latin-American mind' — proffered un-solicited advice on a wide range of topics, including the question of amnesty after the negro revolt of 1912, a contract for harbour development, and a concession for the reclamation of the Zapata swamp. During the 1912 revolt United States naval forces were sent to Cuba, and marines landed, in order to protect American property; and the demands made upon the Cuban government on behalf of resident Americans materially hampered the government's efforts to suppress the revolt. The State Department did not, however, regard this action as amounting to intervention, and explicitly denied the intention to intervene. Obviously, so long as American advice, backed by an implied threat of intervention, was accepted, official intervention was unnecessary. Wilson's administration showed a somewhat less open interest in Cuban internal affairs, exerting its influence through its ambassador in personal conversations rather than through minatory notes; but Wilson also sent marines to Cuba in 1917. This was to protect American lives and property believed to be threatened by a liberal revolt against the administration of Menocal, a sugar magnate who had been elected president in a notoriously corrupt election. The American refusal to go behind the Cuban election results was entirely proper, but had the effect, in this instance, of supporting the authority of an extremely unpopular government. The United States was fast drifting into war with Germany, and Cuba must be quiet. The State Department communications with Cuba were at least frank: 'As the Allied Powers and the United States must depend to a large extent upon the sugar production of Cuba, all disturbances which interfere with this production must be considered as hostile acts.'

Cuba was the first American country, after the United States, to enter the First World War; and at the end Cuba sat at the conference table at Versailles. The war brought Cuba an increased sense of nationality, an opportunity to vindicate her international personality. On the other hand, the end of war brought sudden wealth, equally sudden financial collapse, and increased economic subjection. As always, Cuban-American relations were governed by the state of the sugar industry. The United States government feared — wrongly but persistently — a sugar shortage, and endeavoured to stimulate home production, while at the same time fixing prices to prevent profiteering. Cuba, in urgent need of food, coal and shipping — all controlled by Americans — , was in no position to bargain, and accepted a price fixed with reference to the figure at which the leading American beet-sugar producers agreed to sell. As it worked out, the price, though less than Cuba would have received in an un-controlled market, was fair, and allowed reasonable profit and rapid expansion. It was considerably increased the following year — again, indirectly, through the insistence of the beet-sugar producers and their farmer allies; and in September 1918 the newly established Sugar Equalization Board contracted to buy the whole 1918–19 Cuban crop. This amounted to 4,000,000 tons — about 25 per cent of the world's supply. Ten years before, Cuba had produced 1,500,000 tons, or about 10 per cent of the world's supply. In 1909 sugar amounted to 54 per cent of Cuba's exports; in 1918, 89 per cent. Cuba had become even more dependent upon the market for her sugar than the world was dependent upon Cuba for its supplies. Expansion caused an acute demand for labour, and set in motion a steady stream of immigration, both from Europe and (for a time at least) from the rest of the West Indies. Jamaica, especially, profited in-directly by the temporary employment of some of its surplus population in the Cuban canefields.

Two months after the 1918 contract the war came to an end. The demand for sugar continued to rise. The Sugar Equalization Board sold the 1918–19 Cuban crop at a profit of $42,000,000, to the accompaniment of growing protests from Cuban producers, and an epidemic of investigations in Washington. As a result, the 1919–20 crop was thrown upon the world free of controls. There ensued the wild scramble for the available sugar which Cuban journalists called the Dance of the Millions. The price, which had been fixed at 5½ cents a pound at the end of the war, reached four times that figure, after many fluctuations, in May 1920. Before 1920, although the expansion of the sugar industry had depended upon the North American market and had been carried out, in part at least, with capital borrowed from North American banks or other investors, the actual production of sugar had remained largely in Cuban hands. Estates and mills had belonged mostly to Cubans, and the peculiarities of the *colono* system had ensured that small cane-farmers shared in the increased profits. Now, North American refiners, distillers, confectioners and others, seeking to safeguard their supplies of sugar, rushed to buy mills and estates in Cuba, offering unheard-of prices for all kinds of sugar property. Some fifty large factories changed hands during the boom; thousands of *colonos* sold their rights and their standing crops; and those who resisted the temptation to sell made immense profits, with sugar selling at 20 cents a pound.

But since the sugar shortage which caused the boom was largely imaginary, the boom itself was short-lived, the reaction swift and catastrophic. By October 1920 sugar was down to 7 cents and still falling, and many sugar producers, who had borrowed heavily to expand their business, were in serious difficulties. To add to their distress, the United States government in February 1921 introduced an Emergency Tariff Bill raising the duty on Cuban sugar by about 60 per cent: a tribute levied upon Cuban producers at the moment when they could least afford to pay. More and more mills and estates fell into North American hands, now through forced sale or fore-closure. The Havana banks, which had vied in lending money on sugar, mills and standing cane, now found themselves faced with disastrous withdrawals. They begged government for a moratorium, and when it was granted closed their doors. Most of them failed early in the spring of 1921. Government, heavily indebted, and pledged to an elaborate public works programme, found its revenues dwindling and its treasury almost empty. Only foreign assistance on a large scale, it seemed, could save the republic itself from bankruptcy.

The solution of the financial crisis was made more difficult by the fact that Cuba experienced a serious political crisis at the same time. As usual, the trouble arose from a disputed election, in which the 'government' candidate, General Zayas, was elected president, and his predecessor, Menocal, was accused by the Liberal opposition of rigging the polls. It was partly the entreaties of the Cuban Liberals, and partly the outcry of American bankers and merchants, who were prevented by Menocal's moratorium from collecting their debts, which induced the United States government, early in 1921, to send General Crowder 'to confer with President Menocal with respect to the political and financial condition of Cuba'. Crowder — in the words of Leland H. Jenks, a severe critic of his country's policy in Cuba — was 'the personification of that aggressive altruism which has given the world its great proconsuls'. He knew Cuba well, and had twice before been employed to advise the Cubans about electoral arrangements; but he spoke no Spanish. Crowder's arrival — in a battleship, unheralded and uninvited — began an intervention, in fact if not in name, which lasted for three years. Briefly, Crowder used the urgent Cuban need for a North American loan to compel the judicial tribunals to make decisions on the election results, in order to obviate the need of American intervention, and then to induce President Zayas to retrench government spending, to reform his administration, to expel from public office a large number of expectant political adherents, and to appoint a cabinet whose competence and honesty conformed to Crowder's own exacting standards. In the autumn of 1922 a 5 per cent loan was negotiated with J. P. Morgan and Company, and appropriate taxation imposed for meeting the interest and amortization payments. To that extent, Crowder's mission was a success, however unwelcome his authority may have been to some Cubans, and however dis-illusioning the ultimate results to his own idealism. He left Cuba in 1923, to return shortly afterwards as the first United States ambassador — a friendly gesture. The price of sugar, and with it the economic health of Cuba, improved markedly in 1923. Public revenues increased again, and the year ended, almost miraculously, with a budget surplus. Zayas, president now in fact as well as in name, lost no time in dismissing Crowder's 'honest' cabinet and replacing a number of its members by others, reputed to be equally honest, but unembarrassed by the stamp of Crowder's public approval. Politics returned to normal.

The ultimate result of war, crisis and intervention was to concentrate the economic control of the island more firmly in the hands of a relatively small group of New York financiers, both through the increased part played by the sugar industry in Cuban economic life and the increased part played by foreign capital in the Cuban sugar industry. Jenks estimated that of the 1926–27 crop — some 4,400,000 tons — 62½ per cent was made by American-owned mills, 8 per cent by mills jointly owned by Cubans and Americans, and 4 per cent by Canadian-owned mills. Most mills, both native and foreign owned, were in debt to American bankers and sugar merchants for short-term loans. The total value of American permanent investment in the Cuban sugar industry was about $600,000,000; of such investment in all industries in Cuba, including railways, public utilities, tobacco and so forth, about $1,150,000,000. This great volume of investment involved a steady increase in production, a constant pressure to reduce unit cost of production, and a continued tendency to increase the size of factories. For the Cuban countryman it meant higher wages, regular payment, improved housing, living conditions, and facilities for recreation. At the same time the unbalanced condition of the Cuban economy, the increasing amount of food, clothing and amenities which had to be imported, made — and still make — the cost of living extremely high. Moreover, the economic freedom of the peasant was largely destroyed. Unless he happened to possess a *vega* in one of the favoured tobacco areas he was more and more caught up in the machinery of industrial enterprise, in vassalage to a foreign giant.

Paradoxically, the war, the Dance of the Millions, and the Crowder mission produced, or fostered, a greatly strengthened sense of Cuban nationalism, a new willingness to subordinate family and faction to nation, a new reluctance to seek foreign backing for the sake of party advantage. This change of feeling became apparent in Zayas' time, particularly over the dismissal of Crowder's cabinet. It accounted partly for the support given to the brutal but businesslike dictatorship of Zayas' successor Machado. As if in response, there grew in the United States a new determination to respect Cuban feelings and to refrain from political meddling. After 1923 even veiled interventions ceased. Possibly political purists in Washington shared with Crowder a sense of disillusion over the results of intervention. It is unlikely that, twenty years earlier, the United States government would have tolerated a Machado in Cuba. With all the patriotism and vigorous competence of his early administration, Machado's methods were those of a small-scale Mussolini. They included imprisonments without trial, torture of prisoners, political assassinations, and all the highly developed modern apparatus for preventing the expression of opinion. During the hard years of the depression discontent was met by the employment of hired gangs of gunmen. For two years the University of Havana, a notable centre of learning with roots in Spanish times — it had been founded in 1721 — was closed for fear of student demonstrations. Through all this Washington held its hand and Machado ran his course until armed mutiny and revolution turned him out in 1933. The United States government, probably wisely, did not recognise the short-lived revolutionary government which succeeded Machado, but it extended prompt recognition to the more solid administration formed in 1934 by the scholarly and respected Mendieta, and — more important still — in the same year it gave public evidence of the permanence of its policy by the formal abrogation of the Platt Amendment and the voluntary renunciation of all right to intervene in Cuba. It is true that tolerance and respect for Cuban interests were less evident in the economic field; in 1930 the United States dealt the Cuban sugar industry one of the hardest blows it had ever suffered — the Hawley-Smoot Tariff — at a time when the Cubans were least able to bear pressure. Even this, however, was brought to negotiation in 1934; the rate of duty was lowered, by mutual agreement, from 2.5 cents a pound to .9 cent, and a fixed quota of Cuban sugar guaranteed admission to the United States. Both the United States and Cuba had travelled a long way, in political maturity and mutual respect, since the days of the 'big stick'.

The other two independent republics of the West Indies have differed from Cuba in the present century in that they have been much less dependent economically upon the United States, whether as a market or as a source of capital. Being somewhat more free in that respect, they are both — but especially Haiti —

poorer. The population of Haiti, except for a small, French-educated mulatto group in the towns, consists of negro peasants. The country has little industry and its only considerable export is coffee. Its rural economy is largely one of direct subsistence. The Dominican Republic has a considerable sugar industry, but its economic life is more diversified, and sugar is relatively much less important there than in Cuba. A considerable amount of the sugar crop, moreover, is sold outside the United States. American capital did not enter the country, except in very small amounts, until the occupation by American troops. Bankers and financiers in New York were understandably reluctant, in the first decades of the century, to invest in these disorderly little states; when they did so, it was partly at the insistent urging of their own government. While it is true that the history of both countries, from 1900 to 1936, was largely the history of American interventions, it is also true that those interventions were not made at the behest of American investors. The motives of government were principally political and strategic.

The murder of Heureaux left the Dominican Republic in a state of political and financial chaos, and there was a real possibility of European governments seizing custom-houses and other sources of income, on behalf of creditors who were their nationals. In 1905 the United States government, to forestall this possibility, negotiated — or demanded — an arrangement for the collection of the customs by American officers. This arrangement, and a second one which followed in 1907, were from an administrative point of view highly successful. Similar but more comprehensive suggestions were made a few years later in Haiti, but several presidents, who followed one another in rapid succession at the time, refused to consider the proposal. Knox, however, while Secretary of State, pursuing a policy of transferring the foreign indebtedness of Caribbean countries from European to American creditors, had persuaded the National City Bank of New York to take a part of the stock of the Haitian Bank. Thus the United States government had financial excuses for intervention both in Haiti and the Dominican Republic. During the First World War anxiety over the intentions of Germany in the Caribbean, and chronic disorder in both republics, combined to alarm the State Department, and armed intervention in both countries was the result. In Haiti the occasion was an incident in 1915 in which a Haitian president, who had been driven from office by revolution and had sought refuge in the French legation, was seized, dismembered, and his mutilated body paraded through the streets of Port-au-Prince. In the Dominican Republic the occasion was a disorderly interregnum in 1916, when President Jiménez, pressed to accept a greater degree of American control, refused, resigned, and left the country without a government.

The occupations brought with them great advantages to both countries, of which the most important, perhaps, were the maintenance of order and the reorganization of finances. In each case arrangements were made for the service of the public debt, and measures taken for the adjudication, and inevitably the reduction, of foreign claims against the governments. These arrangements were of more immediate benefit, perhaps, to the foreign investor than to the Haitian peasant or Dominican cane-cutter; but the development of any country must depend upon the soundness of its credit, and to that end United States help has been highly effective, especially in the Dominican Republic. Other physical improvements have been the construction of motor roads (which in Haiti hardly existed); the organisation of public health services, water supply, and sewage disposal; and the provision of schools. This last endeavour, with the aid of educated local people, achieved considerable success in the Dominican Republic. It was less effective in Haiti, owing to the twin difficulties of finding prospective teachers among an illiterate peasantry, and persuading members of the 'élite' group to take an interest in peasant schooling; but the efforts made were not entirely wasted, and have continued since the American withdrawal. Finally, in both countries the occupying power prepared for its own departure by establishing, training, and arming a disciplined local police force. The wisdom of creating a potential praetorian guard of this kind has been questioned by some enthusiasts for democracy. It is true that the commanding officers of the constabulary can use — sometimes, later, have used — their office as a route to political power; and that in the hands of a strong president a loyal constabulary can be an instrument of dictatorship. The relation both of the police and of the army with the civil power has never been satisfactorily

s

settled in either state; but in both the basic need at the time of the occupation was domestic order, protection against a constant cycle of revolutionary violence; and this a constabulary can provide. Dictatorship is a price often exacted, especially from small nations, for their national independence, and it is a price which, within reasonable limits, some at least of the Caribbean peoples seem willing to pay.

In making these considerable (if unsolicited) gifts the United States discovered the truth of a remark which an observant student of imperialism — Kipling — made, years earlier, about a not entirely dissimilar situation in the Sudan: 'It is a hard law, but an old one — Rome died learning it, as our western civilisations may die — that if you give any man anything that he has not painfully earned for himself, you infallibly make him or his descendants your devoted enemies.' The occupations were deeply resented. In the Dominican Republic persons described by the American Press as bandits put up considerable resistance, and in 1917 and 1918 the military government undertook extensive operations against them, especially in Seibo and Macoris provinces. Inevitably, unauthorised acts of violence were sometimes committed by the occupying troops, and acts of repression by the government. The trial of the poet Fabio Fiallo for making some indiscreet remarks about the occupation caused a considerable stir. Full use of such incidents was made by the enemies of the United States in Latin America, who at that time were many. In Haiti feeling was even worse. American officials, having failed to secure the effective co-operation of social or political leaders, encroached more and more upon the powers of the Haitian administration. Also, in order to hasten road construction and relieve unemployment, the old *corvée*, which was still lawful but which had not been enforced within living memory, was revived in 1916. The manner of its enforcement led in 1918 to an armed rising led by an irreconcilable *caco* chief, Charlemagne Péralte, which dragged on throughout 1919 and into 1920. Some two thousand Haitians, seven U.S. marines and twenty-seven *gendarmes* were killed in this fighting.

A permanent policy of intervention, with its implication of bullying, was no more popular in the United States than in the occupied countries, and in the nineteen-thirties the strategic necessity for it was past. The government was anxious to be rid of an expensive and unpopular responsibility; but it would have been highly irresponsible to have abandoned a task of reconstruction half completed, because of a change of political circumstances. The Americans naturally, and rightly, wanted some assurance that their efforts would not be wasted, that the work they had initiated would be continued after their withdrawal, and above all that just debts would be paid. All this meant careful and patient negotiation. In the Dominican Republic the negotiations between Mr. Sumner Welles, General Vásquez, and other political leaders were successful, and in 1924 the American occupying forces were withdrawn. Only one outward mark of tutelage remained: the customs of the island were left under American administration. In Haiti the required assurances were more difficult to obtain. It was not until after the Havana Conference of 1929 had revealed the almost universal unpopularity of the United States in Latin America that negotiations for withdrawal were begun. The occupation — though not, once again, the control of the customs — ended in 1934. By that time the 'Roosevelt Corollary' had been explicitly disavowed; the United States had embraced the policy associated with F. D. Roosevelt and described by him as that of a 'good neighbour'.

The ending of North American control left a political vacuum in the Dominican Republic which was capably and brutally filled by General Rafael Trujillo. From 1930 to 1961 the country was governed by a dictatorship — under various titles — which made no pretence of lip-service to representative, scarcely even to constitutional, practice, and which was probably the most efficiently ruthless government, in both foreign and domestic politics, that the country had ever had. Trujillo's first major task was the rebuilding of the ancient capital — founded in Columbus's time and famous for four and a half centuries by the name of Santo Domingo — which in 1930 was partly destroyed by a hurricane. After the rebuilding, Trujillo renamed the city in commemoration of himself. His activities were not confined, however, to public window-dressing and repression. Improved communications, land colonisation, the encouragement of rice and corn growing (by bounties and protection) and modest advances in social legislation were among the features of Trujillo's administration. Thanks to these efforts, and perhaps even more to the expansion of the sugar industry and the influx of North American capital, the country was relatively prosperous by Caribbean standards. A large share of its increased wealth went to swell the private fortunes of the Trujillo family and their immediate associates; but enough remained in peasant hands to keep the mass of the people reasonably contented. Opposition — repressed by an extremely brutal secret police — came chiefly from an urban middle class denied any part in political life, and, in the dictator's last years, from the Church.

Trujillo's assassination, long awaited in other American capitals, took place in 1961. The United States Government, its sympathies long since alienated, was vigilant to prevent, on the one hand a violent revolution, and on the other the transfer of Trujillo's military dictatorship intact to a successor. The problem of an alternative government was an intractable one; though newly-formed political parties abounded, Trujillo's thoroughness in eliminating his political opponents had left alive few men with administrative experience who were not associated with his régime. Early in 1962, a Council of State of seven men, including two of Trujillo's assassins, under the presidency of Dr. Rafael Bonnelly, assumed the task — with United States' approval and the support of a substantial United States credit — of leading the country back to some kind of lawfully constituted government.

The Dominican Republic in Trujillo's day maintained an army and an air force extremely formidable in relation to the size and resources of the country. These forces both served the purpose of internal repression, and supported an aggressive interference in the affairs of neighbouring states. Ciudad Trujillo was an open asylum for exiled dictators and provided a base for their conspiratorial activities. For such dangerous meddling — specifically for supporting an assassination plot in Venezuela — the Dominican Republic was indicted in 1960 by the Organization of American States and subjected to damaging economic sanctions. Its relations with the neighbouring state of Haiti have been particularly and consistently bad. Haiti is overcrowded, the Dominican Republic relatively empty; but the Dominicans, for reasons economic, cultural and racial, are resolutely — indeed ruthlessly — opposed to Haitian immigration into their territory. The frontier runs through wild, mountainous and sparsely inhabited country, and many Haitians in the past have wandered across, either to seek work on the sugar estates or to settle in remote valleys as peasant squatters. In 1937, a large number of these immigrants — 10,000 according to some estimates — were rounded up and massacred; and though an indemnity was assessed by an international tribunal and eventually paid, the resulting hatreds remained as another potential danger to peace in the Caribbean.

In Haiti itself, though the country's credit was restored by the North American occupation, comparatively little was done to provide a more stable economic foundation for the life of an independent people. Haiti is an over-populated country, with no resources except its exhausted, eroded soil, and its people remain miserably poor. Politically, its history has been relatively peaceful since the occupation. The United States government has refrained from further intervention and tolerated — 'supported' is too strong a word — a series of inefficient and corrupt, but not unduly oppressive, presidential dictatorships. There has been one transfer of government by constitutional process and several by palace *coups*. The mulatto 'elite' has long ceased to play any prominent part in politics. There has been a significant growth of Haitian nationalism of an African type, distinct from the European culture of the 'elite' group. This nationalism tends to prefer créole French to the French of France, and Voodoo cults to catholic Christianity; and one of its features is the growth of a primitive and vigorous school of local painting.

Nationalism in all its forms has become an increasingly prominent feature of the Caribbean scene. Even in Cuba, by far the largest and richest of the islands, the consciousness of economic dependence and relative powerlessness imparted a shrill emphasis to outward expressions of national pride and exclusiveness. The hardships of the great depression accentuated the tendency. From 1931, legislation placed increasing difficulties in the way of immigration, and of the employment of foreigners in many industries. The chief victims of this policy were West Indians, who competed for rural jobs at a time when chronic unemployment was general, and who were regarded in some quarters as a 'cultural liability'. During the 'thirties a considerable number of Jamaicans and Haitians were rounded up and deported.

The general lines of Cuban economic development seemed firmly established. The Second World War, however, damaged the tobacco trade by cutting off the Cuban cigar-maker from his

European customers, especially in England and in Spain. Great upheavals must always hurt an industry which exists to supply products of high excellence to a discriminating market, and the trade in fine cigars has never fully recovered from the ravages of war. On the other hand, war once again encouraged an increase in sugar production; but this was achieved rather by a more efficient use of existing machinery than by any radical change in the structure of the industry. The peak year was 1946, with a production of 5,225,000 tons. There was also a significant increase in mining. Cuba has considerable deposits of iron and manganese; but as it lacks fuel, the presence of these minerals has not led to any great industrial development. The product of the Cuban mines, like the product of the sugar mills, was exported, until 1960, to the United States.

In political affairs, the *Machadato*, and the spontaneous violence of the revolution which brought it to an end, revealed in the Cubans an unsuspected depth of hatred for arbitrary rule. On the whole, the Cubans throughout their history have been long-suffering people, prepared to accept from their rulers a great deal of incompetence, of personal dishonesty, of unconstitutional procedure, for the sake of peace. In these respects the first decades of the republic probably did not differ much from the Spanish régime in the nineteenth century, except that more of the proceeds of graft stayed in the country. In their reaction to Machado, however, the Cubans demonstrated with remarkable unanimity the limits of their tolerance. They would not endure brutal repression and senseless cruelty. The rising of 1933 had no previous parallel in Cuban history. It was followed by a return to elected government and, for a time, by an improvement in the competence, the honesty and the scope of administration. This was a Cuban achievement. The United States government scrupulously observed its undertakings, both explicit and implied, not to meddle in the internal affairs of Cuba; though probably no administration which Cubans were likely to accept could command the entire approbation of North American doctrinaires. Cuba already had a Communist movement — probably the only serious organized Communist movement in the West Indies — apparently imported by Spanish immigrants in the 'twenties. The avowed Communists were not very numerous; but the left-wing government of Dr. Grau San Martín secured office in 1944 with the support — among other parties — of the Partido Social Democrático, which was described by foreign observers as 'frankly Communist', and which certainly contained some Communists. The Partido polled some 122,000 votes in 1944. It was well represented in trade-union circles, especially in the Confederation of Cuban Workers which, like many West Indian trade unions, had become a powerful factor in local politics.

At the other end of the effective political scale from Grau San Martín stood the remarkable figure of Sergeant — later President — Batista, the chief architect of revolutionary success in 1933–34, with his skill in organizing the non-commissioned-officer element in the army for political ends; with his flair for picking and supporting respectable presidents for years before he sought that office himself; with his genial (and therefore tolerable) periods of personal rule between 1934 and 1944. Batista's political strategy was both opportunist and flexible. He even accepted, for a time, a working arrangement with the Communists. Throughout this period, however, he never repudiated the political principles of his revolutionary days. His influence did not prevent the adoption of an orthodox liberal constitution in 1940 and the promulgation of a strict and explicit electoral code in 1948. In 1944 he went into a voluntary and strategic exile, and in 1952 stood constitutionally for election as president. When the election seemed likely to go against him, however, he resorted to a military *coup*, which inaugurated a new period of personal dictatorship. During this period Batista, like many other dictators, was chiefly concerned to maintain himself in office as long as possible, and to secure his own private fortune against the danger of revolution. The rapacity of the leadership, the brutality of the police, the corruption of the government and its indifference to demands for social services and economic opportunity, all recalled the last years of Machado. When Dr. Fidel Castro collected his irregular army in the Sierra Maestra and proclaimed an armed revolution, Batista, with his professional army, was able for many months to resist the threat; but his civil support behind the lines crumbled rapidly, and at the end of 1958 he was driven from office. Like other exiled dictators, he fled to the Dominican Republic, leaving the field to Dr. Castro and a group of revolutionary enthusiasts totally inexperienced in the task of government.

The proclaimed objects of the Castro revolution had included traditional liberal items — the restoration of the constitution of 1940 and the electoral code of 1943 — and land reform. After victory, the constitutional objects were quickly forgotten. Like many other successful revolutionaries, Dr. Castro found it necessary to govern by propaganda and police, to shoot large numbers of his political opponents and to imprison many who had supported him against Batista but subsequently differed from his policies. The Communists in his *entourage* — semi-professional revolutionaries in a crowd of amateurs — rapidly extended their influence, monopolising the instruments of mass propaganda and using them incessantly, insisting upon a strict revolutionary orthodoxy in all public speech. The treatment of universities is usually a reliable measure of the tolerance and the self-confidence of a government. The University of Havana had been closed for considerable periods by both Machado and Batista. Under Dr. Castro it was bullied into conformity, in teaching and writing, with the current official doctrine and jargon. Some two-thirds of its staff went into exile.

The economic objects of the revolution, on the other hand, were pursued with great vigour. Confiscation of large properties and distribution of land to peasant co-operatives began on a scale without precedent in the Caribbean, and work was started on impressive schemes for rural housing, rural education and medical services. These radical departures won for the government the enthusiastic support of a peasantry long accustomed to poverty and hopeless economic dependence. They went to the root of rural discontent, and once made they were irrevocable. They entailed, on the other hand, heavy expense and diplomatic and military hazards. Much of the confiscated property belonged to North American concerns; an understandable resentment in the United States against the confiscations was quickened to shrill fury by reports of the Communist sympathies of the confiscators. Such a reaction was understood and expected — indeed positively welcomed — by the more extreme of Dr. Castro's advisers. Anti-American nationalism, an emotional rejection of dependence, was latent in the revolution from the beginning. When Batista fled, another scapegoat was needed. To maintain the momentum of a revolution which had neither a party organization nor a clear-cut programme, it was necessary to represent the United States not only as a past oppressor but as a present enemy. The United

Eighteenth- and nineteenth-century Spanish, twentieth-century American: Calle Tanca, San Juan, Puerto Rico

[Courtesy of U.S. National Parks Service]

An interior staircase in the same house
[*Courtesy of Dr. J. M. Pérez Cabrera*]

An eighteenth-century town house in Cuba: Casa
del Marqués de Arcos, Havana, now a lodging-
house

States government appeared to accept this rôle by the assistance it gave to an inept counter-revolutionary landing at Cochinos Bay in 1961; and its attempt — which met with only limited success — to arraign Cuba before the Organization of American States as a danger to the peace of the hemisphere. More it could not do, without eating thirty years of protestations of respect for Latin-American sovereignties; and without incurring the risk of a war which might spread far beyond the boundaries of Cuba. Cuba, therefore, was not immediately attacked or threatened; but the economic consequences both of American displeasure and prodigal internal spending were serious. Sugar exports to the United States ceased; the tourist trade disappeared; debts mounted; and shortages of imported commodities, including food, became acute enough by 1962 to necessitate rigorous rationing. Inevitably, the Cuban government turned to Russia. From that quarter, help was quickly forthcoming: purchases of Cuban sugar, credits to buy Russian goods, the services of technical, possibly military advisers, proposals to build a Russian fishing harbour on the Cuban coast within ninety miles of Guantánamo. So the Cold War, with its competition in conferring suspect favours, entered the American hemisphere through the internal disorders of a small Caribbean state.

CHAPTER XVIII

THE CARIBBEAN COLONIES
1918–62

THE MOST STRIKING SINGLE FACTOR in the political life of the West Indies in recent times has been the growth of local nationalisms. Feelings of local pride and separateness, the desire of island communities to run their own affairs, are not merely the invention of local demagogues (though such people have sometimes exploited them); they are deep-seated and widespread, and no political arrangements in the West Indies can safely be made without giving them their due weight. On the other hand, no people can live entirely to itself, and the West Indians more than most are closely linked to the outside world by economic, cultural and traditional ties. Most West Indian politicians are well aware of this. Indeed, one of the most difficult problems confronting them is how to utilise the emotional and political advantages of nationalism without suffering the economic disadvantages and assuming the administrative burdens of national independence.

This problem was posed in its most acute form in the island of Puerto Rico. Puerto Rico had been one of the poorest and least considered of the Spanish colonies. Its value had lain chiefly in the great fortresses at San Juan. At the end of the nineteenth century it differed from most West Indian islands in that it had never developed extensive slave-worked plantations and its population was almost entirely white. The island did not rebel against Spain, but nevertheless was ceded to the United States by the Treaty of Paris in 1898, and so lost the autonomy which the Spanish government had tardily conceded in 1897. It again became, like most of the British islands at that time, a colonial possession; but, unlike them, it differed profoundly in language and traditions from its new metropolitan rulers. In the first Organic Act of 1900 Congress created a system of government resembling that of some British Crown colonies; power was to reside chiefly in a governor and officials appointed in Washington; there was to be a legislature, with a nominated upper house and an elected lower house; and a supreme court, also appointed in Washington. These arrangements caused considerable disappointment among those Puerto Ricans who had hoped for admission to the United States, or, pending such admission, for the restoration of an autonomous government such as that of 1897. Their disappointment was not counterbalanced by any obvious or immediate economic gain; for though the inclusion of Puerto Rico within the tariff wall of the United States brought rapid expansion and great wealth to the sugar industry, the industry itself came under the control of three or four American corporations, which acquired in a few years — despite legislation forbidding such concentrations — more than half of the land suitable for cane-growing in the island. The remaining sugar lands belonged mostly to small cane-farmers, who depended on selling their canes to the American-owned mills. A big sugar corporation was in many ways a state within the state. The benefits of economic union with the United States were largely lost to the people of the island. The first enthusiasm for incorporation in the United States quickly evaporated, to be succeeded in the minds of many by vague aspirations to complete independence.

Public opinion in the United States also — when it considered the matter at all — was uneasy about the situation in Puerto Rico. The island was of little direct value to the United States as a possession, except in the negative sense that its use as a potential naval base must be denied to other major powers. Imperial responsibility was a new experience for Americans, whose thinking on the subject still commonly found expression in the concepts of 1776. Elected officials, for example, were associated, somewhat uncritically, with liberty, appointed officials with repression. These considerations affected the amendments to the original Organic Act, enacted by Congress in 1917, creating an elected senate and depriving the governor's executive council of its powers of legislation. Puerto Ricans were declared to be United States citizens, though obviously they could not exercise the full rights of citizenship unless they resided in the continental United States. The constitutional position of Puerto Rico still depended upon legislation by

Congress, and the more senior officials continued to be appointed in Washington. These cautious enactments failed to satisfy either Puerto Rican pride or American conscience. The only possible escapes from an uneasy relationship seemed to be either formal independence — which, in the economic and geographical circumstances, would be largely illusory — or else statehood within the Union, attainment of which depended upon a complex array of political factors, many of which had nothing to do directly with Puerto Rico.

No further constitutional changes of importance were made in the next thirty years; and during that time it became clear that neither of the two ready-made solutions provided exactly what the Puerto Ricans, or at least their leaders, really wanted. The reasons for this were mainly economic. The Puerto Rican sugar industry, which had been of minor importance in Spanish times, grew rapidly under the directing force of the United States tariff and United States capital, until it dominated the entire economy. Not only did it provide the main outlet for employment and investment; it gave the impetus also for the development of a network of ancillary institutions — transport, communications, power, banking, and so forth. Within the limits of this growing monoculture, total output and income grew rapidly under American rule; but population grew more rapidly still. Sanitation and medical services, though not good enough to prevent the prevalence of debilitating diseases, were sufficient to keep the death-rate surprisingly low, considering the economic conditions. The gains in total income were largely absorbed by the increase in the number of consumers; and in the sugar industry, the backbone of the economy, expansion of total income was in any case limited, internally by the amount of land available, externally by the international sugar quota system. The economic situation, never very favourable, deteriorated greatly as a result of the great depression, and throughout the nineteen-thirties most Puerto Ricans suffered serious distress. The federal government did its best to remedy the situation, both through the efforts of the Puerto Rico Reconstruction Administration, and through relief grants and loans which, from 1933 to 1941, amounted to some $230,000,000; but even these large sums only alleviated distress, without doing much to strengthen the foundations of the economy. Federal initiative received relatively little spontaneous support from the Puerto Rican public, among whom the prevailing feelings in the 'thirties seemed to be apathetic dependence and hopelessness.

It was the peculiar merit of the Popular Democratic Party, in making its first bid for office in 1940, that it bravely abandoned the traditional legal-constitutional-political grounds of party difference and set out to rally public support for a programme of economic and social reform. The party's achievement, both political and administrative, in this direction has been remarkable. Its policy has embraced three main features. The first is what may broadly be termed 'social reform', and includes the acquisition of land for smallholdings and 'proportional benefit' farms; the strengthening and regulation of the position of trade unions — usually of weak and tardy growth in a sugar economy; and the beginnings of a social security system. The second feature has been the improvement of the public services and facilities, both to lay the foundations of economic expansion and to encourage social progress. Electric supply, transport, water supply, and sewerage have all been made the concern of separate governmental 'authorities', and the facilities have been greatly improved and expanded. Much money has been spent on education and health services, and large-scale slum clearance and public housing schemes have already made notable progress.

The third, and boldest, aspect of the programme has been the direct promotion of economic development. In the face of the reluctance of private enterprise to take risks in untried fields, the insular government in 1942 created an Industrial Development Company for the purpose of opening up new manufacturing opportunities, and established a Development Bank to provide long-term investment credit. The earlier policy of promoting industrial development through the activities of government-built and operated factories has given way, since the Second World War, to attempts to attract mainland industries and capital to the island by means of tax exemption, industrial services, loans, provision of buildings, and other forms of assistance. Over two hundred manufacturing concerns of various sizes have been established in this way in Puerto Rico, mostly in the textile or clothing fields, or in assembly. Attempts have been made also to promote agricultural development by means of research, land reclamation, the introduction of new crops, and so on; these attempts have been less successful, but some progress has been made. All in all, the Puerto Rican economy has made great gains in the last twelve years. Production of goods and services has nearly doubled; and the material level of living of the average Puerto Rican is higher than it has ever been.

All this represents a remarkable achievement; and most remarkable of all, perhaps, is the evidence which it affords of the administrative competence of the island government, and the extraordinary corporate enthusiasm among all classes of Puerto Ricans which has replaced the apathy of the 'thirties. It represents, among other things, a striking tribute to leadership. Elected politicians who can combine high administrative ability with great political magnetism, and with transparent integrity, are rare indeed. Luis Muñoz Marín would be an eminent figure on a much larger stage; his willingness to accept administrative responsibility as well as political leadership has been Puerto Rico's good fortune. Other parts of the West Indies have suffered much from politicians who would not, or could not, administer. Nevertheless, in comparing the development of Puerto Rico with that of other West Indian colonies it must be remembered that external circumstances have been extremely favourable to Puerto Rico. The high level of economic activity in the United States since the Second World War has been a crucial factor. A strong continental demand has kept up the prices of Puerto Rican agricultural products; high taxes and high wages in the United States have supplied a powerful inducement to American industry to set up factories in Puerto Rico; and — most important of all, perhaps — several hundred thousand Puerto Ricans have found employment in the United States. Air travel is easy and rapid, and the island government has done all in its power to make it cheap. Year by year, over the last ten years, emigration has drawn off between one-half and four-fifths of the natural increase in population. Emigration has been of vital help to an overcrowded island not only demographically, in reducing the pressure of population upon resources, but economically also, because the emigrants send large sums of money back to Puerto Rico. Without the safety-valve of emigration the industrial and agricultural developments which have taken place would have been little more than

Coconuts on an estate

[*Photo: Packer, Kingston*]

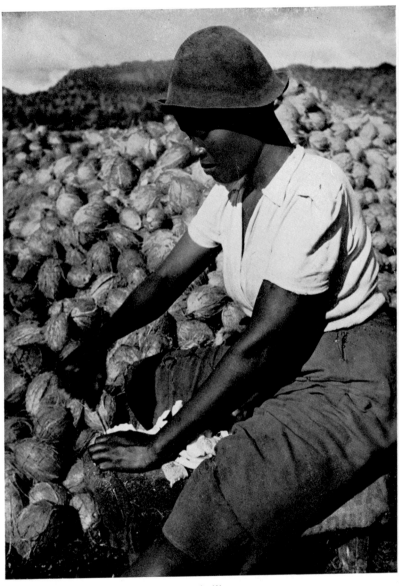

Coconuts: shelling copra

[Photo: Packer, Kingston]

palliatives; for no action has yet been taken to limit population increase, and perhaps no action could be effective in present circumstances. Even with emigration Puerto Rico imports more than half its food, still has a negative balance of trade and unfavourable terms of trade, still bears a heavy burden of unemployment. The productivity of Puerto Rican agriculture and manufacture is still low, partly because of low capitalization and inexpert management; and despite the striking rise in output and level of living, the average per capita income is still less than one-fourth that of the United States. Puerto Rico is still, therefore, a relatively poor country.

These economic considerations go far to explain the peculiarities of the constitutional history of Puerto Rico. In such circumstances complete political independence was out of the question. There is, it is true, a nationalist party, some members of which, in the spring of 1954, made their way into the House of Representatives in Washington and shot five Congressmen. The comparative indifference with which this news was received by the American public contrasted sharply with the shocked horror which it caused in Puerto Rico. Among Puerto Ricans the nationalists are a small and discredited band of fanatics. The traditional alternative to independence was, of course, statehood. Other areas which the United States had at various times annexed from its neighbours had become states after a period of tutelage as 'territories', and this seemed to many Americans an obvious aspiration for the Puerto Ricans. It did not, however, and apparently does not, command the support of a majority of the people of Puerto Rico. Statehood would mean federal taxation, the loss of the peculiarly favoured position enjoyed by the island, under the Foraker Act, since 1900. A decision to enter the Union as a state, moreover, would establish a frame of relations — as American history has abundantly demonstrated — both rigid and irrevocable. A new political form was required which would avoid these disadvantages, while permitting local self-government and self-respect.

In 1947 the governorship of Puerto Rico was made elective. This step, which in other places has so often produced either popular dictatorship, or administrative mediocrity, had a fortunate outcome in Puerto Rico. Muñoz Marín, the first elected governor, and his associates in government, found a way of avoiding the political dilemma by means of a 'Common-wealth' — *Estado libre asociado* — and induced Congress in 1950 to accept it. The concept itself was both ingenious and workable, and ingenious devices were used to give a special symbolic significance to its introduction: referenda in the island, and a revocable 'compact' with the Congress of the United States. The relation so created by Law 600 and the corresponding Federal Relations Statute bears a superficial similarity to the British concept of 'Dominion status'; but the similarity is misleading. The British Dominions are associated but independent kingdoms (or, in one or two cases, republics). Puerto Rico is not independent. It is self-governing in all local matters, but its defence and foreign relations are handled by the United States. The federal government, in its normal sphere of activity, operates alongside the island government, as it does in the states of the Union. Puerto Rico, on the other hand, pays no federal taxes, and all customs duties collected in the island, or on Puerto Rican goods entering the continental states, are refunded to the island treasury. In some ways the constitutional arrangements are nearer to those of the French than to those of the British Caribbean; but whereas the French islands send delegates to the National Assembly in Paris, Puerto Rico — on the principle of no representation without taxation — has no voting representatives in Congress. The *Estado libre asociado* is, in fact, unique. It is a notable example of wisdom and ingenuity, in devising constitutional machinery to suit a difficult social and economic situation.

All the metropolitan governments having interests in the Caribbean have lately, in their different ways, pursued policies designed to develop West Indian self-government and to devolve responsibilities upon local shoulders. Corresponding local aspirations have sometimes preceded, but occasionally lagged behind, metropolitan policy. In almost all cases the main obstacles to genuine self-government have been economic, and this is especially true in the British West Indies. The differences between the situation of Puerto Rico and that of the British West Indies are considerable. The British West Indies are widely scattered; they include one island — Jamaica — which is comparable in size and population with Puerto Rico, but also many others of varying size, down to mere scrub-covered rocks supporting a few families. They vary greatly among themselves. They lie far from Great Britain; British policy and (for the most part) West Indian aspirations have in recent years contemplated not only self-government but also self-reliance and self-support. Puerto Rico lies close to the United States; North American policy and (for the most part) Puerto Rican aspirations, while contemplating self-government, have sought also comprehension within the economic and demographic frontiers of the United States.

These are important differences; but there are also underlying similarities in the two stories. The British West Indies, like Puerto Rico, experienced hopelessness and resentment in the 'thirties, hope and renewed constructive activity in the 'fifties. Their external circumstances have been much less favourable; but like Puerto Rico they have lately received considerable outside help, and their internal reaction has shown a like optimism and vigour. Trinidad possesses, of course, valuable resources of oil and asphalt, which alone make the island relatively rich, and Trinidadians are a lively, cosmopolitan, experimental people. In British Guiana and Jamaica the development of bauxite-mining — chiefly, it is true, by American and Canadian companies — is creating employment and bringing in money, despite the low rate of royalties. In Jamaica and Trinidad a considerable range of local industries has lately been established, including matches, cement, textiles, coconut oil products, glass, and other smaller concerns. Less spectacular, but still substantial, innovations have been made in agriculture. A notable achievement in Jamaica has been the development of stable local breeds of tropically-adapted milk and beef cattle; a development which has coincided most happily with the decline in the demand for draught animals. Even in forgotten British Honduras a determined effort has been made to develop agriculture, notably citrus growing at Stann Creek, in place of exclusive reliance on fishing and the exploitation of natural timber.

Some of the initiative and much of the capital for these developments has come from outside sources, public and private. The Colonial Development and Welfare Acts of 1940, 1945 and 1949 provided funds for the colonial empire as a whole; but a special Comptroller for Development and Welfare, with a technical and research staff, was appointed in 1940 for the West

T

Indies, not to spend the money voted, but to assist governments in framing schemes which, when approved by the Secretary of State for the Colonies, would be eligible for grants. Up to 1950 the West Indies had received, in grants and loans, some £18,700,000 out of a total £76,400,000 granted or lent to the colonial empire as a whole. Private capital investment from outside sources has also been considerable. But a great deal of initiative and a surprising amount of 'risk' capital has been found within the West Indies. Governments have been generous in tax concessions to pioneer industries, and vigorous in encouraging enterprise. In Jamaica, particularly, the Industrial and Agricultural Development Corporations, established in 1952, have already demonstrated their value as centres for collaboration between business and government, and as agencies for intelligent and imaginative economic planning.

As in Puerto Rico, so in the British West Indies only time can reveal to what extent all this optimism will be justified and all this vigour sustained. Meanwhile, one ineluctable fact remains: the central position of the sugar industry. The price of sugar is still the barometer of West Indian prosperity. It had been high in England during the First World War, and mounted higher still after 1920, when price control was abandoned; but it began to fall in 1923, and fell catastrophically after 1929 to reach the lowest figure in its history — less than £5 per ton — in 1934. Lord Olivier, in his report of 1930, urged a substantial increase in preferential protection, but this was not granted until the eleventh hour, in 1934. The industry, meanwhile, strove to set its own house in order and to offset low prices by increased production. It did this by amalgamating factories, by closing small and inefficient units, by reducing the cost of production in field and factory, and, especially in Jamaica, by irrigation, which brought much virgin but arid land into cultivation on the south side. The Moyne Commission in 1939 remarked on the increase of production, from 370,000 tons in 1928 to 620,000 tons in 1938, and added that 'the preferential assistance which the industry had received has been a vital factor'. Limits were set to the increase, however, by the International Sugar Regulation of 1937, which, in a not very successful attempt to raise prices, apportioned world production on a quota basis. In these circumstances increased efficiency combined

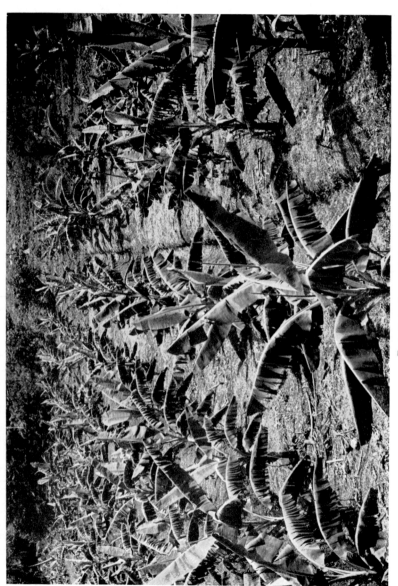

Bananas on an estate
[*Photo: Packer, Kingston*]

Ground provisions in the market
[*Photo: Packer, Kingston*]

Ground provisions on a peasant holding
[*Photo: Packer, Kingston*]

with preference was not enough to guarantee the prosperity of the industry; certainly not enough to guarantee a living wage to those employed in the canefields — a fact to be borne in mind in discussing the riots and disturbances of 1935-38.

As had often happened before, war brought a reprieve. Demand increased and quantitative control was abandoned. The Ministry of Food became in 1939 the sole importer of sugar for the United Kingdom, and remained so until the end of 1952. It became also the agent for supplying Canada and other Commonwealth countries. The price, negotiated from year to year, was increased as costs of production rose, reaching a peak of £42 6s. 8d. per ton (cf. U.K.) in 1953. By that time, however, quantitative controls had been re-established. The Commonwealth Sugar Agreement of December 1951, and the International Sugar Agreement of October 1953, prescribed quotas for the sugar-exporting countries. In the negotiations in 1950-51 the West Indian producers, who were then exporting some 740,000 tons annually, asked for a quota of 1,100,000 tons in the British market. The United Kingdom government in the end agreed to buy 925,000 tons of West Indian sugar, at prices guaranteed to be reasonably renumerative. This was considerably less than the West Indies could produce, given increased guarantees and encouragement; but the neo-mercantilist age could not be expected to last for ever. The agreed arrangements were to last until 1960.

Long-term contracts have given a measure of security to the industry and so to the community. They are essential — as the Moyne Commission pointed out — because 'there is a radical difference between the economic difficulties that face the West Indies today, and those they had to encounter in the nineteenth century. Then the world demand for almost every tropical product was increasing so rapidly as to outstrip . . . the available supply . . . but the development of new productive areas has been carried so far that the productive capacity seems now to be greatly in excess. . . .' The war-time and post-war arrangements have placed the British West Indian industry in a much stronger position than before. It is much more closely organised. During the war, to safeguard the future of the industry and ensure that war-time arrears in maintenance of capital equipment would be made good, mutually agreed reserve funds were established by legislation in the Commonwealth exporting countries concerned. The funds were built up by the payment of a specified contribution in respect of each ton of sugar exported. They were to be used for price stabilisation, capital rehabilitation and labour welfare. At the same time, associations of sugar manufacturers were formed to negotiate prices, pool resources, provide for scientific research, use modern techniques, and act on a regional basis in the interests of the industry.

The same tendency towards common action appeared even earlier in the banana industry in Jamaica, which also faced grave difficulties during this period. Though sugar was the predominant industry in the West Indies, bananas were the principal crop in Jamaica. Sugar is mostly a plantation crop, but banana cultivation could be — and was — undertaken by a large number of smallholders. Moreover, unlike sugar, which offers only seasonal employment to the majority of those engaged in its production, bananas can be harvested throughout the year. Bananas are essential to the well-being of rural Jamaica. In 1929 the Banana Producers' Association of Jamaica was formed to consolidate the producers into one body for protection and co-operative action. This organisation has proved, on the whole, a notable success. Certain local factors helped to counteract monopolistic tendencies and to protect the independence of the banana planters and of the people as a whole. First among these influences was the authority of the government, which ensured stable conditions and respect for law, and rendered the island less vulnerable than the 'banana republics' to coercion by foreign corporations. The United Fruit Company, which has usually taken at least half of the Jamaica crop, nevertheless failed to secure, by threatening to cut its passenger service, monopolistic privileges such as the exclusive use of a new pier and control over a railway. Having good roads and railways, Jamaica was never dependent on a railway run by a fruit company. Having satisfactory retail shops, it was not baulked by the problem of company commissaries competing against local business. With no one company dominating the chief ports, competing companies were able to enter the banana trade. Alone among the banana-exporting countries, Jamaica produced a body of specialised banana buyers who knew the country and were prepared to organise purchase and collection on behalf of any company which cared to employ them. These men served the Association well. By 1931 it handled one-third of the total output and with government assistance it ran a regular shipping service and did its own marketing. The structure of the Association was changed in 1936, when it was transformed into a private trading company; but the company works closely with the All Island Banana Growers' Association, which is itself another example of the growth of primary producer organisations. The value of the Association lay not only in its own marketing activities but in the fact that it maintained a state of competitive buying, so that other fruit companies normally paid considerably higher prices in Jamaica than in countries where they held monopolies. An interesting, and quite unforeseen, outcome of this competition was the discussion between Mr. Norman Manley, as legal representative of the Association, and Mr. Samuel Zemurray, as president of the United Fruit Company, which led to the gift by the company of one cent for every stem exported for the cultural development of the island and its peasantry. This was the origin of Jamaica Welfare Ltd., whose activities and methods have won wide recognition within and outside the Caribbean area.

The Jamaican banana industry showed an astonishing resilience in the face of recurrent adversity. The Second World War, which brought prosperity to sugar growers, brought banana growers near to ruin. Shipments to Great Britain stopped in 1940 and were not resumed until after the war. Disease also — leaf spot (which can be controlled) and Panama disease (which cannot) — entered the island from Central America and caused great losses. The damage due to disease has since been very greatly reduced by spraying and by the introduction of resistant varieties; and after the war exports to Great Britain again mounted rapidly. In 1951, however, a severe hurricane destroyed more than three-quarters of the crop. Once again the industry recovered. A government-sponsored scheme for insurance and rehabilitation kept planters on their feet. The British Ministry of Food agreed to take 85 per cent of the exportable surplus, at least until the end of 1954; and the production of bananas in 1954 already approached the peak years of the 'thirties.

The coming together of primary producers is characteristic of the period throughout the British West Indies. The Nutmeg Growers' Association of Grenada, the associations of cotton

and rice growers, of coconut and citrus producers, of cane-
farmers, and many others, all illustrate the general tendency to
form groups to defend common interests and to secure common
benefits. Their importance is social as well as economic; and
they are not, for the most part, associations of the poor against
the rich, of the peasant against the big planter or factory owner,
for among the cane farmers, the coconut growers and the
banana growers large and small producers have been able to
make common cause. It is not unusual in Jamaica to find the
manager of a big sugar factory taking a prominent and helpful
part in the affairs of the local cane farmers' association. Allied
with the producers' associations are the co-operative groups. A
Trinidad Co-operative Citrus Growers' Association was formed
in 1931, and within five years was handling over 60,000 crates
of grapefruit annually. Tobago formed a lime-growers' co-
operative in 1931. The Jamaica Citrus Growers' Association
runs its own canning factory. The inevitable needs of these
groups for credit is met in part by the development of co-
operative credit societies. A survey in 1950 revealed the existence
in the British Caribbean of 350 savings unions, 207 credit unions,
279 agricultural credit societies, 158 consumer societies and
about 30 marketing societies. Almost all are of relatively recent
growth; their numbers and their influence are steadily increasing.

A similar general tendency may be seen also in the growth of
labour organisations. Trade unionism in the West Indies is
relatively young. A workingmen's association was founded in
Port-of-Spain in 1907, but soon languished. After the war the
association was revived, and a popular figure emerged who was
of stature to assume and exercise leadership — Cipriani, known
to many as 'Tattoo'. The association agitated for a trade union
law, which was passed in 1932, but there was no general union
movement until after the riots which broke out in 1937 at
Fyzabad, a centre of migrant industrial labour. The development of trade unions in Jamaica was similar, for though the
waterfront workers had two registered trade unions in 1919, a
trade-union movement did not begin until after the riots which
broke out in 1938. This was generally true of all the British
West Indies, including British Guiana. Orde Brown, in his
report on labour in the West Indies, said in 1937 that 'trade
unions in the proper sense of the word are non-existent in

Barbados at present'; he said the same of Antigua, though he alluded also to the existence of friendly societies such as the Antigua Workingmen's Association. The Antigua Trade and Labour Union was not registered until 1940 and the St. Kitts trade-union movement is of much the same date.

The situation changed swiftly after the riots that spread through the West Indies in the late nineteen-thirties. The depression which caused such wide distress in Britain and in the United States in the years after 1929 had its effects, as we have seen, in the West Indies, where most industries were in difficulty. To the long-standing problem of intermittent employment in the towns was added the equally serious problem of rural under-employment. Wages were low, there was less work for more people, and the governments were too poor to take effective measures to lessen the depression. At the same time — according to the 1938 Royal Commission — 'the cumulative effect of education, the press, wireless, the spectacle of the standards of living of white people, and the reports of West Indians who have lived and worked abroad, particularly in the United States of America, has been to create a demand for better conditions of work and life. This demand has found expression from time to time in disorders and bloodshed, but it is also strongly in evidence where there has been no resort to violence, and is different in kind from the blinder discontents which in the nineteenth century also led occasionally to disaster.' Further, the population of the British West Indies had increased from 1,719,000 in 1896 to 2,514,000 in 1936, and there were no outlets for emigrants. The 1941 Constitution of the Republic of Panama forbade the immigration of 'the negro race, whose native language is not Spanish, the yellow race and the native races of India, Asia Minor and North Africa'; in 1942 the United States government promised, in recruiting labour for the Canal Zone, to 'co-operate to the extent feasible under present circumstances in meeting the expressed policy of Panama in this matter'. Costa Rica, Cuba and the United States similarly had all either closed the door completely to the West Indian or left only a small space for a few to enter.

The trouble came to a head first in St. Kitts, the powder-keg of the West Indies, in 1935, when sugar workers struck for more wages. Some months later the tension mounted in St.

Vincent, and the St. Vincent Workingmen's Association was formed to press for land settlement and a new constitution. In Castries there were strikes among the coal-heavers, but no violence. It was in the Trinidad oilfields that blood was shed. There Uriah 'Buzz' Butler became the leader of a great mass of workers, and arms had to be used to quell the disturbance and to restore order. Soon after, rioting broke out in Barbados over the deportation of Clement Payne, who had gone to the island from Trinidad to persuade the sugar workers to organise. Finally in June 1938 there were serious disorders in Guiana and in Jamaica originating in economic and in political grievances fomented by inflammatory speeches and sensational journalism.

Out of these disorders there emerged the first enduring labour organisations of the British West Indies. Trade unions sprang up overnight, and often the union was also a political party. In Antigua the unions soon claimed a membership of 12,000, or approximately one-quarter of the population. In Jamaica the 1,089 trade unionists of 1938 had grown to 57,700 in 1947 and 67,000 in 1950. In all the West Indian territories the trade-union movement grew and flourished, and the leaders became important political figures in the community. After 1938 this growth was encouraged by governments. Between 1939–45 some sixty-five trade unions were formed and legislation was passed setting up departments of labour and providing machinery for regulating labour disputes.

The rise of labour to political power has been as swift and dramatic as the rise of trade unions. The leaders who emerged from the period of the riots were capable of formulating the demands of labour, and pressed for political reform as well as for increase in wages. Bradshaw in St. Kitts, Bird in Antigua, Grantley Adams in Barbados, Bustamante and Manley in Jamaica, were foremost among those who made labour an organised and powerful political force. The sustained and widespread nature of the agitation which preceded the disorders points to a growth of political consciousness that makes these risings different in kind from earlier disorders, and that expressed itself in a demand for increased political responsibility. There had been dissatisfaction in the nineteen-twenties over Crown colony government, and constitutional changes had been made in Guiana and Jamaica which gave rather more power to the elected

Coffee: beans drying on a Blue Mountain barbecue

[*Photo: Packer, Kingston*]

Tobacco: harvesting the crop
[*Photo: Packer, Kingston*]

Tobacco: watering the nursery bed
[*Photo: Packer, Kingston*]

members and a little less to the governor, but now the leaders of the new nationalist movement sought the abolition of Crown colony government and the granting of new constitutions and responsible government.

The tendency to express economic dissatisfaction in terms of political reform reflects the remarkable speed of social integration in the West Indies in recent years. Trade unions, producers' associations, co-operative societies and professional societies all play a part in this process and they take action both in local matters and on a regional basis. In each territory the community is becoming organised within itself, and at the same time all the territories make common cause and act together when need arises. The dynamic after emancipation was evangelical and philanthropic, and it manifested itself not only in action to gain security and independence but also through missionary effort, by sending teachers from Jamaica to West Africa to christianise and educate their kinsmen. The dynamic in the West Indies of today is political, springing from the identification of oneself with the West Indies.

Racial considerations have played a part in the national movement. One of its better-known prophets was Marcus Garvey, who, though born in Jamaica, became celebrated more as an international champion of the negro race than as a West Indian. Garvey left Jamaica, as a youth, for the United States, where he came under the influence of Booker T. Washington, and launched the 'Universal Negro Improvement Association' to improve the conditions of negroes everywhere, and to establish a government of negroes in Africa. Nothing practical came of these schemes, but through them Garvey did much to create a feeling of racial pride and unity among negroes in the United States and the West Indies. His return to Jamaica was occasioned by his deportation from the United States, after serving a prison sentence for fraud in connection with his celebrated Black Star Steamship Line. Garvey was a powerful and picturesque figure. His emotional hold over many West Indians was extraordinarily strong. The Garvey cult of the 'thirties showed what power could be acquired by an orator who identified himself with the mass of the people and preserved his emotional links with them. More recent political leaders have not failed to profit by the lesson.

Parallel with the mass appeal of men like Garvey was a different but related factor — the discovery of the West Indies by the West Indian intellectual, of whatever race or colour, and his growing wish and ability to identify himself with the community. The process has been described by one who experienced it (H. W. Springer) in these words: 'During this period [the 'thirties and 'forties of the twentieth century] the slowly gathering discontent of the depressed classes reached bursting point and erupted in an energetic and sometimes violent protest, followed by a spurt of unprecedented political activity which we are still in the midst of. The dust has not settled yet and the outlines are blurred, but it seems plain enough that the West Indian people have come to the end of one epoch and are at the beginning of another.

'It is worth pointing out that the whole process that is going on, of which the spectacular political and economic changes are only the mechanical adjustments, is a social one. It may be described as the absorption of the majority into the way of life of the minority. I hasten to add that such a process can never be complete; it will result not in the absorption of the majority but in the creation of a new way of life. But it did set out in 1834 to induct the majority of ex-slaves into the way of life of the minority of free men, and so far as any conscious direction has been given to the process it has, until very recently, continued in that way. But now there has been a change of direction, or perhaps we might say a complication has been introduced. The majority, with increasing self-confidence, have begun to find merit in their own way of life, recognisably West Indian.'

Making due allowance for patriotic exaggeration, it is clear that factors such as these coloured and influenced the social protests and disturbances of the nineteen-thirties and helped to bring about conditions in which professional men — lawyers like Manley or Adams — seeing the potentialities of trade unions as sources of political power, defied the restrictions which social convention placed upon their class and became labour leaders. They campaigned for constitutional reform, and in 1944 a political change of the first magnitude was made by the grant to Jamaica of a new constitution in which the House of Representatives was to be elected by full adult suffrage. Up to 1944 the majority of people in the British West Indies had been without a vote. It is true that from time to time the franchise had been extended under Crown colony government, but as late as 1934 in Trinidad only 25,000 out of 400,000 people had the vote, and in Barbados in 1937 only 5,000 had the right to vote out of a population of nearly 200,000. Now the Colonial Office publicly announced a policy leading towards self-government for the West Indies, the abolition of Crown colony administration and the adoption everywhere of adult suffrage.

Representative government, as West Indian history has repeatedly demonstrated, can produce only frustration and deadlock unless it is accompanied by corresponding responsibility. The constitutions promulgated in several of the British West Indian colonies in the nineteen-fifties provided, in varying degrees, for systems of ministerial responsibility. The most complete was that inaugurated in Jamaica in 1953 with Mr. (now Sir Alexander) Bustamante as chief minister. Foreign relations and defence remained the responsibility of the United Kingdom; the courts and the civil service establishment (as in England) and the police were excluded from the control of political ministers. Otherwise, the whole range of government departments, including the all-important financial departments, fell within the authority of five ministries, each headed by a minister, advised and assisted by a permanent secretary. The ministers were all elected members of the majority party in the House of Representatives, and responsible to the House. They formed a majority in Executive Council, where they sat with the colonial secretary, the financial secretary and the attorney-general, under the chairmanship of the governor. Somewhat similar arrangements were introduced in Trinidad, Barbados, British Guiana and (with some misgivings) British Honduras. In British Guiana ministerial administration broke down after a few months, and the colony was threatened with financial chaos and serious disorder. In 1954 the constitution was suspended, and an interim government set up with wide emergency powers in the hands of the governor. Elsewhere, the system worked with reasonable efficiency, and afforded a valuable period of preparation for the political independence eventually proposed.

It was clear, however, that the smaller British territories — and perhaps some of the larger ones — could not by themselves support the cost and the responsibility of complete independence. The idea of a West Indian federation was not new, though in the past it had been extremely unpopular. The Leeward Islands were formed into a federal group, against much local opposition, in 1871. Attempts to federate the Windward Islands were unsuccessful. In 1876 the Barbadians rioted against proposals to include their island in such a federation. In 1921 E. F. Wood reported that proposals for federation were so unpopular as to be impracticable. As late as 1936 a commission from the United Kingdom considered the possibility of a closer union between Trinidad and the Leeward and Windward Islands, and reported unfavourably. After the Second World War, however, opinions and attitudes became less hostile to the idea. Many factors contributed to the change — the growth of West Indian national feeling; the spread and inter-connection of labour movements (a labour congress in British Guiana in 1938 urged federation); and the insistent urging of a few respected leaders, notably T. A. Marryshow in Grenada. Encouragement from the United Kingdom also played a part. The establishment of the Development and Welfare organization — though the initiative for it came from London — was a response to a felt need for West Indian rather than purely local planning. The Colonial Office, anxious to create a self-reliant state which would take over all British West Indian responsibilities, warmly supported proposals for a political federation, with the proviso that it could be successfully created only by the efforts of the West Indian governments themselves.

The first conference on British West Indian federation was held at Montego Bay in 1947. By a majority vote it accepted the principle of political federation and set up a Standing Closer-Association Committee to study the possibility of federation and to draft a federal constitution. The Committee produced a report, notable both for wisdom and for ingenuity, which in 1953 was submitted to a second conference in London and accepted, with modifications, for embodiment in the conference's recommendations. It then went back to the individual governments for acceptance. The two mainland territories, British Guiana and British Honduras, had both announced beforehand that they would not accept. In both territories there was widespread fear of a flood of immigrants from the over-populated islands, and the 'East Indians' of British Guiana disliked the prospect of joining a large community, with a population chiefly African in origin, in which they would be a relatively small minority. The mainland attitude robbed the federal project of much of its attraction; nevertheless, Jamaica, under the able leadership of Mr. Norman Manley, by a unanimous vote of both houses accepted the recommendations of the London conference and the other islands followed Jamaica's lead. A period of administrative preparation ensued, during which reports were prepared on federal finance, the future federal public service, and allied matters. A third conference on federation met in London in 1956, and the final decision was then made to federate the island territories and to leave the way open for the inclusion of British Guiana and British Honduras at a later date. The following year, after long and stubborn argument, it was agreed that the federal capital — to be built with the help of £1,000,000 contributed by the Government of the United Kingdom — should be in Trinidad. Lord Hailes was appointed Governor-General of the Federation. The first federal elections were held early in 1958; the federalist party — supported by Sir Grantley Adams, Mr. Manley and Dr. Eric Williams, premiers of Barbados, Jamaica and Trinidad respectively — secured a small majority in the house of representatives, and Sir Grantley Adams became the first prime minister.

Enthusiasm for federation has always been strongest in the small islands. In the larger islands opinion was divided. In Jamaica especially, many people feared that they were being asked to support the poorer territories, and that their progress in local self-government might be delayed by association with less 'advanced' groups. Jamaica, heavily dependent on customs duties for its revenue, refused to consider a customs union; Trinidad as resolutely opposed free movement of population, which Barbados considered to be essential for a federation. To these differences were added traditional insular prejudices and the personal jealousies of political leaders. In consequence, the federal government set up in 1957 was extremely weak. It had no power to raise taxes. Its revenue, derived from 'unit' contributions, was only about £2,000,000 a year. Federal 'subjects' of government were few and in concurrent 'subjects' the federal government was unable, both for financial and political reasons, to take the initiative. Foreign affairs, while awaiting final independence, were to be conducted through London. Apart from functions concerned with its own maintenance, therefore, the principal activities of the federal government were the distribution of grants under Colonial Development and Welfare Acts, the administration of the West India Regiment and the support of the University College of the West Indies.

The Federation lasted only three years. Its end was caused by the defection of Jamaica. Support in that island — which holds half the population of the British West Indies — was confined to a relatively small number of educated people, and Sir Alexander Bustamante, in opposition, was able to persuade an unsophisticated though shrewd electorate that they were being exploited in the interests of remote and indigent islands in the eastern Caribbean. The government — perhaps unwisely — put the question to a referendum in 1961. As a result, Jamaica decided to seek separate independence. On the wave of popular enthusiasm so created, Sir Alexander Bustamante was shortly afterwards returned to power, and Jamaica was formally declared an independent state within the British Commonwealth in August 1962. Trinidad, British Guiana and British Honduras all chose to follow its example. The smaller islands were left to find their own way out, either in association with Trinidad or in a smaller federation of their own. Separate independence for eight separate governments in a total population of 700,000 people would clearly be absurd; and meanwhile the responsibility for these ancient colonies rests upon the United Kingdom.

Of the smaller groups of non-British dependent territories in the Caribbean, one, the Danish Virgin Islands, was purchased by the United States in 1917 to prevent the possibility of German seizure. The administration of these small and indigent islands has been a disillusioning experience. The total population is about 25,000. Most of the sugar plantations ground to a standstill many years ago. Apart from relief expenditure from the United States — which has been on a fantastic scale by normal West Indian standards — the islands live mainly by the tourist trade, specialising, until very recently, in catering for visitors seeking easy divorces. The St. Thomas hotels feed these birds of passage largely on provisions grown by the hard-working peasant population of the British Virgin Islands, and brought in schooners down Sir Francis Drake's channel.

The French West Indies commanded the anxious attention of the Western world during the Second World War because of their adherence to the Vichy government after the capitulation of France; and in 1941 a conference of foreign ministers of the American republics discussed a plan for annexing European colonies whose metropolitan countries had suffered conquest. American and British naval forces in the Caribbean made such intervention unnecessary, and in due course Admiral Robert was induced to hand over to the representatives of General de Gaulle. On the whole, the white people of Martinique and Guadeloupe, and propertied people generally, tended to support Vichy, and so were discredited after the war. Also, the Robert episode cut the French islands off from possibilities of economic help. While Puerto Rico was receiving millions in American grants; while Curaçao was booming with war-time oil refining, and growing towards its present status of self-government within the Netherlands Union; while Jamaica benefited from British price-controls and the high demand for sugar, and also developed organs of self-government; while Trinidad grew rich by the sale of its asphalt and, above all, its oil; while all the West Indies were looking for their cut of war-time profits, Martinique and Guadeloupe languished under an economic and intellectual blockade. Plantations almost stopped production, and the area of cultivated land under canes fell from 37,000 acres to about 6,000. The prices of imported foodstuffs soared and a vigorous black market developed. The result at the end of the war was a series of bitter and disorderly strikes, which raised wages by about 300 per cent in money terms; though in real terms this meant little or nothing, because of the devaluation of the franc and general inflation. It is not surprising that the political life of the islands, under universal suffrage, swung sharply to the left after the war. Communists have predominated both in the local legislatures and among the deputies sent to Paris. The Communists and the Socialists — who are nowadays somewhat old-fashioned and conservative — hurl vituperation at one another in the local, as in the national, assemblies. Martinique and Guadeloupe, indigent, discontented, with decayed economies and not much immediate likelihood of recovery, still remain closely, and enthusiastically, part of the cultural and intellectual life of France. Their system of primary and secondary education — which, for such poor territories, is a creditable one—emphasises this attachment. The islands are tied the more closely to Europe, by being cut off linguistically from a Western hemisphere whose people speak English, Spanish or Portuguese. In 1946 the old French policy of centralisation was carried to its logical conclusion, and Martinique and Guadeloupe became departments of metropolitan France.

In conclusion, there are two aspects of recent West Indian history which affect the whole area and demand brief mention. One is the growth of North American influence in the territories associated with European countries. These territories, which originated in the great movement of the Old World to dominate the New, were left behind as isolated remnants when that movement receded. Their existence must depend, in the last resort, upon the maintenance of reasonable relations with the United States. The United States government has shown, over the last half-century, scrupulous respect for the sovereignty of the metropolitan governments. The British and other European colonies in the Caribbean have not, therefore, been subjected to political interventions by the United States, as most of the Caribbean republics have been; nor do they depend, as Cuba depended, upon the United States as the principal market for their products. Indeed, currency difficulties have tended to reduce West Indian imports from the United States, particularly motor cars, since the Second World War, and North American immigration policies have restricted the further northward emigration of West Indians. Nevertheless, the influence of so large and powerful a neighbour inevitably pervades the whole area. The celebrated agreement of 1941, by which the United States leased sites for bases in Bermuda, Trinidad, St. Lucia, Jamaica, Antigua and British Guiana, emphasised the process whereby the defence of the Caribbean area against aggressors has become primarily an American responsibility. American capital has been invested in the islands, especially in bauxite mining. The establishment of bases during the war, the great expansion of the tourist trade since, and the constant communication between West Indians resident in New York and their relatives in the islands, have all brought American wealth and American ways to the notice of West Indians generally. American films, Coca-Cola, chewing-gum, and tabloid magazines are all regular features, at least of urban life, in the West Indies. There is an obvious ambivalence in the West Indian attitude towards these cultural and economic influences. The West Indian often associates the United States with colour discrimination, of an overt kind which hardly exists in the islands. He is inclined, naturally, to resent the more flamboyant type of tourist; and respectable West Indians deplore, though they seem unable to prevent, the gathering of beggars, importunate taximen and touts of all sorts in the major tourist centres. He derives a certain amusement from the seasonal incursions of sociologists. Educated West Indians dislike the persecution of political dissidents and of 'intellectuals', which has been widely publicised as a feature of American life since the Second World War. On the other hand, the West Indian greatly admires American wealth and business efficiency. He likes the egalitarianism and the generosity ingrained in the American nature. He appreciates the existence in the United States of a great number and variety of university institutions, some of which have conveniently low entrance requirements and offer education of a sort to all comers. For the sake of these advantages he is prepared to put up with exile, with colour discrimination, and with red tape. Many, perhaps most, West Indians cherish an ambition to migrate to the United States, and a considerable number, even today, achieve that ambition. Yet they remain West Indians; they continue, even in Harlem itself, to play cricket; they retain their contacts with home, and some of them — not only the unsuccessful ones — return. The tendency of temporary immigrants, which Americans naturally resent, to treat the United States as an economic convenience, is common among West Indians. The same attitude can be seen among those who stay at home in the islands. Most West Indians — among those who think about such matters — do not desire a complete severance of their connections with Europe. The deep loyalty and affection of most British West Indians towards the Crown, and the wearer of the Crown, was abundantly shown during the visit of Her Majesty Queen Elizabeth II in 1953. Educated West Indians certainly do not desire political government or control by the United States. Nor, it should be added, has public opinion in the United States shown any great wish to take on such responsibilities, especially in view of the somewhat disillusioning experience of the Virgin Islands. Central American states have been less reticent. Guatemala maintains a claim upon the territory of British Honduras, for which there appears to be no reciprocating enthusiasm in the territory itself, and various Latin-American states from time to time propose

U

resolutions at Pan-American conferences against 'colonialism'. These activities have rarely passed beyond the talking stage. On the whole, while American interest in the West Indies has increased since the Second World War, it has tended to take forms other than political. Contacts of an intellectual kind have grown closer and more frequent. Intellectually and culturally the West Indies are becoming a meeting-ground; and in the process of building characteristic communities of their own, West Indians are increasingly in a position to select those European, North American or Latin American ideas and devices which appear to suit them best.

The second general aspect of contemporary West Indian life which calls for special mention is the growth of higher education. The problems which beset the West Indian colonies as they develop into self-governing, autonomous communities are not primarily political. They are primarily administrative. Political leaders emerge naturally and quickly as national consciousness grows; but self-government on the political level alone is an empty pretence unless there exists a reserve of educated and responsible local people qualified to man the public services, to advise the political leaders in the formulation of policy, and to see that policy is carried effectively into action. This means higher education in the colonies themselves. It is not enough to send selected students to the metropolitan country, where a large proportion tend to remain once they are there. Apart from the public service, a growing community needs its parsons, schoolmasters, doctors, engineers, chemists, and so forth, and they too must be — in part at least — locally trained, if self-government is to be a reality. It needs also a focus for its intellectual life, an institution which shall conduct and encourage original inquiry, and establish standards of excellence in scholarly and scientific pursuits. In those parts of the West Indies which are not, or until recently were not, fully independent, there are two university institutions, the University of Puerto Rico and the University College of the West Indies, which is situated in Jamaica but also has a branch in Trinidad, formed from the old Imperial College of Tropical Agriculture. The large sums of money spent on the University of Puerto Rico reflect the great financial advantages which that island enjoys through its special relation with the United States; its income is derived from certain public revenues specifically appropriated to its support. The University College of the West Indies grew up in close association with the University of London. It was built and equipped at United Kingdom expense under the Colonial Development and Welfare Acts, but its recurrent expenses, until the Federation was formed, were a charge upon the contributing governments in the British Caribbean, distributed according to a formula based on population. It is noteworthy that the decision to establish the college was made during a difficult period of the Second World War, when the outcome of that conflict was still uncertain. The foundation of such an institution was an act of faith and a declaration of intellectual independence; but it is also a recognition of inter-dependence, for no country, especially in matters of the mind, can live to itself. It is right and natural that competent scholars and scientists from England or Canada or the United States should work at the University College, and that eminent West Indians should hold chairs at universities in England and elsewhere. A similar exchange of talents with continental America and with Europe enriches the University of Puerto Rico; and the two West Indian universities have everything to gain from co-operation with one another and with the universities of other Caribbean countries. These two institutions are among the hopeful signs for the future happiness and prosperity of the West Indies. They rank high among the means — and are essential conditions — for achieving the aims to which responsible West Indians, Europeans and Americans throughout the area are committed: the development of the old system of imperial administration into one of self-government in association; the change from a relation of colony and metropolis to a friendly and fruitful co-operation between free and (within the limits of their resources) equal partners.

SUGGESTIONS FOR FURTHER READING

Chapter I. DISCOVERY

T. A. Joyce, *Central American and West Indian Archaeology.*
London, 1916.

S. Loven, *Origins of the Tainan Culture, West Indies.* Göteborg,
1935.

S. E. Morison, *Admiral of the Ocean Sea.* Boston, 1942.

Chapter II. THE SPANISH INDIES

C. H. Haring, *The Spanish Empire in America.* New York, 1947.
*Trade and Navigation between Spain and the Indies in the Time
of the Hapsburgs.* Cambridge, Mass., 1918.

A. P. Newton, *The European Nations in the West Indies.* London,
1933.

I. Wright, *The Early History of Cuba.* New York, 1916.

J. H. Parry, *The Spanish Theory of Empire in the Sixteenth Century.*
Cambridge, 1940.

L. Hanke, *The First Social Experiments in America.* Cambridge,
Mass., 1935.

Chapter III. THE CHALLENGE TO SPAIN

A. P. Newton, *op. cit.*

I. Wright, *op. cit.*

Sir J. S. Corbett, *Drake and the Tudor Navy.* 2 vols. London, 1898.

J. A. Williamson, *Maritime Enterprise 1485-1588.* Oxford, 1913.
Sir John Hawkins, the Time and the Man. Oxford, 1927.

R. Hakluyt, *The Principal Navigations, Voyages, Traffiques and
Discoveries of the English Nation* (1589). 12 vols. Glasgow,
1903-5.

C. Fernández Duro, *La Armada Española desde la Unión de los
Reinos de Castilla y León.* 9 vols. Madrid, 1895-1903.

C. B. de la Roncière, *Histoire de la Marine Française.* Paris, 1899.

Chapter IV. THE SETTLEMENT OF THE OUTER ISLANDS

C. M. Andrews, *The Colonial Period of American History.* 4 vols. New Haven, 1934–38.

J. A. Williamson, *The Caribbee Islands under the Proprietary Patents.* Oxford, 1925.

V. T. Harlow, *History of Barbados, 1625–85.* Oxford, 1926. *Christopher Codrington, 1668–1710.* Oxford, 1928.

C. S. S. Higham, *The Development of the Leeward Islands under the Restoration.* Cambridge, 1920.

F. Morales Padrón, *Jamaica Española.* Sevilla, 1952.

G. Debien, 'Les Engagés pour les Antilles', in *Revue d'Histoire des Colonies.* Paris, 1951.

E. Sluiter, 'Dutch-Spanish rivalry in the Caribbean area, 1594–1609', *Hispanic American Historical Review,* vol. 28 (1948), pp. 165–196.

A. E. Smith, *Colonists in Bondage.* Chapel Hill, N.C., 1947.

Père J-B. Du Tertre, *Histoire Générale des Antilles.* 3 vols. Paris. 1667–71.

Chapter V. THE SUGAR REVOLUTION

A. P. Newton, *op. cit.*

Père Du Tertre, *op. cit.*

R. Ligon, *A True and Exact History of the Island of Barbados.* London, 1657.

S. L. Mims, *Colbert's West India Policy.* New Haven, 1912.

N. M. Crouse, *The French Struggle for the West Indies, 1665–1713* New York, 1943.

E. Williams, *Capitalism and Slavery.* Chapel Hill, N.C., 1944.

G. L. Beer, *The Old Colonial System, 1660–1754.* 2 vols. New York. 1912.

M. Herskovits, *The Myth of the Negro Past.* New York, 1941.

C. A. Banbuck, *Histoire de la Martinique.* Paris, 1935.

M. Satineau, *Histoire de la Guadeloupe sous l'Ancien Régime.* Paris, 1928.

A. Whitson, *The Constitutional Development of Jamaica.* Manchester, 1929.

L. A. Harper, *The English Navigation Laws.* New York, 1939.

Chapter VI. THE BUCCANEERS

N. M. Crouse, *op. cit.*

A. P. Newton, *op. cit.*
    Colonizing Activities of the English Puritans. New Haven, 1914.

C. H. Haring, *The Buccaneers in the West Indies in the Seventeenth Century*. London, 1910.

J. Esquemeling, *The Buccaneers of America* (1678). London, 1911.

W. A. Roberts, *The French in the West Indies*. New York, 1942.

Père P-F-X. Charlevoix, *Histoire de l'Isle Espagnole ou de Saint-Domingue*. 2 vols. Paris, 1730–31.

Chapter VII.   THE SLAVE TRADE AND THE *ASIENTOS*

E. Williams, *op. cit.*

G. L. Beer, *op. cit.*

Gaston-Martin, *Histoire de l'Esclavage dans les Colonies Françaises*. Paris, 1948.

G. Scelle, *La Traite négrière aux Indes de Castille*. 2 vols. Paris, 1906.

R. Pares, *War and Trade in the West Indies, 1739–63*. Oxford, 1936.

F. W. Pitman, *The Development of the British West Indies, 1700–63*. New Haven, 1917.

R. Bourne, *Queen Anne's Navy in the West Indies*. New Haven, 1939.

Père Labat, *Nouveau Voyage aux Isles de l'Amérique*. 6 vols. Paris, 1722.

Chapter VIII.   COMMERCE AND WAR, 1739–63

R. Pares, *op. cit.*

F. W. Pitman, *op. cit.*

A Morales Carrión, *Puerto Rico and the Non-Hispanic Caribbean*. Rio Piedras, P. R., 1952.

L. M. Penson, *The Colonial Agents of the British West Indies*. London, 1924.

G. L. Beer, *British Colonial Policy 1754–65*. New York, 1907.

Chapter IX.   REORGANISATION, REBELLION AND WAR, 1763–83

G. L. Beer, *op. cit.*

L. M. Penson, *op. cit.*

L. J. Ragatz, *The Fall of the Planter Class in the British Caribbean*. Washington, D.C., 1928.

F. Armytage, *The Free Port System in the British West Indies*. London, 1953.

H. T. Manning, *British Colonial Government after the American Revolution*. New Haven, 1933.

Chapter X. THE SUGAR ISLANDS ON THE EVE OF REVOLUTION

L. J. Ragatz, *op. cit.*
R. Pares, *A West India Fortune.* London, 1950.
J. Saintoyant, *La Colonisation Française sous l'Ancien Régime.* 2 vols. Paris, 1932.
P. de Vaissière, *Saint-Domingue 1629–1789.* Paris, 1909.
M. L. E. Moreau de Saint-Méry, *Description de la Partie Française de Saint-Domingue.* 2 vols. Philadelphia, 1797.
Description de la Partie Espagnole de l'Isle Saint-Domingue. Philadelphia, 1799.
B. Edwards, *History, Civil and Commercial, of the British Colonies in the West Indies* (1794 — many editions).
J. H. Parry, 'The Patent Offices in the British West Indies', *English Historical Review,* April 1954.

Chapter XI. REVOLUTION AND WAR

J. G. Leyburn, *The Haitian People.* New Haven, 1941.
T. Lothrop Stoddard, *The French Revolution in San Domingo.* New York, 1914.
J. Saintoyant, *La Colonisation Française pendant la Révolution.* 2 vols. Paris, 1930.
La Colonisation Française pendant la Période Napoléonienne. Paris, 1931.
Sir J. W. Fortescue, *History of the British Army.* 13 vols. London, 1899–1930.
R. W. Logan, *Diplomatic relations of the United States with Haiti, 1776–1891.* Chapel Hill, 1941.

Chapter XII. ABOLITION AND EMANCIPATION

W. L. Burn, *Emancipation and Apprenticeship in the British West Indies.* London, 1937.
T. Clarkson, *The History of the Rise, Progress and Accomplishment of the Abolition of the African Slave Trade.* 2 vols. London, 1808.
W. L. Mathieson, *British Slavery and its Abolition, 1823–38.* London, 1926.
D. H. Hall, 'The Apprenticeship Period in Jamaica', *Caribbean Quarterly,* December, 1953.
V. Schoelcher, ed. A. Césaire, *Esclavage et Colonisation.* Paris, 1948.

Chapter XIII. 'THE BEST AND WORST OF TIMES'

W. L. Mathieson, *British Slave Emancipation 1838–49*. London, 1932.

J. Davy, *The West Indies before and after Slave Emancipation.* London, 1854.

W. Sewell, *The Ordeal of Free Labour in the West Indies.* New York, 1861.

A. Caldecott, *The Church in the West Indies.* London, 1898.

Chapter XIV. PATTERNS OF COLONIAL GOVERNMENT

H. T. Manning, *op. cit.*

H. Wrong, *Government of the West Indies.* Oxford, 1923.

K. N. Bell and W. P. Morrell, *Select Documents on British Colonial Policy.* Oxford, 1928.

Sir C. Clementi, *The Constitutional History of British Guiana.* London, 1937.

Report of the Jamaica Royal Commission, 1866.

Chapter XV. THE SPANISH ISLANDS IN THE NINETEENTH CENTURY

S. Welles, *Naboth's Vineyard.* 2 vols. New York, 1928.

R. Guerra y Sánchez, *Manual de Historia de Cuba.* Havana, 1938.
Azúcar y Población en las Antillas. Havana, 1944.

F. Ortiz, *Cuban Counter-point.* New York, 1947.

H. H. S. Aimes, *A History of Slavery in Cuba.* New York, 1907.

H. E. Friedländer, *Historia Económica de Cuba.* Havana, 1944.

H. F. Guggenheim, *The United States and Cuba.* New York, 1934.

L. M. Díaz Soler, *Historia de la Esclavitud Negra en Puerto Rico 1493–1890.* Madrid, 1953.

J. M. Sanromá, *Puerto Rico y su Hacienda.* Madrid, 1873.

R. W. Logan, *op. cit.*

Chapter XVI. THE BRITISH AND FRENCH WEST INDIES, 1860–1918

W. Sewell, *op. cit.*

Lord Olivier, *The Myth of Governor Eyre.* London, 1933.

W. L. Mathieson, *The Sugar Colonies and Governor Eyre 1849–66.* London, 1936.

C. D. Kepner and J. H. Soothill, *The Banana Empire.* New York, 1935.

G. Cumper, 'Labour Demand and Supply in the Jamaican Sugar Industry 1830–1950', *Social and Economic Studies*, vol. ii, no. 4. Kingston, 1954.

Report of the Royal Commission appointed 1882.

D. Nath, *A History of Indians in British Guiana*. London, 1950.

I. M. Cumpston, *Indians overseas in British territories 1835–1865*. Oxford, 1953.

Sir A. Aspinall, *A Wayfarer in the West Indies*. London, 1928.

V. Reid, *New Day*. New York, 1949.

Chapter XVII. THE UNITED STATES AND THE INDEPENDENT ISLANDS

S. Welles, *op. cit.*

F. Ortiz, *op. cit.*

H. E. Friedländer, *op. cit.*

L. H. Jenks, *Our Cuban Colony*. New York, 1928.

R. L. Buell and others, *Problems of the New Cuba*. New York, 1935.

R. Fitzgibbons, *Cuba and the United States*. Menasha, Wis., 1935.

L. L. Montague, *Haiti and the United States, 1714–1938*. Durham, N.C., 1940.

C. Lloyd Jones, *The Caribbean since 1900*. New York, 1936.

Dexter Perkins, *The United States and the Caribbean*. Cambridge, Mass., 1947.

Chapter XVIII. THE CARIBBEAN COLONIES, 1918–62

C. D. Kepner and J. H. Soothill, *op. cit.*

Various authors, 'Puerto Rico, a Study in Democratic Development', *Annals of the American Academy of Political and Social Science*, January 1953.

Lord Olivier, *Jamaica, the Blessed Island*. London, 1937.

K. Pringle, *Waters of the West*. London, 1938.

R. W. Thompson, *Black Caribbean*. London, 1946.

W. M. Macmillan, *Warning from the West Indies*. London, 1938.

A. Lewis and E. Williams, *The Negro in the Caribbean*. New York, 1942.

T. S. Simey, *Welfare and Planning in the West Indies*. Oxford, 1946.

P. Blanshard, *Democracy and Empire in the Caribbean*. New York, 1947.

Sir F. Stockdale, 'The Work of the Caribbean Commission', *International Affairs*, vol. xxiii, no. 2. April 1947.

R. A. Humphreys, 'The Anglo-Guatemalan Dispute', *International Affairs*, vol. xxiv, no. 3. July 1948.

C. W. W. Greenidge, 'The British West Indies', *International Affairs*, vol. xxv, no. 1. January 1949.

M. Proudfoot, *Britain and the U.S.A. in the Caribbean*. London, 1954.

H. W. Springer, 'On being a West Indian', *Caribbean Quarterly*, December 1953.

General Works.

W. L. Burn, *The British West Indies*. London, 1951.

Sir A. C. Burns, *The History of the British West Indies*. London, 1954.

G. Hanotaux and A. Martineau, eds., *Histoire des Colonies Fran-çaises*. 5 vols. Paris, 1930.

N. Deerr, *The History of Sugar*. 2 vols. London 1950.

Sir C. P. Lucas, *Historical Geography of the West Indies*. Oxford, 1905.

J. A. Saco, *Historia de la esclavitud de la raza africana en el Nuevo Mundo y en especial en los Países Américo-Hispanos*. 4 vols. Havana, 1938.

A. W. Acworth, *Treasure in the Caribbean*, a first study of Georgian buildings in the British West Indies. London, 1949.

HISTORIES OF INDIVIDUAL COUNTRIES
(Not mentioned under chapter-headings)

Sir R. Schomburgk, *History of Barbados*. London, 1848.

W. J. Gardner, *A History of Jamaica*. London, 1909.

E. Long, *History of Jamaica*. 3 vols. London, 1774.

H. Breen, *St. Lucia*. London, 1844.

S. L. Caiger, *British Honduras, Past and Present*. London, 1951.

R. Guerra y Sánchez, J. M. Pérez Cabrera, J. J. Remos, E. S. Santovenia, eds., *Historia de la Nación Cubana*. 10 vols. Havana, 1952.

SOME RECENT BRITISH OFFICIAL PUBLICATIONS
ON THE WEST INDIES

Report of Royal Commission appointed 1938. (1945. Cmd. 6607.)

Statement of Action Taken on the Recommendations of the West India Royal Commission. (1945. Cmd. 6656.)

The Colonial Empire, 1939–47. (1947. Cmd. 7167.)

The Colonial Empire 1947–48. (1948. Cmd. 7433.)

Report of the West Indies Committee of the Commission on Higher Education in the Colonies. (1945. Cmd. 6654.)

Closer Association of the British West Indian Colonies. (1947. Cmd.
7120.) (Montego Bay) Conference on Closer Association. Part I,
Report. (1948. Cmd. 7291.) Part 2, Proceedings. (1948. Colonial
No. 218.) Report of the British Caribbean Standing Closer Association Committee 1948-9. (1950. Colonial No. 255.)

Report of the Commission on the Unification of the Public Services
in the British Caribbean Area 1948-49 (the Holmes Report).
(1950. Colonial No. 25.)

Report of the Commission on the Establishment of a Customs Union
in the British Caribbean Area 1948-50. (1951. Colonial No. 268.)

Report by the Conference on West Indian Federation held in London
in April 1953. (1953. Cmd. 8837.)

The Plan for a British Caribbean Federation, agreed by the Conference
on West Indian Federation held in London in April 1953. (1953.
Cmd. 8895.)

Report of the Fiscal Commissioner (Cmd. 9618, December 1955).
Report of the Civil Service Commissioner (Cmd. 9619, December
1955).

Report of the Judicial Commissioner (Cmd. 9620, December 1955).

Report of the Conference on movement of persons within a British
Caribbean Federation, Port of Spain, 1955.

Industrial Development in Jamaica, Trinidad, Barbados and British
Guiana. Report of Mission of U.K. Industrialists,Oct.-Nov. 1952.
(1953. Colonial No. 294.)

Comptrollers' Reports on Development and Welfare in the West
Indies.

 (i) 1940-2. Sir Frank Stockdale. (1943. Colonial No. 184.)
 (ii) 1943-4. Sir Frank Stockdale. (1945. Colonial No. 189.)
 (iii) 1945-6. Sir John Macpherson. (1947. Colonial No. 212.)
 (iv) 1947-9. Sir Hubert Rance. (1950. Colonial No. 264.)
 (v) 1950.   (1951. Colonial No. 269.)
 (vi) 1951. Sir George Seel. (1952. Colonial No. 282.)
vii) 1952. Sir George Seel. (1953. Colonial No. 291.)
    Etc.

Report by the Conference on British Caribbean Federation held in
London in February 1956. (Cmd. 9733, March 1956).

WEST INDIES

Miles
100   200   300   400

A T L A N T I C

O C E A N

OMINGO

Virgin
Is
San Juan   Anguilla
Vieques   Barbuda
PUERTO   Sta Cruz   Antigua
RICO   St Kitts
Montserrat
LEEWARD   Guadeloupe

E A   ISLANDS   Dominica

WINDWARD   Martinique

ISLANDS   St Lucia

St Vincent   Barbados

Grenadines
Bonaire   Grenada

cao   Tobago
Tortuga   Margarita
Trinidad
P. of Spain
Caracas

N E Z U E L A

62°

62°

26°

18°

10°

INDEX

PRINTED BY PURNELL AND SONS, LTD.
PAULTON (SOMERSET) AND LONDON